35613

The Situation of the Novel

The Situation of
the Novel

BERNARD BERGONZI

Macmillan

First edition 1970
Reprinted (with corrections) 1971

Published by
THE MACMILLAN PRESS LTD
London and Basingstoke
Associated companies in New York Toronto
Dublin Melbourne Johannesburg and Madras

SBN 333 10139 1

Printed in Great Britain by
REDWOOD PRESS LIMITED
Trowbridge & London

Contents

Preface

THE title of this book is more ponderous than I like; yet to refer to the 'situation' of the novel, rather than its 'state' or 'condition', seemed the best way of suggesting my intentions. In recent years I have read a good many books – some admirable – which offer a panoramic or comprehensive survey of the novel, or try to define its essence as a literary mode. I have learnt a great deal from them, but I am not now trying to add to their number. My immediate concern is with the contemporary novel as the product of a particular phase of history, in a particular culture. The situation of the novelist is one which he shares with the critic and the general reader, and though literary values lie at the heart of it, any attempt to examine this situation leads towards other questions, which are conventionally regarded as extra-literary. Thus, although there is an extended critical discussion in this book of some English novelists who have been active in the last twenty years, I have become increasingly aware that to write about modern English fiction is also, in some measure, to attempt to define what it means to be English at the present time. I hope I have avoided the naïve error of using novels as 'documentary' sources for illustrating the contemporary scene: the relation between the small world of a novel and the large world from which it draws its life is rarely simple and can be remarkably complicated. It is, however, true that I have become discontented with the customary academic notion of the novel as a complex but essentially self-contained form, cut off from the untidiness and discontinuities of the world outside. Some of that untidiness has undoubtedly incorporated itself into the design of the present book: I begin with general questions about the present state and possible future of fiction, and go on to talk about the cultural attitudes implicit in the recent English novel. There follows a chapter about some modern American novels, which are discussed both for their own sake and to establish a contrast with the English works which are more fully discussed in the next two chapters. I end with further speculative and general questions, though they are focused on particular books and authors. I hope that the issues raised at the beginning will acquire sufficient momentum to be carried through the book, picking up further implications on the way.

There is, I have been faintly dismayed to observe, a hint of cultural determinism in my approach, but it seems called for by the material and the situation, and I do not believe it undermines the possibilities of creativity and freedom. The dominant emphasis in English literary criticism – whatever Matthew Arnold may have said about 'the power of the man and the power of the moment' – is on creation as a solitary and isolated act, and on critical response as a further isolated act by a free and reasonably sympathetic spirit. In the face of such a well-established tradition, I do not think that any over-compensatory reaction I may have indulged in is likely to be dangerous. The total freedom of the great book, wholly surprising and yet wholly true to the world and human nature, is an ideal we can all support. Yet very few writers have embodied it with total plenitude. There is perhaps a sense in which all literature would be *King Lear* or *Anna Karenina* if it could; yet we remain aware of the countless ways in which it usually fails to be anything of the kind. Even the best literature – and specifically fiction – is full of contradictions and even cowardice, shown by retreats into the generic or the culturally conditioned; a tendency to play the little world of art against the large world of human freedom; or a grateful falling back on the stock response when the material gets out of hand. Like people, literature is deeply imperfect. All these failings are certainly to be found in the authors I discuss in this book; much of the time inevitably so, for reasons which I hope to establish as my discussion proceeds.

The debts I incurred in writing this book were manifold; not merely to the distinguished novelists and critics whose ideas I have used, whether in agreement or disagreement, and whose names and works are listed in the notes and index; but also to the friends, colleagues and students with whom I have discussed the novel during recent years. I was greatly helped by a series of radio programmes that I prepared for the BBC in 1967–8 under the title 'Novelists of the Sixties', and in particular by my conversations with Margaret Drabble, B. S. Johnson, David Lodge and Andrew Sinclair; I am also indebted to Antonia Byatt and Julian Mitchell. I will mention one further name : that of my wife, Gabriel, who has freely shared her ideas and patiently listened to mine. Some of the material in this book first appeared in periodicals, though much of it has been rewritten; I am grateful to the editors of the *Critical Quarterly, Listener, London Magazine, New York Review of Books* and *Twentieth Century.*

But just as there was a moment in political history at which the difficulties of action became so great that they could not be directly overcome without reflecting on the situation itself, and just as man was forced to learn more and more to act, first on the basis of external impressions of the situation and afterwards by structurally analysing it, just so we may regard it as the natural development of a tendency, that man is actually grappling with the critical situation that has arisen in his thinking and is striving to envisage more clearly the nature of this crisis.

KARL MANNHEIM, *Ideology and Utopia*

1 The Novel
No Longer Novel

Certain elderly counsellors, filling what may be thought a
constant part in the little tragi-comedy which literature
and its votaries are playing in all ages, would ask, suspect-
ing some affectation or unreality in that minute culture of
form: – Cannot those who have a thing to say, say it
directly? Why not be simple and broad, like the old writers
of Greece? And this challenge had at least the effect of set-
ing his thoughts at work on the intellectual situation as it
lay between the children of the present and those earliest
masters. Certainly, the most wonderful, the unique, point,
about the Greek genius, in literature as in everything else,
was the entire absence of imitation in its productions.
How had the burden of precedent, laid upon every artist,
increased since then!

WALTER PATER, *Marius the Epicurean*

THE novel was described by D. H. Lawrence as 'the one bright
book of life'; by enlarging and directing our deepest currents of
feeling it could help us to achieve a new unity and intensity of
being:

> Books are not life. They are only tremulations on the ether. But
> the novel as a tremulation can make the whole man alive tremble.
> Which is more than poetry, philosophy, science or any other book-
> tremulation can do. (*Selected Literary Criticism*, 1961 : p. 105)

Lawrence meant something much more than the novel as a particular literary kind, which sprang up in bourgeois society at the end of
the seventeenth century, and which was intimately associated with
individualism, class and money. For him the novel was a transcendent entity; not a historically generated mode, but a way of responding to the world that was timeless and absolute, and ultimately to be identified with the essence of all great literature: 'The
Bible – but *all* the Bible – and Homer and Shakespeare : these are the
supreme old novels.' Lawrence, as a major novelist and innovator,
had earned the right to such a confident and unhistorical vision,
even though it is too elevated to be of much help in the everyday

forms of critical discussion. Yet it defines one way of looking at the novel, which is perhaps the only one possible for the practising novelist who wants to take seriously the possibilities of the literary medium to which he devotes his life, however much critics may allege that the novel is declining, or otherwise in difficulties. Thus Anthony Burgess ends his book, *The Novel Now*, with these brave words:

> The contemporary novel is not doing badly. Soon, when we least expect it, it will do not merely better but magnificently. Any one of us may, astonishingly, prove the vehicle of some great unexpected masterpiece which will burn up the world (meaning the people who read). That dim hope sustains us. (1967: p. 225)

One admires such confidence, even while remaining sceptical about the possibility of novels being able to burn up the world any more.

If one thinks about mere production, the contemporary novel is certainly in a healthy state. An enormous number of novels is published each year (and these are only a tiny percentage of the total numbers which are sent to publishers for consideration), and a good deal of space is devoted to reviewing those of them that make some claim, no matter how faint, to serious literary attention. Reviewers give the impression of being eager to find what Mr Burgess calls 'some great unexpected masterpiece which will burn up the world'; there are frequent announcements of a 'major achievement', 'an exciting contribution to the art of the novel', 'the best book this year'. In the arena where novels are produced, publicised, reviewed and, presumably, read, there is every indication that the form is in a state of high vitality. Nevertheless, even this happy state of affairs has its curious aspects. It is well known that the economics of novel-publishing is precarious; that first novels almost always lose money, and very few novels make much; and yet publishers are still remarkably eager to go on publishing them, because the rewards from hitting the jack-pot with a best-seller are so prodigious. Yet it is conceivable that the economic basis of novel-publishing could change in such a way that bringing out novels would cease to be worth while for a publisher who wanted to stay in business: if, say, the relation between the certain loss on run-of-the-mill novels and the possible gains from a best-seller were to alter in a way unfavourable to the publisher, publishing novels at all would cease to be an attractive gamble. In that case, presumably, novels would disappear from the market, and publishers could turn their attention to more profitable kinds of book. The fact that there would still be some remaining demand for novels would not affect the issue, since modern large-scale industry – which is what publishing is increasingly becoming – is quite accustomed to leaving small-scale consumer needs unfilled if it is not profitable to fill them. (There was a comparable situation in the 1890s, when the three-volume novel, which had been the staple of the Victorian fiction market, was killed off almost overnight when the circulating libraries suddenly ceased to purchase it.) There is little that the prospective novelist could do, apart from circulating his work in manuscript, since the printing and distribution of a novel is a complex and expensive business (unlike the case of a book of poems, which can easily be duplicated or, for that matter, recorded on tape), and few novelists could meet it out of their own pockets. Presumably for a few years the flood of unprinted novels would mount higher and higher in ever-increasing frustration, but I imagine that within a generation novels would have ceased to be written, and that some other vehicle would have been found for the 'one bright book of life'.

This is, admittedly, an extreme and highly speculative picture, but it is, I think, worth projecting if only to emphasise the paradox that the novel, which seems so open to life, and to give, as Lawrence saw, a total picture of man in all his variety and fullness, is intimately connected with a particular technology and form of commercial development, neither of which may be permanently protected from obsolescence. There is a further paradox in the fact that despite the commitment of novelists to the power and authority of the fictional form, critics have for a long time been predicting the end of the novel, in tones ranging from cool indifference to apocalyptic gloom. The apocalypticism may, indeed, be inherent in the form. The novel is concerned, above all, with carving shapes out of history, with imposing a beginning, a middle and an end on the flux of experience, and there might be obscure connections between the need for a novelist to find an end for his novel, and the preoccupation of critics with seeing an end for all novels: the larger implications of this question can be pursued in Frank Kermode's *The Sense of an Ending*. Lionel Trilling gave a graphic expression of this critical apocalypticism in 1948:

> It is impossible to talk about the novel nowadays without having in our minds the question of whether or not the novel is still a living form. Twenty-five years ago T. S. Eliot said that the novel

came to an end with Flaubert and James, and at about the same time Señor Ortega said much the same thing. This opinion is now heard on all sides. It is heard in conversation rather than read in formal discourse, for to insist on the death and moribundity of a great genre is an unhappy task which the critic will naturally avoid if he can, yet the opinion is now an established one and has a very considerable authority. (*The Liberal Imagination,* 1961: p. 255)

Ortega y Gasset remarked in *The Dehumanization of Art and Notes on the Novel* that 'anyone who gives a little thought to the conditions of a work of art must admit that a literary genre may wear out'. He went on to argue that by the 1920s this was precisely what had happened to the novel:

> It is erroneous to think of the novel – and I refer to the modern novel in particular – as of an endless field capable of rendering ever new forms. Rather it may be compared to a vast but finite quarry. There exist a number of possible themes for the novel. The workman of the primal hour had no trouble finding new blocks – new characters, new themes. But present-day writers face the fact that only narrow and concealed veins are left them. (1948: pp. 57–8)

In the 1940s Alberto Moravia allowed himself a similar reflection:

> When I think of the number of literary *genres* which seemed likely to live for ever and yet have died out, I cannot help wondering whether the novel, the last in the series, is also doomed to the same fate. (*Man as an End,* 1965: p. 64)

At about the same time Cyril Connolly harshly observed, 'Flaubert, Henry James, Proust, Joyce and Virginia Woolf have finished off the novel. Now all will have to be re-invented as from the beginning' (*The Unquiet Grave,* 1961: p. 21). Most recently George Steiner has argued, with a wealth of dazzling illustration, that the traditional novel is too rooted in a vanishing phase of history and society to be able to grasp contemporary reality:

> Following on the epic and verse-drama, the novel has been the third principal genre of western literature. It expressed and, in part, shaped the habits and feelings and language of the western *bourgeosie* from Richardson to Thomas Mann. In it, the dreams and nightmares of the mercantile ethic, of middle-class privacy, and of the monetary-sexual conflicts and delights of industrial society have their monument. With the decline of these ideals and habits into a phase of crisis and partial rout, the genre is

losing much of its vital bearing. (*Language and Silence*, 1967: pp. 421–2)

One could multiply such instances, all of which have been accompanied by a constant increase in the number of novels written, published and read. Assuming that the critics who make these gloomy prognostications are serious, one must find some way of resolving this paradox. (I am assuming that my speculation about the physical disappearance of the novel as a form of printed literature is not, in fact, likely to be realized in the near future). What is happening, I would like to suggest, is that the novel, while continuing to be a popular cultural form, no longer possesses the essential 'novelty' that traditionally characterised it.

Several of the critics I have quoted use the word 'genre' when discussing the novel. This is a significant usage, since in its origins the novel was marked precisely by its freedom from genre and established literary convention generally. If one believes that the novel offers unique possibilities for the enlargement of consciousness and the intensification of being, then one will resist treating it as a particular kind of literary pigeon-hole, no matter how capacious, and will see the form in a non-generic and ahistorical way, as indeed Lawrence does, when he refers to the Bible and Homer and Shakespeare as 'the supreme old novels'. At the beginning of his celebrated book on eighteenth-century fiction, *The Rise of the Novel*, Ian Watt stresses the form's inherent freedom and originality:

> Previous literary forms had reflected the general tendency of their cultures to make conformity to traditional practice the major test of truth: the plots of classical and renaissance epic, for example, were based on past history or fable, and the merits of the authors' treatment were judged largely according to a view of literary decorum derived from the accepted models in the genre. This literary traditionalism was first and most fully challenged by the novel, whose primary criterion was truth to individual experience – individual experience which is always unique and therefore new. The novel is thus the logical literary vehicle of a culture which, in the last few centuries, has set an unprecedented value on originality, on the novel; and it is therefore well named. (1963: p. 13)

Ian Watt perhaps sees too direct a relation between the novel and philosophical empiricism, but the links between the form and the emergence of individualism are clear enough. The eighteenth-century novel constantly gives the sense of a new and vigorous literary mode emerging almost by accident from the remnants of genre. Richardson's novels, for instance, originated in a collection of letters written for young ladies who wanted a model of the epistolary art. From this unpromising beginning there emerged *Clarissa*, which is a masterpice of psychological realism and moral insight. Again, Fielding may have started *Joseph Andrews* as a parody of Richardson's *Pamela*; and nothing is more of a restricted, indeed parasitic, genre than parody. Yet the story soon developed its own particular energies, and Fielding's original limited intention was abandoned. After *Joseph Andrews* Fielding wrote *Tom Jones*, where a neo-classical epic framework scarcely contains the novel's sense of freedom and irrepressible vitality. The picaresque novel, originally a distinctive genre, soon burst its bounds, and before long the term 'picaresque' lost much of its critical usefulness. Yet if the novel established itself as an anti-generic form, fiction in the broader sense continued to develop generically; the eighteenth century evolved a new and popular literary genre, the Gothic novel, from which descended the horror story in the manner of Poe, and which has had a widespread progeny in subsequent American fiction. Related conventional forms include the old-fashioned detective story, the modern thriller and science fiction. But all these kinds of writing are marginal to that central territory dominated by the novel proper, where, in E. M. Forster's words, 'stand Miss Austen with the figure of Emma by her side, and Thackery holding up Esmond' (*Aspects of the Novel*, 1927 : p. 15).

Taking a synoptic view, one can see the development of the European novel in the eighteenth and nineteenth centuries as the successive opening up of tracts of unexplored territory. After the remarkable but comparatively modest advances of the eighteenth-century novelists, who never wholly freed themselves from the remnants of neo-classical convention, we move into the realm of the great nineteenth-century realists where the image of man, in the hands of Flaubert and Tolstoy and Dostoievsky is remade with an astonishing power and freedom. The novel, in short, soon manifested an intense degree of stylistic dynamism. This phrase may need clarification. The word 'stylistic' might well arouse the suspicions of English critics who see the novel as, above all, a source of moral health, and who regard any talk of 'style' as leading to aestheticism, formalism and the other heresies so elegantly propagated in Susan Sontag's 'Notes on Style' (*Against Interpretation*).

They can be reassured: by 'style' I mean almost anything that is worth talking about in a novel, considered as a unique verbal structure. It is not only aesthetes who believe that form and content go indissolubly together: as Trilling puts it, 'the novel makes some of its best moral discoveries or presentations of fact when it is concerned with form' (*The Liberal Imagination*, p. 277). It will be evident that stylistic dynamism, or steady formal change, has been one of the most noticeable characteristics of Western art, as it has of Western technology. Indeed, one contemporary aesthetician, the American Morse Peckham, has evolved a theory of art which detects its very essence not in any ontological qualities, but in what he calls 'non-functional stylistic dynamism'. The question of how far the artifacts of non-Western civilisations also manifest this dynamism is debatable, and has given rise to argument between Morse Peckham and E. H. Gombrich (see *Innovations*, ed. Bergonzi, 1968: pp. 109–21). It is certainly true that in its short life the novel has manifested a very high degree of such dynamism, and it is a real problem to avoid talking as if the novel went on steadily improving between, say, 1730 and 1880. We avoid confusing technical progress and aesthetic merit when we are dealing with the other arts. We may, for instance, admit that Raphael was technically better equipped than Giotto without in any way implying that he was the greater artist. Yet it is, I think, remarkably difficult to see the eighteenth-century novelists entirely in their own terms, without considering them as in some way foreshadowing the achievements of the next century. Discussion of Defoe, for instance, constantly comes back to the question of how far he was or was not an early exponent of true fictional realism. It can hardly be denied that in a few decades the novel underwent an astonishing technical development, and this development in fact involved more than mere technique, since new areas of experience and new ways of understanding were inextricably tied up with formal change. Thus discussion of the novel has become inevitably historicist and teleological; the early masters of the novel are seen as imperfectly pointing towards the later achievement of Flaubert and Turgenev and James. Such a teleology may be yet one more example of the novel's seemingly inevitable involvement with 'ends'; it is very much part of the critical attitude that we associate with James and Conrad and Ford Madox Ford, and which has evolved into an academic critical orthodoxy in England and America (though there are now signs that its power is slackening). That this tendency is not inescapable is shown by Erich Auerbach's brilliant book *Mimesis*, which ranges over many centuries of narrative prose; and it can be partly resisted by giving due weight to Cervantes, as the founder of the Western novel.

Nevertheless I think it is much harder to see the novel in a purely comparative, ahistorical fashion than, say, poems or paintings. One is forced to return to the image of a new territory being steadily opened up, or to Ortega's model of a quarry whose riches are vast but finite. At what point was the last piece of territory occupied, the last vein of the quarry exhausted? Inescapably the answer must be that it was in the decades between 1910 and 1930, in the work of Proust and Joyce, whom Moravia has referred to as 'the gravediggers of the nineteenth-century novel'. *A la recherche du temps perdu* and *Ulysses* mark the apotheosis of the realistic novel, where the minute investigation of human behaviour in all its aspects – physical, psychological and moral – is taken as far as it can go, while remaining within the bounds of coherence. Attempts to force the exploration still further, whether in *Finnegans Wake* or Beckett's later fiction, have their own remarkable interest *sui generis*, but their relation with the novel as normally understood is problematical.

Ulysses quite clearly *is* a novel, of a kind that would not have been totally unfamiliar to the readers of Dickens or Flaubert or Tolstoy. And yet it will not fit into a genre, its nature is unique and paradoxical to a degree that defeats any attempt to apply a single critical formula to it, no matter how tentative (which has not deterred an ever-increasing number of Joyce critics from trying). It is at once the most 'realistic' and the most 'literary' of novels; the most open to experience and the most tightly structured; the most parochial and the most universal. If ever a novel indicated exhaustive finality and the end of a line of development, then *Ulysses* does. But, such is the paradoxical nature of the book, it is not only the end of a trail, but also – to change the metaphor abruptly – a wheel swinging full circle. In one sense *Ulysses* completes the realistic fiction of the nineteenth century, in a total culmination of naturalism; in another sense, it supersedes it, as is suggested by the very title. *Ulysses* is partly underpinned by a classical myth, in a way which seems to deny the novelist's total freedom from dependence on established literary convention. For a parallel we have to go back to the still partly neo-classical Fielding, whose *Amelia* has deliberate Virgilian undertones in its plot.

The present situation is one in which Proust and Joyce and the other masters of the early twentieth century have, in Cyril Connolly's words, 'finished off the novel', and yet where there are very strong cultural and sociological reasons, ranging from the dedication and aspiration of novelists to the commercial needs of the publishing industry, for the continuation of the novel form. Herein lies the dilemma of the contemporary novelist; he has inherited a form whose principal characteristic is novelty, or stylistic dynamism, and yet nearly everything possible to be achieved has already been done. Nevertheless the search for newness continues, often in a very serious and dedicated fashion. Alain Robbe-Grillet, for instance, is a celebrated practitioner of and propagandist for the *nouveau roman* who is totally committed to breaking with the previous forms of the novel. He wishes to abolish the pathetic fallacy, to sever what he conceives of as the sentimental or pseudo-religious ties that supposedly link man to his environment. For Robbe-Grillet it is nonsense to talk about man being 'at home in the world'; in his novels men and objects exist in complete isolation and mutual indifference. Robbe-Grillet's intention was to revolt against the kind of novel – exemplified in Proust or Virginia Woolf or Sartre's *La Nausée* – where objects exist only as part of a character's sensibility and not in their own right. Such an intention has admirable features, and Robbe-Grillet has embodied it in interesting ways in his own fiction. Yet, taking a long view, it is scarcely original, for this is undoubtedly what Joyce was attempting in the 'Ithaca' section of *Ulysses*, the coldly objective catechism that takes place in Leopold Bloom's kitchen when he and Stephen Dedalus are sitting drinking cocoa at the end of their long day. Here Joyce is precisely underlining the objectivity and apartness of things, after so long an immersion in the consciousnesses of the two principal characters. *Ulysses* also seems to lie behind another admired figure of the contemporary *avant-garde*, William Burroughs: at least *The Naked Lunch* looks very like a detailed extrapolation from the 'Circe' (or Nighttown) section.

No matter how much one claims that contemporary fiction is in a state of commendable health, vitality and promise, one must conclude that the novel has significantly changed its character in the era that followed Proust and Joyce. If one compares the state of the novel in the major Western literatures during the period from 1930 to 1970 with the preceding forty years, it is clear that although in the second period one can observe a good deal of inventiveness and energy, there is not the sense of development and spectacular advance that was apparent between 1890 and 1930; by the latter date the Modern Movement had largely exhausted itself, and the possibilities of the realistic novel had been fully exploited. In the last few decades, the novel has, I think, abandoned freedom for genre, in various important but unremarked ways.

It is true that the novel has never been quite so free and unconditioned as one might imagine from reading *The Rise of the Novel*; no matter how unflinchingly the novelist may try to deal with wholly new kinds of experience, he cannot escape being influenced by the novels that have been written before him; to this extent writing any novel is an implicit literary-critical act. Harry Levin has expressed it very well: 'The novelist must feel a peculiar tension between the words, conventions, and ideas that the masters of his craft have handed on to him and the facts, impressions, and experiences that life continues to offer' (*The Gates of Horn*, 1967: p. 137). The tension is always present: in the nineteenth-century masters, we may say, the pull was most strongly towards life; in the eighteenth-century novel, and again in recent fiction, there is a pronounced pull towards an awareness of craft and convention. At the one extreme we have Tolstoy, who seems to offer not art, but the very substance of life itself, as John Bayley enthusiastically reminds us; at the other extreme we have a devious practitioner of parody and pastiche like John Barth, who has cheerfully remarked that he does not 'know much about reality' (quoted by Robert Scholes, *The Fabulators*, 1967: p. 137).

Recent fiction is, indeed, about life, but scarcely about life in a wholly unconditioned way; the movement towards the genre means that experience is mediated through existing literary patterns and types. This movement is particularly strong in English fiction; the French and many Americans may still feel impelled to strive for novelty, but the English, including the most talented among them, seem to have settled for the predictable pleasures of generic fiction. And so, for that matter, have many Americans: the categories of recent American fiction suggest a truly neo-classical strictness and diversity of genres: the Negro novel, the Jewish novel, the Depression novel, the Beat novel, the Campus novel. The last-named, arising directly out of the circumstances in which many American writers live, forms a thriving literature in itself; the last twenty years or so has seen such novels – of varying degrees of seriousness and achievement – as Lionel Trilling's *The Middle of the Journey*, Mary McCarthy's *Groves of Academe*, Randall Jarrell's *Pictures from an Institution*, Robie Macauley's *The Disguises of Love*, Bernard Malamud's *A New Life*, Jeremy Larner's *Drive, He Said*, and John Barth's *Giles Goat-Boy*.*

A fictional genre may – and probably will – arise out of some new configuration of contemporary experience, but once it has become established it will in turn condition further attempts to reproduce such new experience in fiction : the relation between 'reality' and its literary representation is never a simple one-way process. Kingsley Amis's *Lucky Jim* and the many comic novels stemming from it provide a good example; and there is the instructive case of Malcolm Bradbury's *Eating People is Wrong*, which is an English university novel cast very much in the mould of *Lucky Jim*, but which nevertheless, in its presentation of the hero as a worried academic liberal, also attempts a cross-fertilisation with the American campus novel of the forties and early fifties. An interesting new fictional genre has followed on the fact that an increasing number of Englishmen now visit the United States, often in an academic context. This has been exemplified in books about the Englishman in America such as Andrew Sinclair's *The Hallelujah Bum*, Julian Mitchell's *As Far as You Can Go*, Kingsley Amis's *One Fat Englishman*, Malcolm Bradbury's *Stepping Westward* and Pamela Hansford Johnson's *Night and Silence, Who is Here?* Again, in a very different area, a new aspect of social reality has given rise to a new kind of novel; in our society more and more people are living longer and longer, and old people are increasingly segregated into separate

---

* Generic fiction has, of course, always existed, despite the inherent dynamism of the novel form. A work of illuminating literary history like Kathleen Tillotson's *Novels of the Eighteen-Forties* shows the varities of genre that flourished at that time : the novels of aristocratic life and religious uncertainty; of politics and industrial strife. Yet this was also the decade of *Dombey and Son* and *Vanity Fair* and *Wuthering Heights*, when there was a clear contrast between creative originality and the generic and conventional. In our own time we do not find the conditions for such a contrast, and indeed much fine creative energy now goes into generic modes.

communities, instead of fitting into the larger family unit, as in the past. This situation was explored in a brilliant novel by Muriel Spark, *Memento Mori*, which showed a sensitive yet witty awareness of the predicament of old people and struck a welcome blow against the customary assumption that only the young and healthy are suitable subjects for fiction. One would be tempted to describe it as a wholly original work, if it were not for the way in which its stress on the long memories of the old recalled Proust's *Le Temps retrouvé*. Recently a distinguished first novel, Paul Bailey's *At the Jerusalem*, was devoted to a similar community of old people; although it clearly drew on first-hand observation, one was also inevitably reminded of *Memento Mori* (a work which I am quite prepared to believe Mr Bailey had not read); in this way, even where there is no conscious derivation, fictional genres become established.*

Some novels seem to draw much of their life from a single aspect of some major work of the recent past. Thus I cannot imagine that Anthony Burgess's *Inside Mr Enderby* could have been written without conscious recollection of the scene in *Ulysses* in which Bloom visits the lavatory; nor that the relationship between Radcliffe and Tolson in David Storey's *Radcliffe* does not allude at some level to the relationship between Birkin and Gerald Crich in Lawrence's *Women in Love*. During 1967–8 I interviewed a number of young English novelists for the BBC, and was interested to find that some of them were quite prepared to admit conscious derivation from major novels of the past. David Storey pointed out that the opening page of *Radcliffe*, which describes the hero's first day as a boy at school, was modelled on the opening of *Madame Bovary*. Margaret Drabble said of her first novel, *A Summer Birdcage*: 'A lot of the plot was based on *Middlemarch*, with the two sisters and the honeymoon in Rome, where she realises that she has married a terrible man, and that kind of thing' (BBC recording, 1967: 'Novelists of the Sixties'). Miss Drabble also observed that a scene in her novel, *Jerusalem the Golden*, in which the heroine reads a diary dating from her dead mother's youth, has analogies in Arnold Bennett's *Hilda Lessways* and in Maupassant's *Une Vie*. Such borrowings and allusions have been commonplace throughout the ages in poetry and drama, forms which place less of a premium on originality, but

---

* John Updike's *The Poorhouse Fair* is a distinguished American example of this genre.

to find them in the contemporary novel indicates that the form is losing its total commitment to originality and the immediate unique response to individual experience. (Plagiarism has always been regarded as a far more serious offence in the novelist than in the poet.) David Lodge has drawn particular attention to this state of affairs in his entertaining novel *The British Museum is Falling Down*, in which the hero, a graduate student of literature, constantly interprets his experience in terms of literary parody. In an interview David Lodge observed:

> The *British Museum* book is partly a sort of effort to exorcise the enormous influence that any student of literature feels, the influence of the major modern writers. It's a kind of joke on myself in a way. The basic idea which provokes the parodies in the book is that the hero is a student of modern literature who's so steeped in modern literature that everything that happens to him comes to him moulded by some master of modern fiction, and this is suggested in the shifts of the language of the book into pastiche or parodies of various novelists. This obviously I think has an analogy with the situation of a young writer somewhat intimidated, fascinated and occasionally infuriated by the sense that it's all been done better than you'll ever be able to do it. You could see, I suppose, the parody technique in that novel as a way of meeting ironically that particular problem. (BBC recording, 1967: 'Novelists of the Sixties') *

Authors who do not go as far as parody, but who do make use of conscious allusion, or who derive their plots from other works, are inevitably departing from the premises of the traditional realistic novel. If one is not writing in the realistic tradition, then one can be a good deal more overt about such derivation, as we see in the work of a fabulist such as William Golding: the relationship between *The Lord of the Flies* and R. M. Ballantine's *The Coral Island*, and between *The Inheritors* and Wells's 'A Story of the Stone Age', is well known. There are many possibilities open to writers of fiction who reject the demand for total novelty, and who prefer to write in a conscious relation to other literature; to do this need not invalidate the author's essential originality. *Hamlet* is no less a great and original work for being one more example of a well-worn Renaissance genre, the tragedy of revenge.

---

* Reprinted in *Alta: University of Birmingham Review*, Winter 1968–9.

What is less welcome is the way in which much mediocre contemporary fiction has been unconsciously generic, partly because of the narrowness of the experience which the authors can put into it, but more importantly because of the thoroughness with which they have internalised the formulas of countless other modern novels in a similar vein, and then proceeded to interpret their own supposedly unique experience in accordance with those formulas. I am referring, I should add, to novels which make some claim to literary seriousness, and which get reviewed in the intellectual weeklies; not to avowedly commercial magazine fiction. How often, for instance, does one find a novel about a sensitive young man leaving university and going into advertising, having qualms about it, more or less overcoming them, having an affair with one girl – a secretary, perhaps, or his boss's wife – but finally marrying another? Or about a scholarship boy from the provinces who has climbed up the class ladder, but whose origins continue to trip him up? Or about a very sensitive, rather neurotic girl, living in an Earls Court bedsitter and having sexual difficulties – conventional, or lesbian, or both? There are many more types, given the immense possibilities in contemporary experience – which, as I have suggested, are always being enlarged – but one is struck by the way in which they fall precisely into types. A young and inexperienced writer will work hard at a novel which he or she is convinced is a faithful account of unique experience, only to produce a book which is uncannily like countless other novels by writers in similar circumstances. Fiction reviewers, who generally have to dispose of a lot of books in little space, have evolved a special vocabulary, a shorthand of deliberate clichés, for dealing with the principal genres of contemporary fiction. Thus the three examples I have just described might more briefly be summed up in this fashion :

(1) Lightly written tale of nice young adman with scruples. He overcomes them, sleeps with the boss's wife, but marries the girl from back home.
(2) Dogged account of clever but insecure scholarship boy who falls off the ladder half-way up.
(3) Fey, mixed-up Joanna, in Earls Court bedsitter, has trouble with boy – and girl friends.

Edmund Wilson has condemned book reviewers for their excessive reliance on clichés (The Bit Between My Teeth, 1966 : pp. 561-70). He made some telling points in doing so, but failed to realise that these apparent clichés form a highly conventionalised vocabulary for dealing with an equally conventionalised product. Many such books should, of course, never be published, and are put on the market only because of the complex speculative economics of the publishing business. One publisher, T. G. Rosenthal, has remarked, 'surely fiction publishing is the only form of cultural life where intelligent and serious-minded men and women make available to the public *bad* works of art, knowing them to be bad and knowing also that they will lose money' (*New Statesman*, 22 March 1968). By no means all such books are irredeemably bad; some are the products of modest but interesting talents, whose lack of real originality is compounded by the cultural situation is which they are placed. There is an infinite pathos in the thought of so many aspirants, each believing that he or she is going to produce a further unique version of 'the one bright book of life', and in the event turning out infinitely minor variations on a standard cultural artifact. Granted that most novelists are likely to be teachers or advertising men or journalists or discontented housewives, and that these ways of life will be frequently drawn on for fictional purposes, one must still insist that fiction that is deliberately, even wilfully, generic is likely to be more promising than fiction that is ignorantly and unconsciously generic, while pretending to be free and unconditioned. The American campus novel, which is the most calculatedly generic form of all contemporary fiction in English, has produced several works of real literary distinction. One tends to read such novels rather like Renaissance poems; not looking for newness in the basic topics, situations or motifs, but always ready to appreciate the individual skill and grace with which the writer treats his familiar material.

There are other ways in which the novel seems to have lost its newness, and to be no longer novel. Once, of course, the form of the novel and the sensibility that went with it were radical, even subversive, projecting a bourgeois and individualistic attack on aristocratic values and traditional sanctities. In Martin Green's words:

What would we, as men of taste and principle, have said to *Moll Flanders* and *Pamela*? No; and we would have been right; but it would have been an arid rightness. Sensibility was changing (for the better or the worse is not the only question to ask) and the novel was destined to become a great literary form. ('A New Sensibility', in *Cambridge Review*, Winter 1966-7)

Leslie Fiedler has remarked that in its concern with humble cultural modes and forces the novel was an early version of Pop Art. And by using as its vehicle the printed book, which was the original mass-produced object, the novel became involved with the values of the Gutenberg era; as a cultural artifact it was characterised by wide distribution and private consumption. But over a couple of centuries the novel's radical role has been changed into a moderately conservative one, and the technology with which it is involved, instead of being revolutionary, has now become slightly old-fashioned. So we have Susan Sontag complaining that, in comparison with radically *avant-garde* art-forms in other media, the novel is painfully backward: 'It has sunk to the level of an art form deeply, if not irrevocably, compromised by philistinism' (*Against Interpretation*, 1967: p. 102). She earnestly demands fiction that will be really obscure, challenging and unfamiliar. Alain Robbe-Grillet makes a similar demand for a total break with the past, although he implies that the *nouveau roman* has satisfactorily made such a break. He dismisses out of hand all the traditional attributes of the novel – characters, story, atmosphere – which he sees as linked to an obsolete social, epistemological and ultimately metaphysical frame of reference. Robbe-Grillet shows a forceful tendency to throw out the baby with the bathwater, and it is not clear just how much meaning the word 'novel' could legitimately claim if his demands were fully met. I shall return to this point in the next chapter. He is very insistent that the formal devices of the traditional novel were all ways of reinforcing the basic coherence of the world:

> All the technical elements of the narrative – the systematic use of the past definite tense and of the third person, the unconditional adoption of chronological development, linear plots, a regular graph of the emotions, the way each episode tended towards an end, etc. – everything aimed at imposing the image of a stable universe, coherent, continuous, univocal, and wholly decipherable. (*Snapshots and Towards a New Novel*, 1965: p. 63)

In his reference to the metaphysical implications of the past definite tense, Robbe-Grillet is indulging in a typically French piece of parochialism, by endowing a nicety of French grammar with universal significance, just as Roland Barthes does in *Writing Degree Zero*. Apart from this, many of the features that he attributes to an untenable or otherwise obnoxious *Weltanschauung* look very like the characteristics of the typographical medium, as outlined by Marshall McLuhan: 'the unconditional adoption of chronological development, linear plots, a regular graph of the emotions, the way each episode tended towards an end'. As David Lodge has remarked, the novel, 'of all literary genres, is the one most firmly fixed in the Gutenberg galaxy. It is the characteristic literary product of the printing press' (*Language of Fiction*, 1966: p. 38). If McLuhan is right, the dominance of print-technology brought with it a linear, schematic, and successive view of experience, qualities which seem inherent in the form of the novel. Admittedly, many novelists have tried to break away from these limitations, of which the necessity for simple chronological development has been the most tyrannical. Robbe-Grillet has written cogently about the problem of handling time in a novel: 'Why should we try to reconstitute the time that belongs to clocks in a tale that is only concerned with human time? Isn't it wiser to think of our own memory, which is *never* chronological?' (*Snapshots and Towards a New Novel*, p. 63). Many novelists before him have had similar feelings about the way in which objective chronology falsifies the truth of subjective recollection. As Kierkegaard put it, 'Life can only be lived forward and understood backward.'

Tristram Shandy is a celebrated early revolt against conventional chronology; and at the beginning of the twentieth century the subtle minds of Joseph Conrad and Ford Madox Ford were much exercised by this question. In their endless discussions of the art of fiction they evolved the concept of the 'time-shift', which is dramatically employed in the opening chapters of *Nostromo*, although its most triumphant embodiment is in Ford's *The Good Soldier*, where the narrator unfolds his story in piecemeal fashion, fragment by fragment as his memories come back to him. (Robbe-Grillet's apparent indifference to what had been accomplished in English forty or fifty years before he wrote is further evidence of French cultural insularity.) Other novelists have aspired to the simultaneity of a cubist painting, where the same object is seen from several points of view at once, or to a multiple narrative that recalls a succession of musical chords. There are the superimposed narratives of Philip Toynbee's *Tea with Mrs Goodman*, or the desperate expedient of William Burroughs's 'fold-in' technique, an attempt to achieve by random means the atemporality which Ford and Conrad deliberately sought with the 'time-shift'. One can find instances of authors being uncertain whether or not to employ a rearranged time-sequence, as Scott Fitzgerald was in *Tender is the Night*. James Joyce made a characteristic gesture against the irreversibility of normal chronology by beginning *Finnegans Wake* with the second half of a broken sentence whose opening words appear only 600 pages later, at the end of the novel; thus implying that the work should properly be printed as a continuous strip with no beginning or end, or at least bound in such a way as to have no first or last page, in a very embodiment of Viconian circularity.

One of the most striking and successful recent attempts to meet the challenge of chronology is by another practitioner of the *nouveau roman*, Michael Butor's *L'Emploi du temps* (*Passing Time*), which combines a narrative giving us the hero's present experience with a diary containing his experiences of several months before. Yet the fact that so many different attempts are made suggests that there is a degree of intractability in the problem; no matter how much the writer wants to dissolve conventional chronology, the use of flash-backs and time-shifts seems to go against the grain of the medium. There is often resistance by the reader, which may not be entirely due to laziness, and which the author must consciously overcome. The film, on the other hand, is a medium which has achieved a much greater freedom in the treatment of time, one which audiences accept as a matter of course. The difference lies, I think, in the simple but fundamental fact that the novel is necessarily a book, and that books have numbered pages. An expectation of sequaciousness and inevitable forward movement is set up in the reader that does not occur in the same way when we are watching a film. Poetry, too, as a fundamentally spoken form, can easily escape from the confines of strict chronology. *Paradise Lost* is a good example. Milton's Latinate syntax evades the forward movement of normal English sentence structure, and microcosmically reflects the poem's epic indifference to a conventionally unfolding time-sequence.

In the visual arts, cubism and its derivatives were able to achieve simultaneity of vision and the dissolution of conventional perspective in a far more effective way then anything in printed literature, although in the 'Wandering Rocks' section of *Ulysses* Joyce came remarkably close to it. Again, in poetry, *The Waste Land*, with its frankly cinematic transitions and juxtapositions, was more successful than most novels in creating such an effect. Conrad and Ford and, above all, Joyce, by supreme labours and a virtuoso technique, loosened the grip of lineality and chronology on the novel. Later practitioners of the *avant-garde* novel in France or America have tried to follow them, but I do not think they have surpassed their achievement, or even, most of the time, equalled it. The novel form still remains intractable to radical transformation.

Words themselves are, of course, a conservative and conserving element; inevitably they recall the long generations of human experience that have moulded them, and the writer has always been less radical than the innovator in other arts. In Stephen Spender's words:

> If the literary medium were to become 'new' to the extent that the material a painter works with, or even the instruments for which a composer writes, can be revolutionized for the purposes of his art, then literature would become not merely divorced from 'life', but from language, its own terms, within which writers work. (*The Struggle of the Modern*, 1963, p. 190)

This is pre-eminently true of the novelist, who is not merely tied to words, but to the printed page, unlike the poet who can, if he wishes, by-pass the written word and use a tape-recorder to preserve a poem as a pure aural experience. This simple but crucial limitation must nullify the persuasive demands made by Miss Sontag and others that the novel modernise itself and come into line with other forms of contemporary art. The visual artist need no longer use such antique materials as paint and canvas, since modern technology has put more exciting means in his hands. And the composer of electronic music or *musique concrète* need have nothing to do with living performers and old-fashioned instruments. The most a novelist can do is compose on a typewriter instead of with a pen: but the end-product of his art will still be a small, hard, rectangular object, whose pages are bound along one edge into fixed covers, and numbered consecutively. No matter how revolutionary a novel's content may become, it is still conveyed to the reader by a vehicle that has not essentially changed since the days of Defoe or Richardson. There have, it is true, been recent experiments that have tried to get away from fixed page order by using loose pages or sections, which the reader can rearrange to suit himself, such as Marc Saporta's *Numéro Un* (a book that is known to me only by repute) and B. S. Johnson's *The Unfortunates*. But the practical inconveniences that attend such devices are hardly likely to endear them to readers, and still less to librarians. It might be said that I am overemphasising the role of the book in the existence of the novel, and that the printed medium is no more than a notation, which should not be confused with the work itself, any more than a score in music or a printed poem in poetry. There are large aesthetic questions hovering round this problem, which I am reluctant to raise, but the novel does seem to me different from music or poetry in certain essential respects. The score or the printed poem do undoubtedly exist as notations for an art which in the case of music is certainly aural, and in the case of poetry at least notionally so. Although novels can be read aloud, and often are – one thinks of the recitations from the monthly parts of Dickens's novels, or the serial readings from novels that are so popular on radio programmes such as 'Woman's Hour' – reading a novel is nevertheless in essence a private, individual and silent experience. And from Swift onwards novelists have emphasised the close ties between the novel form and its printed vehicle by the intermittent use of typographical devices, which could not possibly be conveyed in reading aloud. One must conclude, I think, that demands for the total modernisation of the novel are likely to be defeated by the stubbornly traditional qualities of the verbal medium, and by the further limitations that words are likely to assume when they are set down in a printed book. The lesson seems to be that the *avant-garde* novelist will find greater possibilities in other media, notably the cinema. Nevertheless the book is perhaps the most useful of all human inventions, and although it may have lost the supremacy it enjoyed during the Gutenberg era, its sheer convenience is likely to ensure it a prominent place in the electronic age. And although, as I have suggested, it may be the novel's fate to be economically snuffed out, there is a reasonable chance that a literary form called 'the novel' will survive, with a somewhat diminished significance. I do not believe, though, that the future novel will be characterised by stylistic dynamism, by a constant orientation towards novelty; unlike, for instance, Robbe-Grillet, who writes in his essay 'New Novel, New Man', 'the New Novel is merely continuing the process of the constant evolution of fiction'. There is a starry-eyed note about Robbe-Grillet's commitment to constant evolution, for he does not allow for the possibility that roads may have endings. Thus, he remarks, 'there is not the slightest doubt that the exigencies of the anecdote were less compelling for Proust than for Flaubert, for Faulkner than for Proust, for Beckett than for Faulkner' (*Snapshots and Towards a New Novel*, p. 64). 'After Beckett, what?' one is entitled to ask; but Robbe-Grillet does not grasp the evident possibility that Beckett is the end of one particular line. (His argument is in any case questionable, since much of Beckett's fiction is composed of a tissue of anecdotes.)

I have found a useful formula for discussing the possible future of the novel in a recent book by the American musicologist and philosopher of culture, Leonard B. Meyer, *Music, the Arts and Ideas*. Professor Meyer argues that not only contemporary art, but the whole of Western culture, is abandoning the familiar norms of purposive stylistic dynamism, progress and teleological development. He thinks we are moving into a 'period of stylistic stasis, a period characterized not by the linear, cumulative development of a single fundamental style, but by the coexistence of a multiplicity of quite different styles in a fluctuating and dynamic steady-state'. He wishes in fact to substitute the model of 'stasis' (or the 'steady-state') for the model of 'development', although he emphasises that stasis, as he understands it, is compatible with a great deal of local change and movement:

> For stasis, as I intend the term, is not an absence of novelty and change – a total quiescence – but rather the absence of ordered sequential change. Like molecules rushing about haphazardly in a Brownian movement, a culture bustling with activity and change may nevertheless be static. Indeed, insofar as an active, conscious search for new techniques, new forms and materials, and new modes of sensibility (such as have marked our time) precludes the gradual accumulation of changes capable of producing a trend or a series of connected mutations, it tends to create a steady-state, though perhaps one that is both vigorous and variegated. In short – and this is what I hope to show – a multiplicity of styles in each of the arts, coexisting in a balanced, yet competitive, cultural environment is producing a fluctuating stasis in contemporary culture. (1967: p. 102)

I am not certain that I accept the larger cultural implications of Mr Meyer's approach, which is argued at length in his book; it is heavily involved with the assumption that the rate of change of technological development – which in the west has been intimately related to cultural development – is slowing down and may even be achieving its own kind of stasis. Much of Meyer's argument is parochial in a strictly American sense (it is certainly true that a large segment of the American middle class have literally everything they want in life, and have given up the teleological struggle for far-off material goals). He ignores the fact that, taking a global view, as Peter Nettl observes, 'some version of Marxism is the major intellectual orthodoxy of the latter half of the 20th century'. Marxism has no time for the pluralism and relativism implicit in Meyer's view of cultural activity, and it demands a wholly linear and teleological – not to say eschatological – reading of history, in a way which is rooted in Western traditions. And a Marxist would probably see Meyer's phrase about 'a balanced, yet competitive, cultural environment' as a perfect model of neo-capitalist cultural processes. Nevertheless, in its narrower applications, Meyer's argument seems to me substantially true, particularly with reference to the novel.

The situation of the Western novel during the past forty years has been precisely one in which a large amount of local movement has been evident, but no overall development since the achievement of Proust and Joyce and the other major innovators of the early twentieth century. A good small-scale illustration of Meyer's thesis can be seen in the fiction reviews in one of the English weeklies. In an average week the reviewer might discuss several assorted but recognisable types of book: say, a weighty semi-historical novel about family loyalties and industrial strife in a Welsh mining valley in the 1900s; the kind of bedsitter epyllion about fey, mixed-up Joanna that I mentioned previously; a cool, witty, sophisticated contrivance about wife-swapping in the Surrey stockbroker belt; and, from overseas, a translation of the latest gritty version of the *nouveau roman*, and an American study in the comic-apocalyptic vein about the adventures of a psychopathic dwarf with a Ph.D. called Griswold Griswold. None of these books would have anything in common, except the fact that they were all published in the same week (united only by their dateline, as McLuhan observes of the disparate items in a modern newspaper). Certainly the reviewer will have his preferences among them, but he is likely to assume that these books are all representative instances of the contemporary novel, all artifacts of much the same cultural significance, to be given roughly the same kind of attention. Next week the mixture will be different but comparable, and so on through the year. Granted the reviewer may still be looking out for a new *Dombey and Son* or a new *Wuthering Heights*, not to mention a new

Anna Karenina, but the expectation has a somewhat stylized and unreal air about it. Whatever Mr Anthony Burgess may say about 'some great unexpected masterpiece which will burn up the world', no-one seems confident about discovering one. There will be surprises, certainly, but only within a given range of possibilities. Here we have a perfect instance of what Meyer calls a 'fluctuating stasis', taking place within an extensive but closed system of cultural references.

At one point Meyer implicitly answers Ortega's notion about the 'exhaustion' of a given genre:

> the notion of 'exhausting' a style is largely a culture-bound concept, stemming from beliefs in the importance of originality and in the value of individual expression – beliefs important in Western ideology but by no means so in all cultures or in all epochs. (*Music, the Arts and Ideas*, p. 108)

This is undeniable; yet the fact remains that the novel was very much a 'culture-bound' entity, which emerged at a particular phase of history, and was permeated with a belief in originality and the value of individual expression and of individual experience. The ultimate question is whether a movement which, though complicated, is basically circular can have the same significance and value as a forward and linear movement. The novel may, indeed, become generic in the ways that I have tried to indicate, where writers can make conscious use of the fact that they are writing a particular kind of novel; and novels can deliberately draw on earlier novels for their themes or topics or situations. Meyer acknowledges that in a situation of fluctuating stasis, the absolute value of the new, as emphasised by the classical *avant-garde*, becomes impossible: 'the philosophy of the *avant-garde* precludes the possibility of there being an *avant-garde*. For if the world is static and directionless – a perpetual present – how can the forces of art move towards an objective?' One can, of course, turn back to the past and make whatever use one pleases of earlier forms. Meyer gives a valuable account of various ways of utilising previous works of art: paraphrase, borrowing, simulation, and modelling. In literature such usages may be wholly conscious, as in John Barth's adaptation of the eighteenth-century novel in *The Sot-Weed Factor*, or presumably (and lamentably) unconscious, as in C. P. Snow's rewritings of Trollope; no-one has yet gone as far as the hero of Jorge Luis Borges's story, 'Pierre Menard, Author of Don Quixote', who devotes himself to writing a new version of *Don Quixote* in exactly the same words as the original. Such a situation may, indeed, produce much work of merit and interest, as is verifiably the case with contemporary fiction; yet the ideology that sustained the novel for the first two centuries of existence, its belief in unpremediated experience, in originality and individuality and progress, does not seem reconcilable with the aesthetics of fluctuating stasis. If the novel is truly no longer novel, then many of our critical procedures for discussing it will need revision; perhaps, even, we shall do well to think of another name for it.

II Character and Liberalism

Admittedly the English novel has a hard time against such competition. As it stubbornly insists on affirming relations and conflicts between people, on depicting characters and emotions, on developing an exciting plot, on drawing historical and social contexts, and, moreover, on mirroring the individuality of its author, it is not well suited as a model for pseudo-metaphysical programmes.

ALFRED ANDERSCH, in *Times Literary Supplement*,
12 September 1968

W H E N Ortega y Gasset was writing his *Notes on the Novel* in the 1920s he could still take it for granted that the fundamental purpose of the novel was the presentation of character:

> Let the reader recall the great novels of former days that have lived up to the high standards of our time, and he will observe that his attention is turned to the personages themselves, not to their adventures. We are fascinated by Don Quixote and Sancho, not by what is happening to them. In principle a *Don Quixote* as great as the original is conceivable in which the knight and his servant go through entirely different experiences. And the same holds for Julien Sorel or David Copperfield. (*The Dehumanization of Art and Notes on the Novel*, pp. 57–8)

Indeed, Ortega assumed that this interest was being intensified in the work of Proust, which offered opportunities for the ever greater and more leisurely contemplation of character, even if at the expense of dramatically interesting action. And in so far as Proust – like Joyce – represented the culmination of the realistic novel as well as its destruction, Ortega was not wholly wrong. Nevertheless I presume that no intelligent modern reader could read his remarks without some slight incredulity. The notion that character can be considered as an absolute, without necessary reference to a given literary context, is a quintessential nineteenth-century concept; it underlies, for instance, Bradley's *Shakespearean Tragedy*, a celebrated work in which the influence of the nineteenth-century novel is everywhere apparent; it has been pilloried in such a statement of twentieth-century critical orthodoxy as L. C. Knights's *How Many Children Had Lady Macbeth?*

Later opinion has swung sharply in the other direction. The stress is much more on Proust or Joyce in their destructive or innovatory aspects, which seem to make traditional ways of seeing character as an absolute no longer conceivable. Lawrence's well-worn phrase 'You mustn't look in my novel for the old stable ego – of the character' * is frequently invoked. These literary considerations are likely to be backed up by strong but inchoate feelings about the changed nature of reality, the change arising from the decline of religious or metaphysical certainties, the influence of modern psychology, and the public crimes and traumas of the twentieth century. Here, for instance, is Alberto Moravia, in an essay called 'The Man and the Character', written in 1941 (from which I have already quoted his remark about Joyce and Proust as 'grave-diggers of the nineteenth-century novel'):

> This crisis in the character obviously corresponds to a similar crisis in the concept of man. Modern man can be seen as a mere numerical entity within the most terrifying collectives that the human race has ever known. He can be seen as existing not for himself alone but as part of something else, of a collective feeling, idea and organism. It is very difficult to create a character out of such a man, at least in the traditional sense of the word. (*Man as an End*, pp. 70–1)

Moravia was writing during the Second World War, in a country still committed to the ideology of fascism, which took it for granted that man did not exist for himself alone, 'but as part of something else, of a collective feeling, idea and organism'. Fascism may have been defeated, but in the intervening years most advanced societies, whether liberal-democratic or communist, have seen the individual increasingly subject to collective controls, whether by a bureaucratic state apparatus, by the pressures of the industrial urban environment, or by the conditioning apparatus of a capitalist high-consumption society. In such a world the free-standing literary character is indeed likely to be threatened. Moravia, as a traditional humanist, regarded this situation with a certain elegiac tone; his later essays show that he has not lost faith in the future of the novel, but that he regards it as no longer concerned with the presentation of character, but with the inner explorations of the author; the kind of novel, in fact, for which Proust, looked at under another aspect, might serve as a model.

There is a similar analysis in Robbe-Grillet's *Towards a New*

---

* Letter to Edward Garnett, 5 June 1914.

Novel, but the tone is significantly different; there is nothing of the traditional humanist about Robbe-Grillet, who was trained as a scientist before he turned to literature, and whose only concern with humanism is to abolish it. Robbe-Grillet is a brisk operationalist, concerned purely with questions of process and technique, and to my mind an almost perfect exponent of what Marcuse calls the one-dimensional consciousness. (Although underlying the tough modernity of his exposition there is a purely aesthetic concept of the art of the novel that has been inherited virtually unchanged from Flaubert.)

> In fact, the creators of character, in the traditional sense, can now do nothing more than present us with puppets in whom they themselves no longer believe. The novel that contains characters belongs well and truly to the past, it was peculiar to an age – that of the apogee of the individual.
>
> It may not be progress, but it is certain that the present age is rather that of the regimental number. The destiny of the world no longer seems to us to be identified with the rise or fall of a few men or a few families. The world itself is no longer this private property, hereditary and profitable – a sort of prey to be conquered rather than understood. To have a name was no doubt very important in the days of Balzac's kind of bourgeoisie. And to have a character was important too; and the more it became a weapon for hand-to-hand fighting, the hope of achieving success, the exercise of one's ascendency, the more important it was. It was *something*, to have a face, in a universe where personality was at the same time the means and end of every endeavour.
>
> Our world today is less sure of itself and more modest, perhaps because it has abandoned the idea of the omnipotence of the individual, but it is more ambitious too, as it looks beyond it. The exclusive cult of the 'human' has given place to a vaster, less anthropomorphic perception. The novel seems unsure of its step because it has lost what used to be its greatest support – the hero. If it doesn't manage to get back on to a proper footing it will mean that its life is intimately linked to that of a bygone society. If it does manage it, on the other hand, a new path will be open to it, with the promise of new discoveries. (*Snapshots and Towards a New Novel*, pp. 60–1)

Robbe-Grillet's aim seems to be to make the novel a fit occupant of a totalitarian society, where individuals no longer matter; it is not one I find at all congenial. At the same time there is an extraordinary ambivalence in his approach : he sees that the nineteenth-century novel was the historical product of a particular society and set of assumptions about the world which have now largely vanished; yet he also wants the 'novel', as a transcendental entity, to go on existing in a form that bears very little relation to anything previously bearing the name.

At this point I should like to check Robbe-Grillet's theoretical assertions against the way he actually writes novels. *Jealousy* is one of his best-known works; it seems to me a splendid demonstration of Robbe-Grillet's literary power, but a very dubious illustration of his ideas. *Jealousy* is one of those novels – *Emma* is a classical example – which seem significantly different on a second reading. On a first encounter one receives a clear impression of the setting, a bungalow somewhere in the tropics, and of two characters, a woman called A... and a man called Franck, who is a frequent visitor to the house. By degrees one realises that there is an intrigue developing between them, amid the stony indifference of all the natural and man-made objects that form their environment; only very slowly does the reader come to understand there is a third person always present, who observes everything and speculates a great deal, but who apparently never speaks. This can be none other than A...'s husband, who is the narrator. And although Robbe-Grillet radically rearranges the time-sequence, and totally dissolves conventional narration – in ways that owe an immense amount to the methods of the cinema – the story moves forward with a finely sustained suspense. But when one rereads the novel, one knows from the beginning that the narrator is A...'s husband; it is his voice that describes in such meticulous detail the rows of banana-trees outside, the condition of the flaking paintwork on the balustrade, the ice-cubes in the drink, the shape of a squashed centipede on the wall. Why then, one wants to ask, is he telling us all this? Are they significant illustrations of his state of mind? Why has he selected *these* particular images out of all possible ones? At this point, objects lose their autonomy and become incorporated once more into a human consciousness, just as in Proust. *Jealousy* is a brilliant performance, but the fact that it is diminished rather than enhanced by a second reading suggests a crucial deficiency in Robbe-Grillet's method. Even on a first reading. A... and Franck, for all the deliberately fragmentary and elusive fashion in which they are presented, gradually assume the attributes of traditional fictional characters, if only because the mind insists on seeing them in that way. And on a second reading the shadowy narrator-husband assumes a certain substantiality, in terms of the obsessive images that he dwells on and weaves into repetitive patterns.

In fact the whole of Robbe-Grillet's programmatic enterprise – of presenting a 'cleansed' impersonal world of objects, which can be set over against human activity, with the aim of reducing man's domineering place in the universe – is shaky. It rests on a naïve epistemology, which posits a total separation between objects and human perception, whereas it is now a philosophical and psychological commonplace to regard perception as a learnt and active process, so that the objects we see are part of a complex pattern of perception, which is in large measure culturally generated. Robbe-Grillet's notion of avoiding anthropomorphic metaphor in any case stops short in an arbitrary fashion, as Moravia has pointed out. Robbe-Grillet objects to the description of the sea as 'smiling', while approving such a supposedly neutral epithet as 'blue'. But, Moravia observes:

> The very fact of giving a vast expanse of water the name of sea is equivalent to humanising it, for the fact of indicating an object by a word involves withdrawing it from the anonymous objectivity of the pre-human and extra-human world and incorporating it into the human world. In other words the word 'sea' is objective only in appearance; in reality it humanises, that is subjectivises, the object precisely because it names it. So at most the method only allows for allotting limits to the humanising process, such as not allowing us to forget that the sea has properties and characteristics which are not human. (*Man as an End*, p. 187)

Language as well as perception necessarily involves man with his physical environment.

The dehumanisation that Robbe-Grillet looks for is not new in twentieth-century aesthetics: its roots can be found in the programmes and activities of the innovating artists of sixty years ago – those whom Frank Kermode has dubbed the 'paleo-modernists' in distinction to 'neo-modernists' such as Robbe-Grillet himself. One thinks, for instance, of T. E. Hulme's insistence that a truly contemporary art should be 'geometrical' rather than 'organic' or 'vital', and that all obtrusive traces of the human should be diminished. (As Kermode has remarked of this spirit, 'few had any idea of what was going to happen when, having got thoroughly *abstract* about human beings, one might feel that the most appropriate means of dealing with them would be to turn them into lampshades' – *Essays in Criticism*, October 1956.) Over the decades the attempt to achieve a total impersonality, the desire to abolish the traces of the human, has remained a major feature of twentieth-century art: we find the tendency to dehumanisation being deplored in the twenties by a conservative such as Ortega y Gasset and in the fifties by a Marxist such as Ernst Fischer. And it has been linked with fascism, in a crude and naïve fashion, by C. P. Snow and those who think like him. The phenomenon is discussed in Wylie Sypher's book *Loss of the Self in Modern Literature and Art*, which is pervaded by a wistful hope that somewhere, somehow a new humanism will emerge from the ashes of the old, even in the most unpromising contexts. Beckett features inevitably in Mr Sypher's discussion, and offers a convenient point to return to the question of character in the novel. As it has developed from *Murphy*, Beckett's fiction shows a steady decline from character to an almost wholly sub-human mode of existence, ruined creatures with no more life in them than Robbe-Grillet's centipede crushed on the wall. And yet how superbly articulate they all are, how much and how well they all talk; seldom can a movement towards silence and non-being have been so talkatively expressed. It is in the extraordinary vitality of his language that the central paradox of Beckett's art resides: his humanoids all have a very cultivated and fluent way of expressing themselves. They are also, even *in extremis*, irresistibly comic: it may be that in the English-speaking world – or at least in the British Isles – the idea of Absurdity has more comic associations than in continental contexts: the roads to Edward Lear and Lewis Carroll remain open, as the French surrealists were fascinated to discover over a generation ago. Thus, when Georg Lukács remarks of *Molloy*, 'He presents us with an image of the utmost human degradation – an idiot's vegetative existence' (*The Meaning of Contemporary Realism*, 1963: p. 31), we feel that he has rather missed the point. Beckett's characters, or whatever one calls them, *are* images of the utmost human degradation; and yet, to adapt a famous line from Yeats, 'Molloy and Malone are gay!' In Beckett the language itself makes a continued act of defiance. Nevertheless it is appropriate to put questions about the ultimate human worth of what Beckett offers. A great deal of Beckett criticism is narrowly technical, concerned with the endless challenge to explication that his writing presents: to offer a blunt criticism in the language of old-fashioned humanism – in Lukács's case, with a Marxist accent – ought to give the discussion of this strange genius a greater urgency and point.

However we interpret him, we can agree that Beckett has taken the end of the individual, and the supersession of character, to an ultimate point. George Steiner has offered some suggestive though extreme speculations about the end of individualism, and what might replace it. Pursuing McLuhan's ideas about the way in which the electronic media are forming a new global community and affecting the 'retribalisation of man', after the fragmentary individualism of the print era, Steiner suggests that the growing practice of transplanting vital human organs may lead to a diminished sense of the uniqueness of human personality.

> The concepts of human interrelation, or organic community, which we now use superficially or as moral clichés, would come to express concrete realities and felt experience. Man would then pass, for the first time, from the closed sphere of private being into that of collectivity. (*Language and Silence*, 1967 : pp. 418–19)

Cannibalism, presumably, might achieve a similar result. Steiner continues his argument, peering ahead into the collective human future desiderated by the Marxists :

> Our present notion of autonomous identity may be the result of a long, painful process of psychic individuation, of withdrawal from the collective group (the myth of Jacob wrestling with the Angel may be read as a metaphor of the agonizing struggle through which individual members of the species achieved a sense of self, a name). History might then be defined as an episode of personal self-definition, of *egoism* in the proper sense, between much longer pre- and post-historical eras of collective being. Such collectivity would obviously and fundamentally change the nature of art and literature. The voice of man would again be choral. (Ibid.)

In such a situation, it goes without saying, the novel could no longer exist, although other forms of narrative might survive.

After these high-flying generalisations, I would like to pull the discussion back to the question of character in the novel. Although we may truly say that the novel is the characteristic literary form of an age of bourgeois individualism, the novel is concerned with more than simple individuals. The account of an isolated hero, asserting himself in the face of an alien or hostile environment, is, in fact, the typical pattern of American fiction. But in the European novel, character emerges when the unconditioned human organism is placed in a dialectical relationship with a social and moral order that, though intelligible, is complex, stratified and demanding. Again, although it is, I think, reasonable to refer to the nineteenth-century realistic novel as a whole, regardless of nationality, when talking at a certain level of generalisation, one should also make further definitions in terms of national cultural division. In the French novel the relation between the individual and society, although intimate, is apt to be sharp and antagonistic: one thinks of Rastignac's apostrophe to Paris at the end of *Père Goriot*: 'It's war to the death between us now', which Robbe-Grillet may have had in mind in his remark about character being 'a weapon for hand to hand fighting'. In the English novel the tone is gentler, and the stress is on the ties of affection and community, radiating outwards from the family to the larger social grouping. If Rastignac's farewell characterises the French novel, then a comparable epiphany from English fiction would be that tender moment in *Middlemarch* when Mrs Bulstrode takes her husband's hand in a gesture of affection and support, after his misdeeds have been exposed. Martin Green has illuminatingly discussed this division in a recent essay ('British Marxists and American Freudians', in *Innovations*, ed. Bergonzi); he contrasts the stress on the value of 'simple ordinary community life' that we find in Lawrence or Raymond Williams, with Sartre's intense dislike of the same thing, expressed, for instance, in his book on Genet, which attacks the narrowness and viciousness of the peasant community in which Genet grew up. This 'English' attitude, which regards the ideal relation between the individual and the community as one of support rather than conflict is given a theoretical dimension in Raymond Williams's essay 'Realism and the Contemporary Novel'.

On the Continent it seems to be assumed that the realistic novel of character has had its day; while American critics are agreed that it has never properly flourished in the United States. But in Britain it is widely held that such novels can and should go on being written, with few overt concessions to the changed *Weltanschauung* of the twentieth century. If we turn to the recent pronouncements of English novelists and critics, we find ourselves in a different intellectual world from that inhabited by Moravia or Robbe-Grillet. Here character is seen, not as an obsolescent feature of the novel whose existence can no longer be justified – as it is, for instance, by the American novelist John Hawkes, who has remarked, 'I began to write fiction on the assumption that the true enemies of the novel were plot, character, setting, and theme' * – but as something self-evidently essential. And if there seems to be a prevalent decline in the importance of character, then this may be deplored but not regarded as historically inevitable. John Bayley's significantly named *The Characters of Love* asserts that not only should characters exist, but that their creators should love them; a sentiment which, one imagines, would excite the cold derision of Robbe-Grillet:

> What I understand by an author's love for his characters is a delight in their independent existence as *other people*, an attitude towards them which is analogous to our feelings towards those we love in life; and an intense interest in their personalities combined with a sort of detached solicitude, a respect for their freedom. This might be – indeed should be – a truism, but I suppose it to be one no longer. The writers whom we admire to-day do not appear to love their characters, and the critics who appraise their books show no sign of doing so either. For a writer or critic to show delight in a character would seem to-day rather naïve, an old-fashioned response left over from the days of Dickens or Surtees. Characters, it seems, are no longer objects of affection. The literary personality has gone down in the world. (1960: pp. 7–8)

The disagreement about whether character is substantive or merely one element in a complex of literary qualities has become perennial: one thinks of Knights's attack on Bradley's way of interpreting Shakespeare; or the arguments about *Ulysses* between those who see it as an immensely intricate verbal structure, radically unlike traditional novels, and those who insist on regarding *Ulysses* as, before everything else, a realistic novel, about three people called Leopold, Stephen and Molly in the city of Dublin in the year 1904.

Bayley's discussion is important; he has continued it in his more recent book *Tolstoy and the Novel* and several articles. To put his argument in cruder terms than he might wish: he is more interested in content than in form, and he is vehemently opposed to the aestheticism or formalism that is most interested in the shape of fiction, in asserting the presence of art, or in constructing closed

---

* Quoted by Robert Scholes in *The Fabulators* (New York, 1967) p.68.

worlds of the imagination. For Bayley, Tolstoy is the supreme novelist – a judgement from which I presume no-one would wish to dissent – because he presents not *a* world, but *the* world; in Tolstoy's fiction the experiences of the novel flow inevitably into our own experiences, and the characters we meet have the freedom, the opacity, the unpredictability of the people we ourselves know and love. All else is 'pastoral', where experience is cut down to size, structured and otherwise interfered with in the interests of some formal irrelevance. Even so great a novelist as Proust is inevitably limited, by tidying up life and imposing moral formulas on it: 'Tolstoy is like life and Proust is like a vision of it ...' I accept this particular insight, while feeling disturbed by Bayley's need to press home such dichotomies. He regards the great novelist – who is mostly though not exclusively Tolstoy – as marked by his total acceptance of and openness to life in all its aspects; an acceptance which in some moods, it seems, is Franciscan, and in others Stoic. Again I feel partial agreement, then sharp disagreement. What Bayley seems to be asking for is contemplation, while overlooking the fact that contemplation is usually something we direct towards art rather than life, which so often involves us in action of welcome or unwelcome kinds. There are times when Bayley's reasonable preference for Life becomes so emphatic that one wonders why he wants to bother with objects called novels at all : in the words of the *avant-garde* composer John Cage :

> Our attention is to affirm this life, not to bring order out of a chaos nor to suggest improvements in creation, but simply to wake up to the very life we're living, which is so excellent once one gets one's mind and one's desires out of its way and lets it act of its own accord. (Quoted by Ihab Hassan, in *Innovations*, ed. Bergonzi, p. 101)

It is certainly true that Bayley is not interested in novels as achieved wholes, shapes carved out of time and experience, for to profess such an interest is the mark of the formalist. His intention is directed to fragments and sudden illuminations; moments which offer some sharp or poignant epiphany of character, and brief revelations of the resilient facticity of the world, of which he provides some engaging lists. 'Ransome in *The Shadow Line* with his weak heart; the bottle of quinine that has been filled with sand; Captain Mac-Whirr and his barometer; the great flake of rust that springs off the bulkhead of the pilgrim ship and persuades Lord Jim that she is sinking – these things have an existence which is not to be got behind' (*The Characters of Love*, p.267). 'What becomes of Achilles's armour, Alison's arse, Othello's handkerchief, Vronsky's mare, Bloom's kidney?' (*Essays in Criticism*, April 1968). Such an approach makes one inclined to call John Bayley the Longinus of neo-realist criticism. There is no awareness in his writing that it is at such moments when, as one readily agrees, the novelist seems to offer us the very stuff of life itself, not part of a pre-arranged artifact, that the fictional illusion rises to new heights of epistemological and moral *trompe l'œil*.

In so far as the novelist must mediate experience to us through words, then we can never touch the stuff of life through him, no matter how intense an illusion we may have of it. The problem of the distance between words and the reality they are supposed to stand for remains as stark as when Wittgenstein wrote the *Tractatus Logico-Philosophicus* (whatever direction his subsequent thought may have taken), and it is appropriate that Harry Levin should have used propositions from that work as the epigraph to the final chapter, called 'Realism and Reality', of *The Gates of Horn*, his admirable study of the French realists. To say that a novel is made out of words is not to call it a species of symbolist poem – even if some novelists may be quite happy at such a prospect – for words themselves are made up out of lived human meanings, which is a complementary lesson we may learn from the later Wittgenstein. Yet the gap between words and reality, and the inevitable distortions and refractions that go with it, inevitably remains, though the achievement of the great novelist is to narrow it considerably, and to persuade us that it has disappeared.

These dilemmas spring from a perennial dichotomy. At one extreme is Mr Bayley, wanting the fictional medium to be reduced to a total transparency, through which one may contemplate the excellencies of life itself; at the other extreme is someone like John Barth, who has remarked, 'If you are a novelist of a certain type of temperament, then what you really want to do is reinvent the world. God wasn't too bad a novelist, except he was a Realist.' *
Since I find Barth's totalitarian aestheticism even more alarming than Bayley's naïve moral realism I suppose that if pressed hard enough I would opt for the latter. But I would strive to avoid such

---

* Quoted by Robert Scholes in *The Fabulators*, p. 136.

a disastrous choice. To my mind the tensions between the real world of shared human meanings and experience, and the multitudinous forms of fiction, must be preserved and not allowed to collapse towards either pole.

On particular works and points of interpretation John Bayley is a very much better critic than these stringent comments on his general stance might imply, but that stance seems to me so significant, and so representative of a peculiarly English way of looking at literature, that I have allowed myself to discuss it in some detail. In *The Characters of Love*, which is the book I have been most concerned with, Bayley appears as a remarkably ahistorical writer, who is happy to discuss a poem by Chaucer, a play by Shakespeare, and a novel by Henry James in the same context; in *Tolstoy and the Novel*, however, he adopts a different approach and places Tolstoy in the context of nineteenth-century Russian intellectual and literary development, even to the point of being very free with Russian turns of phrase, quoted in the original. Yet, although Bayley has a keen and widely ranging mind, and despite his confessed orientation to life rather than art, his approach is rather narrow. The interest is exclusively literary, quite as much so as that of the aesthetes whom he castigates; one has little sense of the way in which literature is often messily involved with history, politics and the whole spectrum of human behaviour; nor, for that matter, of how it can be subversive as well as reassuring. To say this of John Bayley may be unfair; for if it is true of him, then it is true of most English critics, not excluding the present writer. Bayley's dedication to a Tolstoyan openness to, and acceptance of, experience is very attractive on an ontological plane. Yet it can rather easily be translated into simple complacence. Bayley finds fault with Michel Butor, who claims that the *nouveau roman*, by enabling us to have a new vision of reality, can help us out of that 'profound malaise, the night in which we are all struggling'. Bayley tartly comments that 'any theory of the novel must be crude which starts from the premise that we are all struggling in the night of a profound malaise', and associates it with the baneful influence of socialist realism (*Tolstoy and the Novel*, 1966: pp. 157–8). But it could be, initially, a conviction about life, not merely a theory of the novel, and if it were, then it could find Christian as well as Marxist ratifications. Life *is* intolerable a great deal of the time, and Keats was not writing as a socialist realist when he said that he would 'reject a petrarchal coronation – on account of my dying day, and because women have cancers'. Michel Butor is certainly wrong if he believes that the *nouveau roman* will give us a new sense of reality; yet he is writing in an established continental tradition that sees literature as a potentially revolutionary and subversive weapon, as well as an object for contemplation. On the Continent, literature is taken with the kind of seriousness that means that writers are, on occasion, persecuted, imprisoned, or even shot, a state of affairs inconceivable in England.

A similar concept of character to John Bayley's was presented by Iris Murdoch, in an influential essay called 'Against Dryness', published in *Encounter* in 1961. Her approach is more overtly philosophical: she argues that in the face of the failure of traditional liberal philosophy to develop an adequate concept of man, the novel can give us a full sense of the uniqueness and mysteriousness of human personality. She finds these qualities exemplified in the great novelists of the nineteenth century, particularly the Russians, and contrasts their kind of novel with the typical fictional modes of the twentieth century: the 'journalistic' novel of accumulated fact and information, a degenerate descendant of literary naturalism which is often a formless, inflated daydream; and the 'crystalline' novel of dry aesthetic concentration, which is more concerned with an ideal of form than with conveying the variousness of reality. A normative note emerges at the end of Miss Murdoch's essay:

> Real people are destructive of myth, contingency is destructive of fantasy and opens the way for the imagination. Think of the Russians, those great masters of the contingent. Too much contingency of course may turn art into journalism. But since reality is incomplete, art must not be too much afraid of incompleteness. Literature must always present a battle between real people and images; and what it requires now is a much stronger and more complex conception of the former.

There is a clear consonance between Iris Murdoch's ideas and John Bayley's, and, again, the contrast between these ideas and the characteristic utterance of the continental or American *avant-garde* is striking. Yet it will be evident to the readers of Miss Murdoch's innumerable novels that she has conspicuously failed to put her ideas into practice, at least since *The Bell*, which came out in 1958. Her later novels have increasingly turned into fantasies or myths, full of complex manipulative patterns in which the contingency of life is subdued by the rigid will of the author. They are very far removed from the Tolstoyan openness to which she aspires. One might, I suppose, argue that if, as is almost comically the case, any given character in a Murdoch novel is likely to have sexual relations with any other character or characters, regardless of age, gender or kindred, then this is not really authorial manipulation and pattern-making, but rather an insistence on contingency, a clear recognition of the fact that one never really knows what people might be up to. As arguments go, this could be worth attending to, but what it implies is not so much contingency as a willed idea of contingency.

In 'Against Dryness' Miss Murdoch insisted on the need to respect the 'opacity of persons', by which she means their impenetrability and unpredictability, their resistance to any form of appropriation, whether political or aesthetic. But the characters of her own fiction are opaque in ways that suggest primarily the limitations of their creator. Although Miss Murdoch has some striking literary gifts, she is largely lacking in the essential novelistic ones – in her own formulation – of insight, sympathy and true imagination (as opposed to an endlessly ramifying fancy). In the world, or worlds, of Miss Murdoch's novels, characters, often of considerable complexity, are presented to us and can, indeed, be made to look and sound very real; but they can relate to each other only by some form of arbitrary sexual encounter, or an act of violence, or by involvement in the complicated or dangerous physical activity that Miss Murdoch describes rather well. One thinks, for instance, of the farcical account of stealing the cage containing the film-star dog, Mister Mars, in *Under the Net*: the episodic structure of this novel allowed it to contain a high proportion of such incidents, which provided some admirable entertaining passages. Again, there are the antics on the tower in *The Sandcastle* and the scene in the same novel where a car falls into a river; or the passage in *The Unicorn* where Effingham Cooper is lost at night on the moors; or the graphic episode in *The Nice and the Good* in which two characters are trapped in a cave by the rising tide and narrowly escape drowning. It is in such extreme situations that Miss Murdoch seems most at home, rather than with the quieter but more central forms of human behaviour, about which she seems to know or care remarkably little. But a recent radio interview with Iris Murdoch suggested that since 1961 she has tended to bring her ideas about the novel more into line with her own practice. In 'Against Dryness' she expressed her distaste for fantasy which produced 'small myths, toys, crystals'. But in 1968 she stressed her own concern with pattern-making in a way that looks like no more than a belated recognition of the truth, but which undercuts her own previous convictions:

> I think it's true that the patterns which keep up the structure in my work – I think this is true of a lot of novelists writing today – are sexual, mythological, psychological patterns, and not the great hub of society which a nineteenth-century writer relied on. Of course, in writers like Dickens and many others one could think of, both sorts of structure obviously exist together. I regard my difference from them as a shortcoming – this is something I wish I could solve or get over in my own work. But the whole question of structure is harder – there are probably other reasons, but certainly for the reasons we've discussed: the nature of society having changed, and one's confidence in it having so largely evaporated.
> I think myself that pattern in a novel is very important. This is something which writers vary about: some want a very clear pattern and others don't mind. I care very much about pattern, and I want to have a beautiful shape, an apprehensible shape. (*Listener*, 4 April 1968)

Miss Murdoch is, perhaps, trying to get the best of all possible worlds, but her statement is pleasantly honest. And the fact that she has changed her mind in view of her own practical difficulties in novel-writing does not destroy the importance of the ideas she advanced in 'Against Dryness'.

There is a comparable discussion of character in the late W. J. Harvey's book, *Character and the Novel*, published in 1965. His ideas are similar to those of John Bayley and Iris Murdoch, although his book contains more argument and aims to be more theoretically systematic. It develops an ambitious attempt to understand the nature of fiction by describing the novelist's interpretation of reality in terms of four Kantian 'constitutive categories', through which he mediates and structures experience: Time, Identity, Causality and Freedom. Harvey's discussion is ingenious, exacting, and full of incidental illuminations, but not, I think, altogether convincing. Yet for my present purpose his significance lies in the way in which he approaches the novel primarily in terms of character; his book contains many vigorous defences of the necessity of character, and he quotes approvingly Iris Murdoch's remark: 'When we think of the works of Tolstoy or George Eliot, we are not remembering Tolstoy and George Eliot, we are remembering Dolly, Kitty, Stiva, Dorothea and Casaubon.' Harvey also brings out the ideological implications of the centrality of character. He directs our attention back to the origins of the novel, and its individualistic, free and unconditioned response to experience:

> We may fairly say that the novel is the distinct art form of liberalism, by which I mean not a political view or even a mode of social and economic organization but rather a state of mind. This state of mind has as its controlling centre an acknowledgment of the plenitude, diversity and individuality of human beings in society, together with the belief that such characteristics are good as ends in themselves. It delights in the multiplicity of existence and allows for a plurality of beliefs and values; as Presswarden [sic] notes in Durrell's Clea. 'At each moment of time all multiplicity waits at your elbow.' Tolerance, scepticism, respect for the autonomy of others are its watchwords; fanaticism and the monolithic creed its abhorrence. (p. 24)

Harvey asserts that the novel is the essential vehicle of a liberal, pluralistic world-view, and suggests that good novels are unlikely to be written by anyone totally committed to an absolute and monistic pattern of beliefs, such as Christianity or Marxism; such believers are more likely to write forms of fiction that are peripheral to the true novel, like romances, fables or novels of ideas. Although committed to pluralism and liberal values, Harvey acknowledged, in a crucial passage, that such values may be on the wane:

> It may well be, of course, that we are moving towards a form of society where such a state of mind is no longer viable, that liberalism is a luxury rarely allowed by history. In this case the novel will, like other art forms in the past, cease to be an available imaginative mode and will be supplanted by other art forms, either entirely new or drastic mutations of the novel itself. Considered in this way, the radical experiments of many modern novelists may be seen as the first attempts at such a mutation, the first imaginative responses to a changing world view which involves the gradual death of liberalism. (p. 26)

This passage chimes significantly with the remarks by George Steiner quoted earlier in this chapter.

At this point, various strands in my argument should begin to converge. Certainly, to speak for myself, I agree with John Bayley (despite my criticism of aspects of his approach), Iris Murdoch and

W. J. Harvey about the supremacy of character in the novel; a humanistic view of literature should enjoin both writer and reader to respect and even love the characters of a novel. This, at least, is true about the novel as I have always known and understood it; the contemporary English novels which I most admire are precisely those which offer the greatest plenitude of character. Yet I also feel that this attitude, which still comes naturally to English readers, is historically conditioned, and that its end may be in sight for precisely the reasons Harvey indicated. The liberal and individualistic virtues so marvellously preserved and crystallised in the traditional novel are, indeed, on the retreat over a large part of the globe, and have been continuously on the defensive ever since 1914. There is a good deal of evidence – none of it, happily, quite conclusive – for a human future that will be anti-individual, collectivist and, in effect, totalitarian. One sees it predicted, variously, in McLuhan's ideas about the retribalisation of man by means of the electronic media, in George Steiner's reflections on the supersession of individual awareness; and in Marcuse's analysis of the 'happy consciousness', where a vast complex of social controls maintains a state of affairs in which the given social reality is absolute, and there are no longer any intellectual or volitional possibilities of transcending that reality. And the active movements in the western world that are opposed to the monolithic forces of corporate society – whether capitalist or communist – are also quite vocally opposed to the liberal virtues. It was, for instance, a somewhat chilling moment when, in the spring of 1968, a group of student activist leaders from all over Europe who were assembled in a BBC television studio for a discussion of their aims, burst into derisive laughter at the mention of the word 'liberalism'. The recent wave of student-power movements, with their instinctive belief in the rightness of violence and their contempt for tolerance and free speech, indicates that among a powerful segment of those who are young, articulate, and highly educated 'the gradual death of liberalism', as W. J. Harvey called it, is no longer very gradual.

This opposition to liberalism usually has a *marxisant* basis, where it is not overtly anarchistic: from a Marxist point of view the liberalism that describes itself as a pure respect for persons, untainted by ideology, is in fact very much an ideology, a mystification or form of words, which conceals the crude social realities of exploitation and economic oppression. There is an attempted answer to Harvey – and to a lesser extent to John Bayley and Iris Murdoch – in a long and remarkable essay by an able young Marxist critic, John Goode, called ' "Character" and Henry James' (*New Left Review*, November-December 1966). Goode relates the ideas of these three critics to what he describes as 'a developing ideology in English literary criticism . . . which we might call neo-liberalism'. Proceeding by an exhaustive and not always lucid analysis of the late novels of Henry James, Goode sees the 'neo-liberal' idea of character, the opaque, autonomous, self-determining organism, as actually a typical product of the competitive individualism of the capitalist ethos, where the relations between characters will consist, not in mutual respect and love, but in antagonism and acquisitiveness. He refers to Harvey's claim that liberalism eludes 'the categories of any ideology', and continues:

> The work of the later James might have enabled him to avoid this evident contradiction, for James is saturated in the values of capitalism, in its metaphysical notions of the substantial self as well as its ethical notions of human relationship. The great point about the late novels is that they implicitly celebrate these notions at the point of head-on collision. The intrinsic self can only exist in the conditions in which others are contextual; to protect herself against the threat to her own intrinsic self, defined by its possession of her father, Maggie has to turn her back on Charlotte, on the Prince and even on her father as real, intrinsic others. In order not to be owned she has to become an owner, and what she becomes is the owner of others in the same sense that the author owns his characters in a well made little drama: 'they might have been figures rehearsing some play of which she herself was the author: they might even, for the happy appearance they continued to present, have been such figures as would, by the strong note of character in each, fill any author with the certitude of success, especially of their own histrionic'. The opposing self opposes self.

Much of what John Goode says about Henry James seems to me true in a pragmatic way, and not only about *The Golden Bowl*. I recently reread *The Portrait of a Lady* and was forcibly struck by the way in which the whole texture of the novel is pervaded by images of property, and particularly of works of art considered as portable property – metaphorically prefiguring *The Spoils of Poynton* – and by the extent to which the relations between the characters are so acquisitive and manipulative.

Nevertheless Harvey's essential point still seems to me to stand.

He does, as Goode points out, indulge in a certain sleight of hand when he insists on seeing liberalism as not 'a political view or even a mode of social and economic organisation but rather a state of mind'; the connections between all three are not so easily suppressed. At the same time Mr Goode needs to remember that liberalism *is* a state of mind, whatever else it may be, and that it is perfectly possible to be either a liberal and tolerant Marxist or an illiberal and intolerant one. The novel is still pre-eminently about free individuals, even if one wants to adjust the focus somewhat so as to stress the competitiveness that their freedom necessarily involves, rather than the spiritual cosiness that John Bayley dwells on. The point can easily be picked up, without ideological directives, by reading Stendhal and Balzac as well as Dickens and George Eliot. It is salutary to bear in mind that the novel did not come into existence in a social vacuum and, as I have stressed, has been implicated throughout its existence with social, ideological and even technological factors; I have no objection, even, to describing the liberalism that pervades the novel as an 'ideology', providing that one does not take this to mean that liberal values are thereby automatically dismissed as illusory. The value of Marxist criticism is in letting us see that many traditional novels have a richer moral texture than a relaxed interpretation may have suggested, with freedom and the autonomous personality paradoxically but inevitably involved with exploitation and competitiveness. But when it tries to be normative Marxist criticism loses rigour and even credibility. For instance, Lukács's earnest, hopeful and tortuous reflections on 'Critical Realism and Socialist Realism' are the products of a very remote cultural situation and seem to me to have no conceivable relation to any of the literature in which I am most interested.

If one agrees with the Marxists that the novel is a historically conditioned form, the vehicle of a liberal ideology which exalted the individual and the individual apprehension of experience, and which in practice drew most of its strength from the dual tension between individuals and each other, and between individuals and society; then one is entitled to ask them if they expect the novel to go on existing when our present phase of history is over; when the utopian future is established, and, as the ringing phrase has it, the exploitation of man by man is no more. One assumes that the answer is 'no'. One kind of contemporary Marxist analysis would, in effect, abolish the creative tension between individual and society by collapsing both concepts:

> 'Society' and the 'individual' are both essentialist abstractions, based on the notion that persons and institutions are closed, demarcated *beings*, with fixed boundaries between them. In reality, there are no such separate, autarchic beings – there is instead a continuum of human *actions*, which collide, converge and coalesce to form the whole personal and social world we live in. (Quoted by Brian Wicker in *First the Political Kingdom*, 1967: p. 52)

This statement, by Mr Perry Anderson, is of a curiously significant kind; one notes, initially, its totalitarian implications; it could readily fit into a fascist world-view as well as a Marxist one. One also needs to ask what the depersonalised 'human actions' are which Mr Anderson refers to, if not further examples of 'essentialist abstraction'. Presumably some such formulation as this underlies John Goode's attack on the conception of fictional character upheld by English 'neo-liberal' critics; yet, translated into literary terms, it is hard to see what its positive implications would be. One cannot imagine it being reconcilable with Lukács's desire to see the realistic tradition of the novel continue sturdily in being, albeit as socialist realism, and with his incessant preoccupation with the relation of the individual and the type. Yet there is a sense in which Anderson's desire to abolish the idea of the substantive individual does have literary suggestions, of a familiar kind. It recalls the familiar concept of the dehumanisation of modern art, deplored by traditionalists such as Ortega y Gasset, and by Marxists, of an older and more humane stamp, such as Lukács and Ernst Fischer. A world in which there are no solidly established persons, but only 'actions, which collide, converge and coalesce' is surely that of the twentieth-century *avant-garde* novel, whether represented by the subjectivity of Virginia Woolf or *La Nausée*, or the willed objectivity of Robbe-Grillet. One returns with fresh insight to W. J. Harvey's phrase about seeing 'the radical experiments of many modern novelists' as 'the first imaginative responses to a changing world view which involves the gradual death of liberalism'. Despite the assertiveness of tone, contemporary Marxism is full of uncertainties and contradictions on aesthetic questions, as on most others, and is riven by scholastic factionalism. Nevertheless, if liberalism is in its last days, and the future belongs to one of the several possible varieties of totalitarianism, there is at least a chance that a Marxist future might preserve more humane values than some other varieties, even though novels with characters in them will have perished along with the bourgeois ideology which gave rise to them, and, in George Steiner's uninviting words, 'the voice of man would again be choral'.

III The Ideology of Being English

> For just as life in England was teaching me what class
> meant as a concrete condition, studying with Leavis was
> opening my eyes to the particularism and historicity of
> literature – and, by extension, of culture in general. The
> more I listened to him and the more I read him, the more
> uneasily aware I became of the Englishness of English
> literature, and the more I studied that literature itself, the
> more unfamiliar it paradoxically came to seem.
>   NORMAN PODHORETZ, *Making It*

IN the autumn of 1966 I had a conversation in Budapest with a
sharply intelligent critic and editor who had an extensive knowledge of modern English and American literature. Courteously but
firmly he complained that many English novels were parochial and
inward-looking and dealt with questions that were trivial or unintelligible to the outsider. American fiction, on the other hand, com-
municated directly and forcefully: he instanced Saul Bellow's
Herzog, which he greatly admired. I asked him if he saw *Herzog* as
an example of the plight of the bourgeois intellectual in late-
capitalist society, but he replied, not at all, he read it as a univer-
sally valid statement about the human condition. I heard similar
remarks elsewhere; the staff of the Europa publishing house, who
were responsible for finding books for translation into Hungarian,
were full of good will towards English literature, but had difficulty
in finding suitable novels to translate; American literature offered
more scope, they apologetically remarked, and that week the book-
shop windows were displaying the Hungarian edition of John Updike's *The Centaur*.

I had to admit that there was something in these charges. For
complex historical and cultural reasons, English literature in the
fifties and sixties has been both backward- and inward-looking, with
rather little to say that can be instantly translated into universal
statements about the human condition. There are, of course, notable
exceptions: William Golding's *Lord of the Flies*, for instance, seems
to have been as much admired in Hungary as in America. Such
conversations might be painful for the Englishman, but they are

salutary, in so far as they remind one that in literary terms, as in political ones, Britain is not a very important part of the world today. The global unimportance of Britain is not consciously realised in this country, though I suspect that unconsciously it is grasped very well, and is the cause of many current national neuroses and traumas. When visiting America, one is shocked, until one gets used to it, to see how remarkably little news about Britain appears in American newspapers.

The English have been spared a great deal: they have not undergone the foreign invasions and the totalitarian rule that most other European countries have suffered and they know nothing of the pervasive violence that is so noticeable in American society. Yet throughout the twentieth century the English have had to make a long and painful process of adjustment from being the rulers of the most powerful Empire in the world to being a moderately important power of the middle rank, undergoing chronic economic difficulties and with few cultural achievements to offer the world apart from the strident trivialities of the pop scene. The process of decline has been very evident during the last twenty years, despite the intermittent pronouncements from public men about this or that British 'achievement', whose transparent desire to cheer up the people is contemptibly obvious. The incompetence and dishonesty of politicians, combined with the knowledge that the country has little real sovereignty, has produced a generally depressed state of mind that was exacerbated by the failure of the hopes briefly aroused when the Wilson government took office in 1964. There are times when to be English is, it seems, to be destined for endless humiliations. In these circumstances I do not think it surprising that many English writers, and some of the most talented among them, have exhibited the classical neurotic symptoms of withdrawal and disengagement, looking within themselves, or back to a more secure period in their own lives or the history of their culture, making occasional guesses about a grim and apocalyptic future. If I refer to these writers in this clinical way it is not to dismiss them; it is rather in the spirit of those modern psychologists who suspect that the schizophrenic may be right and the society in which he has grown up wrong, and who urge us to listen to his apparent babblings, since he may have something urgent to tell us. If England is still a country less dominated by totalitarian structures – whether of the state or of capitalism – than most others, where liberal values are still more alive and the individual worth more, and where novels still contain characters, then this is something on the credit side.

We may now look at the slightly tendentious title of this chapter. As I suggested in the last chapter, I am quite happy to follow the Marxists in using the word 'ideology'. It does not come easily to English lips, though it has respectable antecedents in the writings of Karl Mannheim. Leonard Meyer writes:

> The most deep-seated beliefs, attitudes, and dispositions which form the fundamental basis of an ideology are not as a rule rationally arrived at, nor are they usually consciously held. Rather they are the unconscious premises, the basic categories, which channel and direct our perceptions, our cognitions – in short, our understanding of ourselves and the world. (*Music, the Arts and Ideas*, p. 129)

For the Marxist, 'ideology' implies a mystification or sham, a pattern of beliefs, ideas or attitudes which conceals its dependence on some underlying socio-economic reality (this is, I am aware, a simple or 'vulgar-Marxist' explanation; in later versions the relations between the economic base and the cultural superstructure become more and more complex and are even, in some revisionist models, reversed). I would accept that what I call the ideology of being English – that is to say, the unconscious beliefs and attitudes which it is difficult not to hold if one is English – is far more dependent on the accidents of history, economics and geography than we often think; but to say this does not, I think, render the ideology invalid. Since the English are a deeply untheoretical people, it is not easy to formulate the contents of the ideology, although one may be dimly aware of the pressures they exert. There is, however, a brilliant statement of these ideas in a series of three broadcast talks by John Holloway, published in January 1967 in the *Listener*, under the general title of 'English Culture and the Feat of Transformation'; they are so admirably relevant to my present purpose that I can do no better than summarise some of their central points here. For Holloway, the most important fact about contemporary English life – and one says 'English' advisedly, for Wales and Scotland have different traditions – is that it did not undergo the radical transformations that took place in countries which underwent the traumatic experiences of totalitarianism and defeat in war. Ancient traditions and continuities remained undisturbed; there is still a visible stress on the idiosyncratic and the amateur, and a corresponding distaste for the systematic and doctrinaire. In cultural matters we find an unrepentant insularity and an involvement with native elements and traditions, as against the cosmopolitan innovations of the Modern Movement. In intellectual debate there is a hallowed preference for 'sense' as against 'reason', and a lack of hard research and verifiable information about many important areas of intellectual life. Philosophers incline towards 'everyday styles of thought', and there is a tendency to gauge the tone or 'feel' of an argument rather than get to grips with its intellectual content. There is a general avoidance of both the 'abstract-analytical' and the 'visionary-daemonic' as modes of thought – say, Hegel at one extreme, Dostoievsky at the other. Contemporary literature is pervaded by nostalgia, and there is a dedication to myths of the past, and in particular to an ideal of vanished brotherhood in the past. There is domination by what Holloway calls the 'moralized consciousness', which is particularly noticeable in literary criticism, where 'marked moral intensity' is the cardinal virtue. This consciousness heavily stresses certain private virtues, such as inner strength and integrity: Alan Sillitoe's *Loneliness of the Long Distance Runner* is a striking embodiment of these attitudes. Holloway illustrates his argument by a comparison between English and French academic methods and attitudes:

> In France, the seminar as a teaching method has been advocated by reference to Sartre's philosophical theory of the seriality of groups: with a vengeance, the intellectuality I spoke of last time. Our own approach is moralized instead. We do not think in the first place that it increases the rate at which the subject is mastered, or if we do it is because we see mastery of the subject itself in a distinctive light. What we think of, in the first place, is a fostering of the independently developing inward man.

Holloway's generalisations are, admittedly, impressionistic, but to a great extent his impressions are my impressions, and I think he gets to the heart of a large number of interlocking English attitudes. Underlying his talks is the assumption that the English are evading the necessary 'feat of transformation' that other societies underwent forcibly by war, and which we shall have to accomplish voluntarily if we are to keep up with the rest of the twentieth-century world. Thus, although the 'moralised consciousness' has a great deal to recommend it, and certainly leads to a higher level of civic amenity than that of societies dominated by the ideals of efficiency or abstract rationality, Holloway is concerned that it may obstruct transformation, since the moralised consciousness is likely to see any process of adaptation as a sell-out. I think Holloway may have somewhat reified the notion of transformation, seeing it as something both total and all of a piece, and in his grave insistence on regarding it as a necessary medicine that may be nasty but will have to be swallowed by the English for their own good, we have, I think, a remarkably clear example of the moralised consciousness that he analyses so effectively. I think it is possible, even probable, that the English – who are by no means incapable of radical transformations, as the political and cultural revolutions of the seventeenth century, and the industrial revolution of the nineteenth indicate – may have decided against further total transformations, while still being capable of local ones. Thus we may well see important changes in industry and economics, without any necessary accompanying changes in literary or philosophical attitudes. I doubt if all the elements of an ideology have to change together; only those elements that are positively required to change will change.

Holloway's ambivalence about the English ideology indicates that it is one thing to describe and analyse it, and quite another to escape its influence. I have not tried to do so myself. It will be obvious that the stance of such critics as John Bayley, Iris Murdoch and W. J. Harvey, and their belief in the novel of character stems directly from the English ideology, which insists on seeing the nineteenth century as still a going concern. So, at least, it would seem to a French or American observer, and it is hard not to use such phrases without an implied sneer or note of condemnation. Yet this is not at all my intention; I should like, rather, to maintain a difficult balance between the position that unthinkingly regards English cultural and literary attitudes as self-evidently right, and the opposite position, that dismisses recent English literature as flat, tame and hopelessly rooted in the past. I should like, in a provisional way, to adopt the cultural relativism of the modern anthropologist, who avoids making value judgements about one society as against another (carrying, as it seems to the outsider, such tolerance to absurd and even sinister lengths, regarding both suttee and widows' pensions as equally 'valid' ways of dealing with the same problem). The English ideology is, one might argue, right for the English, since it is their way of coping with conditioning factors that have affected them throughout the centuries. At the same time no-one could deny that elements of that ideology may no longer be viable, as Holloway suggests, and will have to be abandoned in the interests of survival. Certainly the English have been remarkably fortunate in their history – whatever their current humiliations and collective neuroses – in so far as they have been spared mass violence, invasion and the visible collapse of national institutions and traditions. The existence of an unarmed police force is still perhaps the most single significant fact about English public life. Compared with other nations, the English are a remarkably innocent people, who scarcely know what violence, crime or civil disorder is: many American cities have as high an annual murder rate as the whole of the United Kingdom. In an essay on Arthur Koestler, written in 1944, George Orwell sardonically remarked: 'In Europe, during the past decade and more, things have been happening to middle-class people which in England do not even happen to the working class' (*Collected Essays*, 1961: p. 237). As Holloway has pointed out, there is a stark contrast between the references to wartime torture in the writings of Sartre and the unreality of William Golding's treatment of the same thing in *Free Fall*. There is also the extreme difficulty of being in a meaningful way a radical in English politics, still less a revolutionary; again one needs an outside viewpoint to make this clear. The young expatriate Hungarian writer Paul Neuburg, going home as a tourist after ten years, reported a conversation with a hitchhiker: 'Asks me about the British. Is Wilson a real socialist, a radical? I try to explain that a British radical is a contradiction in terms ...' (*Partisan Review*, Summer 1967). Hence, the baffled impotence of the English far Left, whether reflected in the endless neo-Marxist hairsplitting of the *New Left Review*, or Raymond Williams's exasperated lurchings between his vision of an egalitarian future and the cherished memories of the working-class community in which he grew up.

To describe the English ideology in these terms is not to suggest that human nature is somehow different in England, and physically incapable of the excesses observable in other countries; one need look no further than the history of Ireland or the inhumanities of the industrial revolution to see that the English are as capable of cruelty and oppression as anyone else, provided it happens decently off-stage. Yet the accidents of history have provided the English with fewer opportunities than other people for inflicting large-scale atrocities on themselves or on others, and their record lags well behind the twentieth-century average in these matters. They do, of course, have their own peculiar forms of domestic horror, like the national addiction to cruelty to children, but we can acquit ourselves of the charge of being a society in love with the gun, like America. It may be in bad taste to stress this point, but it is apt to come into one's mind when defending English culture against American attacks on its general boringness and deadness.

Not long ago I was entertaining two American academics – one a distinguished critic – in my house, and towards the end of the evening conversation became sufficiently relaxed for them to speak frankly about English cultural life; they both deplored its lack of 'excitement'. I knew what they meant: there is a sense in which the very air of America seems more highly charged, more oxygenated, than the atmosphere in England. Nevertheless, I wanted to know why excitement should be regarded as the supreme good; is there not something absurd about rational adults demanding larger and larger doses of excitement from art and literature? My guests were unable to give me a satisfying answer, since it is uncommonly difficult to explain and justify the categories one habitually thinks with. Nor is it only Americans who think in this way: Professor A. R. Jones concludes an article on Robert Lowell, Sylvia Plath and Anne Sexton by using the word 'exciting' three times in the last dozen lines ('Necessity and Freedom', in *Critical Quarterly*, Spring 1965). It is not, perhaps, wise for Americans to be so hooked on excitement, since their society as a whole could use a little English tranquillity.

It will already be apparent that my attempt at an anthropologically 'neutral' stance is breaking down; as a mental exercise and a corrective to over-hasty judgements it has its uses, but it is too unreal to sustain for long. Yet I am very conscious of a difference of emphasis that may indicate a real contradiction. As an English writer and teacher who, in general, likes it here, I am naturally conscious of the positive qualities of the English ideology. Looked at from inside, the society, and its culture and literature, can seem a happy enclave of tradition and liberalism, a living fragment of the nineteenth century, which, given a minimum amount of intelligent adjustment, might go on existing indefinitely. Yet, on a global view, if one tries to see England through the eyes of an American or Frenchman or Hungarian, there is something precarious about the survival of English values, for all their amenity: as a cultural phenomenon the country has all the pathos and unreality of an Indian reservation, full of busily cultivated and exhibited native crafts and customs. (Which is precisely the impression given by the travel posters and advertisements that urge foreign tourists to visit England.) On this view it is only a matter of time before these quaintly preserved liberal *mores* succumb to the totalitarian global pressures that are destined to abolish them. In the attempt to combine both views one arrives at the idea that the present forms of English literary culture are a kind of justifiable neurosis, macrocosmically enacting what has been said of the poets of the Movement in the 1950s:

> They withdrew from politics and fighting, and tried to celebrate the inviolate quality of their emotions in lucid, disciplined verse ... . Larkin often makes the point that for him withdrawal from life is necessary for the preservation of the self. (C. B. Cox and A. R. Jones, in *Critical Quarterly*, Summer 1964)

In the final chapter of *The Characters of Love* John Bayley makes a fruitful distinction between the literature of Nature and that of the Human Condition. The former is, perhaps, more characteristic of drama and poetry, particularly of the Renaissance. It sees man as existing in a given hierarchical relation with other men (the concept of 'society' not being invented until the end of the eighteenth century), with his physical environment and with God. The relation is essentially a harmonious one, with a belief in norms and traditions and laws. In literary terms it means that a writer and his readers have a shared sense of the nature of reality and the values that permeate it. The rule of Nature accepts without question the givenness of the world, in all its diversity. On the other hand, in the literature of the Human Condition, we are concerned with a particular vision of the world, with a writer's capacity to make momentary sense of the incoherence of ordinary living; with his capacity, in Kermodian terms, to invent a fiction. There are no norms or shared values in the Human Condition; man is basically alone, living in a problematical relation with his fellow men, and at odds with society and his physical environment. The author cannot merely accept life; he must adopt a definite attitude towards it. This is, as is well known, the characteristic world of American fiction. In Bayley's words:

> We might begin by observing that there is no Nature in American literature. How could there be? – when America became a nation the word was already beginning to lose its force and authority. The processes of living which give their substance to the literary idea of Nature of course existed in America as much as anywhere

else, but they were not available to the emergent American writer. Indeed, the complex kinds of traditional authority that Nature implies were specifically disowned by the American idea and left out of the American dream. For America, Nature had to become the Human Condition. (p. 270.)

As Bayley admits, the distinction is not and cannot be absolute. Even Shakespeare, the very embodiment of the accepting spirit of Nature, preferred some kinds of behaviour to others. If English novels were traditionally concerned with Nature, French ones have always had a certain bias towards the Human Condition. Yet in the twentieth century, following on mass public horror and inner break-down, an existentially oriented fiction of the Human Condition has become general. To quote Bayley again :

The novel whose world is exceptional because it is the indi-vidual's world is not the vehicle of Nature, and it is this kind of novel which has become the dominant American literary form. To write such a novel is part of the American dream, and the idea of the American novel has conquered Europe. (p. 270)

Bayley's distinction is, as I say, frutiful; though I am not prepared to take it as far as he does; as I have already argued, his dedication to Nature seems to me to take him to a point irreconcilable with the existence of any kind of fiction as a literary art. Nevertheless I am happy to adapt this distinction for my own purposes; 'Nature' obviously has a good deal in common with what I have called the English ideology, and only in England does the concept of Nature seem alive : although there is also a Marxist version of it in Lukács's idea of Socialist Realism. In the process Nature has shrunk into an English Nature, something quaint and marginal in the eyes of the rest of the world.

It is time to make more explicit the confrontation between Eng-lish and American literary attitudes which I have been hinting at. It can be graphically illustrated by opposing two quotations. First, Professor Leslie Fielder offering his reflections in the New States-man (14 June 1968) after an academic year in England :

There is no scene in the arts in England . . . what small activity I have found among younger artists in poetry, painting, the novel, has tended to follow foreign models, occasionally French, more usually American, when it is not actually carried out by Ameri-can expatriates.

Second, Karl Miller in the Introduction to his Penguin anthology, Writing in England Today: the last fifteen years:

The fever for American literature which succeeded the 'French flu' in this country has resulted in a philistine condescension towards native writers. To the extent that it embraces the work done in the mid-fifties, this is quite misplaced, and might almost seem to be a matter of thinking that American writers must rule the waves because their nation does. That the search for new form hasn't prospered in Britain lately is not very alarming: a great deal of the new form that *has* been found, here and elsewhere, is an illusion (William Burroughs's collage technique, for example), and the original abstention from experiment strikes me as having been both comprehensible and rewarding. (1968: p. 26)

One could go on multiplying examples of this opposition, though they are seldom so sharply explicit. If American critics – and those Englishmen who imitate them – are likely to greet the appearance of some new artistic phenomenon with an eager though uneasy cry of 'exciting', British critics are equally likely to utter a crisp dismissal, such as 'rubbish'. This illustrates the distinction between the Human Condition, with its concern for authenticity, exploration and the assertion of an individual vision; and Nature, with its emphasis on tradition and shared values. The regard for native values and traditions, and the parallel suspicion of experiment and the pursuit of newness for its own sake, can be readily seen in the critical writings of Philip Larkin and Graham Hough, Robert Conquest and C. P. Snow, to name four very different though representative writers. The English spirit was well summed up by the young novelist Margaret Drabble in the course of a radio interview:

I don't want to write an experimental novel to be read by people in fifty years, who will say, ah, well, yes, she foresaw what was coming. I'm just not interested. I'd rather be at the end of a dying tradition, which I admire, than at the beginning of a tradition which I deplore. (BBC recording 1967: 'Novelists of the Sixties')

On the American side, one can find similar dismissals to Fiedler's, though usually in less explicit forms. There is often an assumption that modern English literature is not worth bothering with, or even worth mentioning. If it is, it will be dismissed as academic, parochial, small-scale and, inevitably, unexciting.

I must admit to finding a certain fascination in an opposition so forcibly expressed, which, indeed, appears all the more starkly because of the near-identity of language and the countless close personal and cultural ties between the two nations. At the same time, there is, as Fiedler remarks, a noticeable movement of dissent among young English intellectuals, who for largely sociological reasons dismiss the work of admired English writers such as, say, Philip Larkin or Angus Wilson, which they regard as preserving an obsolete strain of middle-class social and literary values, and turn instead to American writing, to find spiritual refreshment in Faulkner or Charles Olson. The way in which the popularity of American culture co-exists with a loathing of American political behaviour is an interesting global phenomenon. The poet Adrian Mitchell has remarked:

> The disease of the British artist since 1945 has been a compulsion to stay small, to create perfect miniatures, to take no major risks. Stay small and the critics will handle you with as much care as a glass paper-weight. Get big and they're forced to drop you.
>   In America writers take greater risks, still attempting to assume bardic or prophetic responsibilities, to run for President, to work out their own language, to bet everything on one book. This American sense of daring is the main reason why the strong American influence on the British Underground should be welcomed. (*Guardian*, 12 October 1967)

The more one pursues this dichotomy, the more one sees that its implications are not merely literary. The question is ultimately sociological, or even anthropological. For a long time the Americans have made the study of their literature part of a multivalent cultural activity, in which literary, historical and sociological approaches are merged. Thus American novels or poems are read, not so much for the literary experience they offer, as for the insights they afford into the American Myth or Dream or Nightmare. This procedure partly stems from the American historical situation; but it also entails a prudent strategy which emphasises the total uniqueness or unlikeness of American literature from any other, and sets up innumerable tactical obstacles to the English reader who wants to try to decide for himself, on the basis of his own literary experience, just how good Hawthorne or Melville, or Dreiser or Ellen Glasgow, or other masters of the tradition, really are.* His own assumptions, it will be insisted, are quite irrelevant when it

---

* One American writer has expressed doubts about his own tradition: 'I never much liked the classical canon in American literature. I always thought that our great novelists were minor provincial writers. Our great classic canon now being taught at Sussex and so on really isn't much good, and I think I have known this all along . . . that *Moby Dick* is a very bad novel. I think I could prove it, given 5,000 words' (Gore Vidal, *Listener*, 26 September 1968).

comes to making any such judgements; and judgements will, in any case, not be encouraged, for any specimen of American writing, no matter how wretchedly bad, can be pressed into service in the interests of the unified American cultural myth (one need only check some of the titles published by the lesser or middle-grade American university presses to see the truth of this; the most unlikely works or authors are subjected to critical analysis and historical investigation). American cultural chauvinism has, it must be admitted, been remarkably successful in imposing on English universities Departments of American Studies, of a thoroughly divisive kind, where American literature is separated from English literature, and American history or politics from any other history or politics. To the English reader, William Carlos Williams's desire to separate American poetry from all British influences, and to use the American language as it came 'from the mouths of Polish mothers', is a cultural rather than a literary decision, but one imagines that to the American reader the two aspects are not to be distinguished. In which case the English may need to make a similar claim for their own literature.

For the Americans, engaging in constant attempts to explore, or assault, the Human Condition, the only tradition is to have no tradition, or to have, in Harold Rosenberg's phrase, a 'tradition of the new', at least in principle. (In practice, as I suggested in my opening chapter, American fiction has exhausted its basic impulse to originality, and has become noticeably generic, though American poetry may be in a genuinely different situation). And, as John Bayley has said, it is the fiction of the Human Condition, of existential isolation and alienation, of efforts at self-definition and vain sisyphean struggles, that for good historical reasons has the most direct appeal throughout the world today. In this situation English literature will undoubtedly seem a backwater, parochial and archaic.

There is one crucial way in which American procedures seem to me clearly superior to English. It concerns attitudes to language. At his best the American author will take nothing for granted; he has to forge his own style as a basic act of self-definition. The process has been well described in Richard Poirier's *A World Elsewhere*; he shows how the first task of any American writer has been to forge his own unique verbal environment. The process has, admittedly, been stylized and to some extent falsified by schools of creative writing, which tend to teach ready-made solutions to unique problems.

Nevertheless they do at least show that there are problems to be faced, and the talented writer will always modify the style he has been taught into a genuinely personal idiom. American novels, even where they are patently mediocre in content, are usually well written; in starting to read an American novel one begins with a sense of language being used with a real openness to its possibilities, something remarkably rare in English novels. The experience of acting as a prize judge has recently involved me in reading a good number of novels by young English writers; they conveyed a general feeling of flatness and banality in the writing, and a complete unawareness of the problems of constructing a novel. Here, again, one can refer to the English ideology. Novel-writing is seen as a visible and established tradition, the niceties of which can be picked up as one goes along. It can even be regarded as a natural process like breathing, in which no conscious thought need be given to questions of style or construction. Irving Howe has summed this difference up very well. After stressing that 'the very best American writers always are involved in defining the terms of their own existence' he remarks:

> By contrast, reading certain English writers from a distance, what strikes me is that for them the modes of expression are – to some extent – given, available, ready. This makes for economy, I think, but sometimes of course it makes for a certain conventionality. (In *Under Pressure*, ed. A. Alvarez, 1965: p. 162)

English novels tend to be, in John Bayley's formulation, a kind of Nature, in which one effortlessly participates, without will and without directing intelligence. Hence the countless, as it seems, first novels by young English writers that all seem to begin in much the same way:

> Janet was tired when she got in from the office that evening. She ran up the stairs to the flat, desperately hoping there would be a letter from Simon. There wasn't, of course, only a boring-seeming invitation to a party given by some dull friends of her sister's. She slumped down miserably in the kitchen, lit a cigarette, and wondered if she could muster up enough energy to put the kettle on to make some coffee . . .

Und so weiter, for seventy or eighty thousand more words of comparable nullity. The depressing thing is not only that such books should be written and seriously offered for publication, but that, because of the peculiar economics of the publishing industry, they should quite often be accepted, printed, bound, distributed, reviewed, presumably bought, and even submitted for prizes. (The above example is, by the way, wholly invented; my apologies if it inadvertently reproduces what someone has already written, or is thinking of writing.)

American first novels do at least show signs of trying hard, of energy and invention. Here for instance is the opening of one such, the late Richard Farina's *Been Down So Long it Looks Like Up to Me*:

> To Athené then. Young Gnossos Pappadopoulis, furry Pooh Bear, keeper of the flame, voyaged back from the asphalt seas of the great wasted land: oh highways U.S.40 and unyielding 66, I am home to the glacier-gnawed gorges, the fingers of lakes, the golden girls of Westchester and Shaker Heights. See me loud with lies, big boots stomping, mind awash with schemes.

This is, in fact, a thoroughly bad piece of writing, a generic version of the inflated prose one has read in many other American novels;* nevertheless its badness is, as it were, the product of conscious effort and has something tangible about it, in contrast to the prevalent English non-style. One would be glad, now and then, of an English first novel that opened with comparable panache. Whereas young American writers think that novels must be *written*, with a full concentration of resources, young English writers seem merely to exude them.

In this situation I am firmly on the side of the Americans. The school of creative writing is often sneered at from this side of the Atlantic, and there can be no doubt that it is a vulnerable institution. Nevertheless such institutions do at least indicate that using words is a conscious process about which something can be learned. In this connection I shall quote a very relevant article by the English novelist Thomas Hinde on his experiences of teaching writing in an American university. He is most interesting when he describes the effect such teaching has had on his own attitude to his craft, as a writer from England where, as he says, 'writers tend to work by intuition and concern themselves little with theory or technique'. He says:

---

* There is an effective parody of this kind of writing in Doris Lessing's *The Golden Notebook*: 'The fellows were out Saturday-nighting true-hearted, the wild-hearted Saturday-night gang of true friends, Buddy, Dave and Mike. Snowing. Snow-cold. The cold of cities in the daddy of cities, New York. But true to us. Buddy, the ape-shouldered stood apart and stared.'

My own feeling was that never again could I write the innocent books I had written before. I sensed I had been blundering about in my writing in a way which was both dangerous and improper. Any success I had had seemed necessarily to have been an accident and therefore not deserved. For English writers who, I believe, persist in a dilettante attitude to their writing – as well as to their reading – long after they should, this is an important moment of understanding and seems to lie at the core of the second part of the problem of the writer at the university : the effect his students and his teaching will have on himself and his own work. (*Times Literary Supplement*, 25 July 1968)

This is admirably honest and direct. Hinde goes on to mention the dangers of this directing of full consciousness onto a process that has previously been habitual and amateur : that it can lead to 'sterile cleverness and works created mainly for other writers or, worse still, other critics'. That this is a real danger is obvious from some of the most admired works of modern American fiction. Nevertheless Hinde firmly concludes that the novelist should understand the critical implications of what he is doing :

A writer cannot block all analytical or critical thoughts about his craft. He necessarily accumulates them as he works. Indeed, an acute sense of self-criticism is his most essential quality. Can it seriously be argued that he should stay with this home-made critical sense, augmented by stray droppings picked up second-hand from reviews, and not find out what a wide group of highly intelligent people who have made the study of literature their life work are thinking about it? (Ibid.)

Hinde's conclusion points to a possibly fruitful association between the novelist and the critic, of a kind that exists, though it is not particularly common, in the United States, where many writers have some kind of academic connection, but is almost unknown in England. Talking to practising novelists I have been depressed to discover that in their work they were feeling their way semi-consiously around problems that have been already well formulated and are the subject of current critical discussion. For instance, Dan Jacobson, who although a South African is representative of, prevalent English attitudes, appears to have had a less profitable experience of teaching in American universities than Thomas Hinde. In an article called 'Muffled Majesty', published in the *Times Literary Supplement* in October 1967, he objected to the idea, which he found still academically dominant, that novels should be impersonal, wholly dramatised structures, with everything 'shown' rather than 'told', and the author conspicuous by his absence; the kind of fiction, in fact, that can be associated with the precept and practice of the late James and of Joyce. Jacobson argues, very plausibly, for a return of the author as narrator and commentator, with a right to let his own voice be heard, and for a restored place for 'telling' as well as 'showing' in fictional narrative. Yet it is surprising that Jacobson advances these ideas as if they were wholly new and subversive, as though the dominance of the critical orthodoxy of impersonality in fiction were total and unchallenged. Perhaps it was at the American university where Mr Jacobson was teaching; nevertheless, during the last ten years there has been a general acceptance in the academic criticism of fiction of the ideas he advances. A crucial work in this process was Wayne C. Booth's *The Rhetoric of Fiction*, published in 1961 : it is sad that Jacobson showed himself so unaware of the arguments put forward in this book, and the subsequent critical response to them. Nor is this a purely academic development: the role of the narrator and the relation of the narrator to the author have been most interestingly opened up in a number of recent novels. I shall return to this question in the final chapter.

I shall conclude this discussion of the the English ideology by looking at some particular novels. That there is a crisis in the English sense of cultural identity is obvious, and what I have called the neurotic stance of much recent literature is one way of responding to it. But two novels, one of the fifties and one of the sixties, seem to me outstanding, both as works of fiction and as attempts to face directly the question of identity. The first of these is Nigel Dennis's *Cards of Identity*, published in 1955 and surely one of the most brilliant novels of its decade. I had thought that its reputation was firmly established, but it may be declining; I was sorry to see no reference to it in Anthony Burgess's generally comprehensive study *The Novel Now*, and no extract from it included in Karl Miller's anthology *Writing in England Today*, which in other respects is so perfect a monument to the taste of the mid-fifties. In its most universal sense *Cards of Identity* is a very funny and penetrating fable about the problem of identity, a problem that is, of course, familiar in many of the most distinguished works of the Modern Movement: one may refer, for instance, to Kafka or Pirandello. In sociological terms this topic ravages a large part of the Western world, particularly America, and is capable of endless commentary and explanation. In American fiction the paradoxes of identity are constantly invoked, and provide central themes for the novels of Barth and Pynchon. *Cards of Identity* appeared some years before their work, and is one of the few English treatments of this topic, which, because of the protective influence of the English ideology that traditionally made sure that everyone knew his place, has been less acute in this country than in others. (Yet there is a classic earlier treatment of it in *Alice in Wonderland*, which is interestingly echoed here and there in *Cards of Identity*.) Nigel Dennis's novel is set in an English country house, where a body called the Identity Club is holding its annual meeting. In some ways it reflects the conditions of the late forties and early fifties, a period of ration-books and identity cards and continuing post-war privations. The case-history delivered by Father Golden Orfe about an ex-communist turned monk, writing his memoirs in a monastery, all of whose intimates have had a similar communist past is, though entertaining, very much a product of the era of Whittaker Chambers and *The God That Failed*. On the other hand the story of the Co-Wardens of the Badgeries, and the sad farcical events that took place while they were ceremonially leading a symbolic stuffed badger across London in the funeral procession of the Lord Royal, is still a valid satire on the more absurd manifestations of English public traditionalism. Yet where *Cards of Identity* transcends the treatment of individual forms of identity-crisis, and looks at the problem of English cultural identity as a whole, is not in the case-histories that are read to the club, but in the narrative framework of the novel. At the beginning of *Cards of Identity* the handsome country house of Hyde's Mortimer has long been empty, but it is taken over by Captain Mallet, the nephew of a former occupant. Mallet is an imposing English gentleman who has moved in with his second wife and his dashing son, Beaufort, in order to make the place ready for the forthcoming meeting of the Identity Club. Nearly all the action takes place inside the mansion, whose architecture and contents are described in loving detail, and it plays the kind of central symbolic role familiar in many English novels; one thinks of Bladesover in H. G. Wells's *Tono-Bungay* or Evelyn Waugh's Brideshead and, on a smaller scale, E. M. Forster's Howards End. Mallet and his wife and son proceed to abduct various of the local inhabitants and by unspecified but infallible means transform them into typical denizens of the traditional country house, such as the butler, the cook and the eccentric gardener. The agents of the Identity Club deftly erect a simulacrum of the comfortable, timeless milieu of a large segment of traditional English fiction (particularly characteristic of such a popular sub-genre as the old-fashioned detective novel). Yet one is left under no illusion about the way in which the social values that sustained such novels have been undermined in post-war England. Consider, for instance, Lolly Paradise, who makes a living by buying and selling whatever he can find:

> What also shocked his uncle and aunt was Lolly's indifference – indeed, absolute ignorance – in matters of social class. Descriptive terms such as 'gentry', 'middle-class', 'squire' were, to him, the equivalent of 'sith' and 'eftsoons' to the student of purely contemporary literature. Lolly did cash business with anyone, and it no more occurred to him to consider their social status than to open a bank account or make an income-tax return.

The point is enlarged on in the impassioned speech which Captain Mallet makes to the opening session of the Identity Club:

> This sort of house was once a heart and centre of the national identity. A whole world lived in relation to it. Millions knew who they were by reference to it. Hundreds of thousands look back to it, and not only grieve for its passing but still depend on it, non-existent though it is, to tell them who they are. Thousands who never knew it are taught every day to cherish its memory and to believe that without it no man will be able to tell his whereabouts again. It hangs on men's necks like a millstone of memory; carrying it, and looking back on its associations, they stumble indignantly backwards into the future, confident that man's self-knowledge is gone forever. How appropriate it is that these forlorn barracks, these harbours of human nostalgia, should now be in use once more solely as meeting places for bodies such as ours! How right that we should assemble this summer in one of the last relics of an age of established identities!

At the end of the novel, when an obtrusive policeman appears, the members of the Identity Club are rapidly transformed into a party of tourists being shown round the house by the impoverished but aristocratic owner, who is Captain Mallet in yet another manifestation. Hyde's Mortimer, it appears, is distinguished from other country houses by displaying not only paintings, furniture and other *objets d'art*, but living exhibits:

> A man with a twitching face is sitting at the writing-table near a window. He rises from a heap of papers and gives the tourists a courtly bow. His face is lined, his brow high and furrowed. The footmen run in just in time to corral the tourists with a crimson cord.

'Here is one of the family at work', explains the duke. 'In the passing of these old houses, nothing is to be more regretted than the loss of the library – and, with it, the sort of occupant you now see. Before we discuss the room, I would like you to look very closely at this individual. His bent shoulders, his pinched and nervous face, his tremulous grasp of his quill pen indicate that he will not be in contemporary society very much longer. I am not *too* well up in these matters, but I am assured that without him and his predecessors we should not have any culture at all.'

In its comic, inventive and somewhat heartless fashion, *Cards of Identity* probes at contemporary dilemmas: its satirical examination of the way in which the traditional symbols of English identity are losing their validity is an important part of its meaning. Nigel Dennis is one of the most accomplished and idiosyncratic of living English novelists, and in his most recent novel, *A House in Order*, he continues to dwell on the question of identity in a way that is at once more personal and less culturally specific than in *Cards of Identity*, though it is an equally distinguished work. The subject could not be more restricted: during a war between two unnamed powers a prisoner is kept confined in a greenhouse near a building which houses a minor army administrative unit. He cannot be moved, as he is an object of contention between two branches of the military establishment, though neither side is interested in his personal welfare. In civilian life this man's hobby was gardening, and with immense patience he starts cultivating the small plants he finds in the greenhouse and the garden outside where he is allowed to take exercise. In time the prisoner becomes attached to his place of confinement, despite the physical privations he undergoes, and he uses the plants to keep not only his house but his mind in order, and to preserve his sense of self. The story has, of course, many symbolic or allegorical implications about the Human Condition in general, but Dennis advances them without destroying the credibility of his narrative. The humour which distinguished *Cards of Identity* is, though necessarily subdued, certainly present in *A House in Order*. The book is noticeable for the way in which it depicts the prisoner's plight without any sense of nightmare. He preserves his sanity, and at the end of the novel he is restored to his own country and a greenhouse of his own, although he looks back nostalgically to the days of his incarceration as to some vanished ideal order. Dennis may have manifested a certain English loss of nerve, or kind-hearted regard for his character : I can imagine a French or American novelist keeping the man a prisoner for good.

Both these novels by Nigel Dennis can be loosely regarded as fables, a kind of writing which has become increasingly popular with the decline or loss of stature of the conventional realistic novel. One thinks of the rise to popularity during the last twenty years of such English novelists as William Golding, Iris Murdoch, Lawrence Durrell, Muriel Spark, David Storey and John Fowles, who are writers of strikingly varied talents, and by no means all entitled to their current reputations, but who, in some or all of their books, are at a considerable distance from the well-made realistic novel as conventionally understood. The impulse to myth has produced some interesting writing. Yet, to speak for myself, I prefer the mythopoeic impulse when it enters into an active relation with cultural and historical realities, and does more than arrange private imaginative counters in an aesthetically agreeable pattern. An ambitious and accomplished example of the latter mode is John Fowles's *The Magus*, published in 1966. This is a long and elaborate fiction set on the Greek island of Phraxos, where a rather caddish young Englishman called Nicholas Urfe has gone to teach in a boys' school. He gets into the clutches of a sinister, elderly Greek, Conchis, and a succession of appalling things happen to him. Fowles writes with stylistic brilliance, and there are some fine descriptive passages. But the whole novel is not much more than a highly inventive series of fantastic or cruel episodes, comprising such varied elements as black magic, occultism, brainwashing techniques, lush Mediterranean travelogues, forgery, flagellation, Nazi atrocities, voyeurism, hypnotism, battle scenes, *fin de siècle* naughtiness, and venereal disease. The mixture is too rich, and as the novel develops the mystification gets more and more involved; Fowles likes tormenting the reader as well as his characters, and is constantly setting traps for him. At the end the elaborate, pretentious glittering structure collapses into anti-climax and absurdity, in which the reader's dissatisfaction may be a final product of the author's sadistic animus. *The Magus* is contributory evidence of the way in which some modern English fiction is getting more like American fiction, and it shows that Fowles has literary gifts far in advance of most young English novelists, just as his book of aphoristic reflections, *The Aristos*, shows an unusual, speculative intelligence. Yet the novel is vitiated by its basic pointlessness, its inability to relate to anything except itself as a centripetal imaginative entity.

I will conclude this chapter with an account of another recent English novel, an equally complex product of the mythopoeic imagination, which has elements in common with *The Magus*, but which I find a generally more impressive work. It uses myth to lead one's imagination back to the public world of shared human experience. I am referring to Andrew Sinclair's *Gog*, published in 1967. Sinclair is an immensely industrious and prolific writer; during the last ten years he has published several novels and books on American history; but one would hardly have expected the large achievement of *Gog* from such amiable but light-weight relics of the late fifties as *The Breaking of Bumbo* and *My Friend Judas*. One must, however, remark that Sinclair now regards all his earlier novels as no more than stylistic exercises. The name 'Gog' comes from one of the legendary giants of British mythology, and in Sinclair's novel he is personified as a huge rugged-featured man who is washed up naked and unconscious on the Scottish coast in the summer of 1945. He is revived and is assumed to be a seaman from a ship sunk in the aftermath of war. The man has lost his memory, but he knows that his name is 'Gog', and the names 'Gog' and 'Magog' are tattooed on the backs of his hands. He senses that he is in some way a representative of the British people, and he sets out to walk to London to claim their inheritance: the book follows his long walk in a loose, picaresque fashion, describing Gog's many adventures on the way, some of which are comic, others horrible, but all of which indicate Sinclair's extraordinary imaginative exuberance. Gog's journey takes him to many sacred places, such as York Minster, Glastonbury and Stonehenge, and it becomes an exploration of the multi-layered English past, almost like the excavation of an archaeological site.

While preparing to write *Gog*, Sinclair covered much of the ground of Gog's journey himself on foot, and in a radio interview he has given a vivid account of his impressions:

> If you sleep out on Hadrian's Wall in a gale, looking towards Scotland, your actual physical experience compared with the Roman sentries' two thousand years ago is exactly the same. The weather has not changed, the view has not changed, the experience of cold and wind has not changed. At two in the morning all men are equal; it's equally black and equally hard. And it was a pilgrimage, like for Gog. I assure you that to walk a week and

reach the Five Sisters Window at York, stand in front of it, makes it a holy experience. To go there by car, it is five windows of grisaille glass. (BBC recording 1967 : 'Novelists of the Sixties')

What prevents *Gog* from being merely a pleasant fictional travelogue is the almost obsessive quality of Sinclair's concern for the English past, and his feeling for myth, which he sees as overtaking history; he has remarked, 'personal obsession must to a large extent influence the facts you are choosing from in history, even if you can establish those facts'. Underlying *Gog* is an intense concern for the question of national identity, which is why I think it appropriate to link Sinclair's book with Nigel Dennis's, even though Sinclair's fable ranges far more widely and is far less controlled. Sinclair has said :

I think as we lose our place in the world we're forced in on ourselves far more, and there's a lot to be said for losing that power and that one might discover Britain at the end of it instead of diffusing it over an imperial tradition. But the question of national identity is certainly on, and *Gog* is certainly to do with it, as a man seeks for his own identity from some mythological tradition. For instance, I do not understand why every child in this country is not given Geoffrey of Monmouth's *History of the Kings of Britain* to read . . . (Ibid.)

Sinclair's enthusiasm for the British legends is infectious, and they are coupled in his admiration with Kipling's *Puck of Pook's Hill*, which contains an imaginative journey into the English past in the guise of a children's book. In *Gog* he puts the Arthurian and associated material to a brilliant imaginative use, in the many passages where he sees a given landscape as a nexus of geography and myth. The only contemporary writer who has a comparable feeling for the legendary strata of the English past is David Jones, in *In Parenthesis* and *The Anathemata*, books which Sinclair had not read when he was working on *Gog*. Not all of Sinclair's dominating myths seem to me equally compelling; his vision of Gog as a representative of the English people against the dominant power of London – symbolised in the novel by the shadowy counter-force of 'Magog' – points to a strain of romantic populism which it is hard to justify historically, no matter how loosely one reads history.

The technique of *Gog* shows the kind of eclecticism that denotes a highly conscious attitude to writing, and which tends to be more characteristic of American writing than of English; Sinclair diversifies, or amplifies, his narrative with interpolated documents, and extracts from film scripts or comic strips. He has emphasised the influence of the cinema :

> *Gog* says there are only three types of truth, a background, a face, and words. There's no psychological motivation whatever, the one thing film can't show. It tries to substitute an incredibly rich evocation of the past. (Ibid.)

Sinclair has spoken of his admiration for Thomas Pynchon's *V.*, an equally elaborate and exuberant fantasy, full of mystifications about identity, whose general influence on the concept and form of *Gog* is not hard to detect. Sinclair's reference to an American author as an influence is, I think, significant. *Gog* seems to offer a mirror-image of much American fiction. The disorientated naked hero without memory whom we encounter at the beginning is reminiscent of the central figures of many American novels. Yet the development of Sinclair's book points in the opposite direction. Whereas American literature has to deal, traditionally, with an alien and history-less landscape, where myths are created by men only in the act of subduing it, Sinclair attempts instead successive penetrations of a rich and deep past. The concern with identity in *Gog* is at the opposite pole to the disembodied though vividly rendered fantasies we find in Pynchon's book and in many other American novels. Yet Sinclair's acknowledgement of Pynchon's influence is one more sign of the way in which many English novels, or more accurately fictional fables, are finding an affinity with American works, an affinity which is not, I think, ultimately to be defined in purely literary terms. With the demise of the unquestioned idea of Nature, English literature, too, is becoming consciously concerned with the Human Condition and with establishing the categories of identity, even though in a characteristically English form.

Sinclair's novel is one way of coping with the sense of collapse of the traditional bourgeois novel, and of a large complex of attitudes and assumptions about the nature of English life and cultural identity. I must confess that I prefer his recourse to the myths underlying our history to the retreat into private myth, which we might call the American alternative. At the same time *Gog* is radically undisciplined and very prolix over large areas, and I dislike its dwelling on violence, which may indeed be an ineradicable part of Sinclair's personal obsessions, but which does not seem altogether free from the dictates of current literary fashion. Quite clearly *Gog* is an intensely personal book, whose approach could not be followed by writers who do not share Sinclair's preoccupations, knowledge and temperament. It does not offer support for anyone who claims that a large-scale recourse to the mythic fable is the appropriate answer for other English novelists facing a cultural impasse.

IV America: The Incredible Reality

> I said: 'I suppose you are writing that great American novel, young hero in search of an identity.' 'Right', he said. 'But I'm not prepared to take that tone of voice from inhabitants of the old world who for some reason I don't understand never have a moment's doubt about their identity.'
>
> DORIS LESSING, *The Golden Notebook*

THERE is a passage in Kingsley Amis's *One Fat Englishman* which sums up English suspicions of American fiction:

> What was in one way most galling to Roger about *Blinkie Heaven* was that it was not, as he had first suspected, entirely staffed by the kind of character America had made its primary fictional concern. There were blind people, true, and the odd Negro, but they were not backed up by the expected paraplegic necrophiles, hippoerotic jockeys, exhibitionistic castrates, coprophagic pig-farmers, armless flagellationists and the rest of the bunch. People like shopkeepers, pedestrians, New Englanders, neighbours, graduates, uncles walked Macher's pages. Events took place and the reader could determine what they were. There was spoken dialogue, appearing between quotation marks.

Conversely, an expatriate British critic, Paul West, has projected a common American counter-image of British writing:

> The British idea of a challenging novel is *Lucky Jim*, which incensed Somerset Maugham but which, as a portrait of society, comes nowhere near Thomas Pynchon's *The Crying of Lot 49* for penetration, originality and something I call the transcendent stare. (*Commonweal*, 17 November 1967)

Paul West makes his comparison between Amis and Pynchon in the course of an article full of eloquent though predictable attacks on the modern English novel for its flatness, gentility and unwillingness to take imaginative chances. The English, Mr West remarks with expatriate severity, are very much in love with their own society, even when they are seemingly satirising it: 'They love it for an absurdity which, for them, reflects nothing universal or even international.' I think this is a fairly accurate observation, although by now it will be apparent that I think the phenomenon it refers to could be treated with more anthropological tolerance than Mr West seems capable of mustering. Nevertheless, his juxtaposition of Pynchon and Amis is potentially illuminating.

Modern English fiction may not, in fact, be as limited as hostile critics such as Mr West allege, but some acquaintance with recent American work can help one to understand why such judgements are so often made, and not only by Americans. Similarly, in my own experience, one understands English life and attitudes infinitely better after a spell in the United States: the kind of enlightenment it can bring has been effectively described by Martin Green in his *A Mirror for Anglo-Saxons*. In this chapter I shall take for granted much of the basic critical discussion about the Americanness of American literature: the ground has already been well covered by such distinguished critics as Leslie Fiedler, Richard Poirer, R. W. B. Lewis and many others. We are familiar with the way in which the heroes of American novels are defiant solitaries, preserving their precious burden of innocence and freedom, establishing, however precariously, their own world around them like the early pioneers: everything, in fact, that John Bayley means when he refers to American literature as being peculiarly concerned with the Human Condition. We know, too, about the persistence of a strain of Gothic fantasy as a central element in American fiction, and, like Kingsley Amis's Roger Micheldene, we expect to meet a high proportion of freakishness and eccentricity. We have been shown at length by Leslie Fiedler how the characters in American novels persist in moral childishness or at best adolescence, and find it very difficult to establish and maintain normal, mature sexual relations. Above all, we have been reminded of the lack of fictionally rewarding social density in nineteenth-century America, in a celebrated passage from Henry James's life of Hawthorne, full of resounding negatives:

No State, in the European sense of the word, and indeed barely a specific national name. No sovereign, no court, no personal loyalty, no aristocracy, no church, no clergy, no army, no diplomatic service, no country gentlemen, no palaces, no castles, nor manors, nor old country houses, no parsonages, nor thatched cottages, nor ivied ruins; no cathedrals, nor abbeys, nor little Norman churches; no great universities nor public schools – no Oxford, nor Eton, nor Harrow; no literature, no novels, no museums, no pictures, no political society, no sporting class – no Epsom nor Ascot!

Some such list as that might be drawn up of the absent things in
American life – especially in the American life of forty years ago,
the effect of which upon an English or French imagination, would
probably as a general thing be appalling.

Richard Poirier has glossed this passage by remarking that nineteenth-century American novelists made determined efforts to evade
even the slight amount of social density that existed at that time in
their country, by habitually retreating in their work into real or
imagined wildernesses, where metaphysical values were more important than social ones. Again, American novels are lacking in the
kind of substantial fictional character admired by English critics. As
Lionel Trilling has remarked:

> I think that if American novels of the past, whatever their merits
> of intensity and beauty, have given us very few substantial or
> memorable people, this is because one of the things that makes
> for substantiality of character in the novel is precisely the nota-
> tion of manners, that is to say, of class traits modified by per-
> sonality. (*The Liberal Imagination*, pp. 261–2)

He goes on to point out that the great characters of American fiction,
like Ahab or Natty Bumppo, are mythic embodiments of ideas
whose 'very freedom from class gives them a large and glowing
generality'.

All these considerations are very relevant to the American novelists of the 'absurdist' or 'comic-apocalyptic' school, who have
emerged in the last few years and whose most brilliant representative is, I think, Thomas Pynchon. Other names would include Joseph
Heller, John Barth, Terry Southern, Stanley Crawford, Jeremy
Larner and Richard Farina. There are, of course, many differences
between them, sufficiently so for one to hesitate to apply the word
'school' at all: nevertheless, to the English reader, their similarities
are more striking than their differences. In such fiction the tragic,
the violent and the comic are interwoven. The conventions of the
realistic novel may be upheld, but only for as long as it suits the
author; at any moment they may be undermined by some unashamedly fantastic or surrealist device. The characters are in no
sense 'rounded' or 'substantial'; they are presented like the boldly
drawn, two-dimensional figures in a comic-strip, with no question of
'freedom' or 'opaqueness' about them. The author is a whole-hearted
manipulator, whose consciousness of what he is doing dominates
the whole novel. And his powers of manipulation frequently

extend to the reader, who is likely to be involved in every kind of trap and mystification. There is often a pervasive sense of disaster, that may or may not be brought to fruition : the film of *Dr Strangelove*, co-scripted by Terry Southern, gave a vivid impression, in another medium, of the quality of such novels. The whole genre has been discussed at length in a splendid essay by R. W. B. Lewis, 'Days of Wrath and Laughter', included in his book *Trials of The Word*. Lewis shows the preoccupation with the biblical apocalypse evident in much nineteenth-century American fiction, and relates it to the absurdist visions of Southern, Heller, Barth and Pynchon.

Leaving aside the nineteenth-century precursors of the comic-apocalyptic school, one finds an immediate ancestor in Nathanael West, who is one of the masters of modern fiction in English. Although very much in the tradition of American prose fantasy, West was one of the few novelists – English or American – to have been successfully influenced by the techniques of continental surrealism. His first work, the novella called *The Dream Life of Balso Snell*, reads like a surrealist five-finger exercise. In West's later novels, notably *Miss Lonelyhearts* and *The Day of the Locust* he evolves stylised fantasies that are frequently absurd but rarely funny. The pressure of actual human misery is always felt : the New York of *Miss Lonelyhearts* is a real city full of real people, whose sufferings drive 'Miss Lonelyhearts', who is actually a male journalist writing an advice-column, steadily mad. Similarly, one could say that the Hollywood of *The Day of the Locust* is 'real', if it were not that such a term has no meaning in the context that West establishes : a veritable Waste Land of houses built in every conceivable style, and film sets that look solid but would collapse at a touch. (It is significant that West places his most powerful novels in the elaborately unreal settings of two of the major mass media : newspapers and the cinema.) One does not find substantial characters in West's fiction; yet if his people are two-dimensional figures, an immense pathos surrounds them. One thinks, for instance, of the seedy Chaplinesque clown, Harry Greener, in *The Day of the Locust*, going through his old theatrical routines like a steadily running-down clockwork toy. The sense of real pain manifested by cardboard or mechanical characters produces some of West's most striking effects; and it is, I think, paralleled in Evelyn Waugh's *A Handful of Dust*, published in 1934, the year after *Miss Lonelyhearts*. In his laconic fashion West is not merely bleak but despairing; the despair rises from his baffled sense of outrage at the intolerableness of the human condition. Unlike the later proponents of comic-apocalyptic fiction, West is a very uncool writer; and it is this that importantly distinguishes him from them.

Another major writer who has affinities with West is Ralph Ellison, whose *Invisible Man* appeared in 1952 : like *The Day of the Locust*, this novel ends with a riot, a vivid image of apocalyptic destruction. *Invisible Man* is a novel of such complexity and distinction, and is so multi-layered, that it would need a lengthy analysis to bring out its full implications. But one can say at once that although it resembles West's work, it is more genuinely comic, and draws on a broader spectrum of emotion. *Invisible Man* is about a latter-day Candide, a clever young coloured boy who is expelled on a pretext from the Southern Negro college where he is a star pupil; he goes to New York, is involved in a variety of odious jobs, and becomes the protégé of a radical political movement that in the end betrays him. *Invisible Man* is, of course, a major example of the literary genre known as the 'negro novel', but one would not do it justice to discuss it only in those terms. If one regards *Invisible Man* as a novel that ultimately refers to the Human Condition in general, one is not selling short its origins in the particular historic and cultural situation of the American Negro – whose plight is manifest in every line that Ellison writes – but is simply following the centrifugal implications of the whole work. For all its elements of sheer fantasy, *Invisible Man* is involved with many areas of human activity : history, politics, sociology. And in the successive dehumanisation of his hero, Ellison links West and the younger novelists I shall shortly be discussing. In the novel's opening paragraph Ellison explains its title : the invisibility is not merely that of the Negro whom white people are accustomed to 'looking through', but points to the common state of individual alienation in mass urban society (already foreshadowed by H. G. Wells in his own novel of the same name).

> I am an invisible man. No, I am not a spook like those who haunted Edgar Allan Poe; nor am I one of your Hollywood-movie ectoplasms. I am a man of substance, of flesh and bone, fibre and liquids – and I might even be said to possess a mind. I am invisible, understand, simply because people refuse to see me. Like the bodiless heads you sometimes see in circus side-shows, it is as though I have been surrounded by mirrors of hard, distorting glass. When they approach me they see only my surroundings,

themselves, or figments of their imagination – indeed, everything and anything except me.

Nor is my invisibility exactly a matter of biochemical accident to my epidermis. That invisibility to which I refer occurs because of a peculiar disposition of the eyes of those with whom I come in contact. A matter of the construction of their inner eyes, those eyes through which they look through their physical eyes upon reality.

The multiple collision of history, violence and absurdity is, if anything, enlarged in Joseph Heller's Catch-22, which appeared in 1962 and already looks like a classic of war literature. Catch-22 is a novel of even greater intricacy than Invisible Man, and has been the subject of good essays by John Wain and Norman Podhoretz.* It is the story of an airman called Yossarian, flying with the U.S. air force in Italy during the latter stages of the Second World War; he thinks he has done enough fighting, but he cannot get out of combat duty, partly because of the malignancy of his commanding officer, who keeps raising the number of missions Yossarian must undertake, and partly because of the general impenetrability and stupidity of the military bureaucracy. Yet any such summary does serious injustice to the complexity and wildness of Heller's novel, which is full of minor characters all busily filling subsidiary roles in the ridiculous drama, and which is written with extraordinary imaginative energy and inventiveness. As Norman Podhoretz has said:

Though ostensibly about an air force squadron in the Second World War, Catch-22 is actually one of the bravest and most nearly successful attempts we have yet had to describe and make credible the incredible reality of American life in the middle of the twentieth century.

Podhoretz writes appreciatively of Heller's achievement, but towards the end of his essay he puts his finger on the central weakness of Catch-22, considered as an exposure of the bloodiness, absurdity and pointlessness of war: does Heller in fact believe that the war against Hitler was nothing but a fraud, with no real values or principles involved? Podhoretz believed that Heller shrinks from giving the affirmative answer that the whole book implies. Its underlying value is the supreme importance of survival, and it insists that the immediate danger to survival comes from one's own military

* John Wain, 'A new Novel About Old Troubles', in Critical Quarterly, Summer 1963; Norman Podhoretz, 'The Best Catch There Is', in Doing and Undoings, 1964.

machine rather than the enemy. The kind of pacifism posited in *Catch-22* seems most sympathethic and plausible when it deals with the victims of an absurd and inhuman military bureaucracy; it is hard to imagine a book like *Catch-22* being written about, say, the French Resistance, rather than the U.S. air force. In such contexts the traditional values of bravery and self-sacrifice that are ridiculed in *Catch-22* preserve their credibility.

Podhoretz makes an important point when he says that Heller is 'trying to make credible the incredible reality of American life in the middle of the twentieth century'. It has been amplified by Norman Mailer when he compares the Vietnam War with the nightmare visons of William Burroughs :

> If World War II was like *Catch-22*, this war will be like *Naked Lunch*. Lazy Dogs, and bombing raids from Guam. Marines with flame throwers. Jungle gotch in the gonorrhea and South Vietnamese girls doing the Frug. South Vietnamese fighter pilots 'dressed in black flying suits and lavender scarves'. (*Cannibals and Christians*, 1967 : pp. 85–6)

It seems to me that in absurdist or comic-apocalyptic fiction there are two opposed impulses at work. The first of them is, in its own way, realistic; that is to say, it grapples with the 'incredible reality' and tries to understand it, if not make it wholly credible. The difficulty is, of course, that American reality is constantly transcending itself, moving to heights of absurdity or horror that leave the most extravagantly inventive novelist lagging behind. What work of comic-apocalyptic fiction, for instance, could rival the vast and growing volume of writing, whether speculative or factual, about the events in Dallas in November 1963, full of fantastic suggestions of conspiracy and counter-conspiracy? Again, one's immediate response to hearing of the assassination of Robert Kennedy was that this event had the sick inevitability of an episode in a tightly plotted absurdist novel.

Even in far less dramatic ways, passages that strike the outsider as wildly exaggerated can in fact be no more than straightforward descriptions of a bizarre reality. Consider, for instance, this description from Stanley Crawford's *Gascoyne*. The eponymous narrator, an eccentric tycoon who spends his whole life driving around in battered old cars, pulls in at a gas station that he happens to own, but where he is not known to the staff :

But first I need gas and so I pull into the next BIG DADDY SERV-

UR-SELPH STATION and stop the car and hop out and flip open
the gas port and unscrew the gascap. Then I stick the nozzle in
and let go with BIG DADDY PURPLE CROWN HIGHER OCTANE
ETHYL and tell the boy to shove three quarts of BIG DADDY
ROYAL GRADE IMPERIAL 30 SAE SLUDGE BANISHING DE-
TERGENT LUBRICATING LIQUID into the engine and add a
little can of Garfield F. Geen's Original Friction Stopper because
I've got about seven clackety valves ...

The guy hands me my bill for fifteen dollars and eighty-nine
cents along with thirty-two BIG DADDY PURPLE PAISLEY
STAMPS which can be redeemed at the end of the year for the
appropriate number of cases of BIG DADDY SUPER KRAZY
KOLA which cannot be otherwise obtained or bought from any
source whatever. I pull out my BIG DADDY BIG CHARGE CARD
and present it to the attendant and he goes through the usual
facial gymnastics upon looking at it and of course when he goes
into the office I can see him rounding up the rest of the staff to
come and take a peek at the BIG DADDY HIMSELF IN PERSON.
When he comes back I have only one criticism to offer him on
how the place is run, which is, 'Son, I think you'll inspire more
customer loyalty and make people feel at home here if you do
not erase what they write above the toilets.'

It is presumably in the desperate attempt to get beyond any conceivable reality that Crawford introduces into his novel such surrealist touches as a young man with an octopus tentacle growing
out of his left ear (one can compare the character with a four-inch
petrified homunculus inside his body in another recent example of
this genre, Stanley Elkins's *A Bad Man*). Passages that look as if they
ought to be satirical often turn out to be charmingly whimsical,
simply because one is quite unsure of just how they relate to the
actual possibilities of American life. Or, quite often, of Californian
life; both the next two instances are set in that state. First, the
electronic music bar in Pynchon's *The Crying of Lot 49*:

A sudden chorus of whoops and yibbles burst from a kind of
juke box at the far end of the room. Everybody quit talking. The
bartender tiptoed back, with the drinks.

'What's happening?' Oedipa whispered.

'That's by Stockhausen,' the hip graybeard informed her, 'the
early crowd tends to dig your Radio Cologne sound. Later on we
really swing. We're the only bar in the area, you know, that has a
strictly electronic music policy.'

Next, the campus chapel at Subliminal University of Los Angeles,
in *John Goldfarb, Please Come Home!* by William Peter Blatty (Mr
Blatty is, I believe, a citizen of the Lebanon, but he writes as a

skilled practitioner of American absurdist fiction). The chapel must be built in a form that would 'eschew even the remotest suggestion of forms or symbolisms associated with any particular creed or persuasion'. The difficulty is that any conceivable shape seems to have some associative significance:

> Spires were Gothic and Thomistic; squares Aristotelian; circles Confucian; and triangles clearly insinuated a Star of David. Even ellipses were out, for one of the trustees, who fancied himself as a whiz at Rorschachs, had espied in them an irresistible link to Holy Rollerism.

In the end, the architects in collaboration with the School of Chemistry design the chapel as a scale enlargement of an uncrystallised crystal: 'i.e. an *actual amorphous mass*'. This is described as a marvel of ambiguity, which can offend no-one.

> Unfortunately, however, no one had ever been able to find the entrance; except, of course, the original planners and designers, who were last seen entering it two days prior to its formal opening and had yet to re-emerge. Like ancient Egyptian tomb builders, they were permanently sealed in and the School of Chemistry was now being petitioned to do something about the smell.

One aspect of American reality which these novelists have seized upon is the motor-car: the sensations of driving, and the way in which the motorist is turned into a mechanised centaur, are lovingly exploited. Although cars are becoming nearly as common in England as in America, there is little sign of this element in English fiction; perhaps because driving in American cars offers a different kind of experience from driving in English ones. As Marshall McLuhan has remarked, in America one is in the car; in Europe one is on the road. *Gascoyne*, in which much of the action takes place in cars, offers some fine examples of the pleasures of driving, notably the mini-apocalypse of the car crash, or what Gascoyne calls a 'freeway spectacular':

> About then some idiot coming the opposite direction on the Skyway jumps the centre strip and goes end over end clear across into our slow lane and piles into a moving van and the whole shooting match plows through the side railing and sails off the Skyway into the SKYWAY VIEW HOMES FOR FAST-LIVING FAMILIES TRACT and the last I see of them is an orange glow down below out the rearview, somebody down there's going to have something to talk about over breakfast. That's about the fanciest one I've seen in a long time and I get to see quite a few

because one of the advantages of being on the road all the time is you pretty often find yourself in a front row seat for freeway spectaculars.

Such passages illustrate the cool relish of disaster which is a noticeable feature of absurdist fiction. In Terry Southern's *Flash and Filigree* there is a virtuoso piece of writing which describes how Dr Eichner regularly beats a traffic light by driving at ninety miles an hour, and how narrowly he escapes a fatal accident when someone tries to edge him off the road. In Jeremy Larner's aptly named *Drive, He Said* (the title comes from a poem by Robert Creeley) there is a similar episode: 'He floored his accelerator, his tires yelping as they jerked from the road. Because it was four years old, too old for the good of the country, the automatic transmission bucked, and that one buck was enough for the faster Caddy to jump right back on his bumper.' This kind of writing clearly derives from the descriptions of car chases and other examples of wild driving in thrillers; in fact, much American absurdist fiction relates to thrillers, comic strips and cheap science fiction in ways that make it a literary equivalent of Pop Art. Significantly, writers with literary pretensions, such as Crawford, Southern or Larner, seem to me to offer a more authentic account of driving than a British thriller-writer such as Ian Fleming, whose works are full of similar episodes and knowingness about cars generally. A different kind of relationship with the car is indicated by a scene in Pynchon's *V.*, in which Benny Profane overhears Rachel Owlglass talking to her MG sportscar as she washes it:

'You beautiful stud,' he heard her say, 'I love to touch you.' Wha, he thought. 'Do you know what I feel when we're out on the road? Alone, just us?' She was running the sponge caressingly over its front bumper. 'Your funny responses, darling, that I know so well. The way your brakes pull a little to the left, the way you start a shudder around 5000 r.p.m. when you're excited. And you burn oil when you're mad at me, don't you? I know.'

This is an early example of the symbiosis between human beings and mechanical objects that is a dominant theme in *V*.

One could go on multiplying examples of the way in which American novelists try to make 'credible the incredible reality of American life', by a variety of stratagems; whether by exaggeration or distortion that tries to be satirical; or merely attempts at a particular form of black or heartless humour; or by using the reality as the basis for a virtuoso stylistic exercise. We may now develop the analogy with Pop Art. Throughout the existence of this form of painting, critics have veered between explanations that see it as a new mode of figurative art, satirising the artifacts and icons of commercial mass culture, and those more austere accounts that see Pop Art as essentially unconcerned with figurative and still less with satirical elements, being interested in iconic elements only as part of an organisation that is purely formal and aesthetic. There is a comparable division in absurdist fiction, between the writers of whom one can posit some kind of relationship to American reality, or reality in general, and those who are much more concerned with establishing their own individual reality, in a self-contained verbal universe. The latter is the second and opposed impulse to which I have referred : the novelist, who must use words with meanings, cannot construct a self-contained aesthetic monad, or write as an activity of pure style, whatever the promptings of neo-aesthetes such as Susan Sontag. But, like many writers of the Modern Movement, he may see such autonomy as an ultimate goal. At this point I should like to glance back at my previous discussion of John Bayley's preference for novels which are concerned with Nature, and are transparent to life, or experience, or reality; and those which, like American novels, are about the Human Condition, and which must begin by adopting an attitude to experience, and making an act of pioneering self-definition. Within the fiction of the Human Condition there is, I think a distinction between the wish to reach outward, centrifugally, as it were, to a shared world of experiences, whether these are treated satirically, derisively or elegia-cally; and the opposed, or centripetal, desire to stress the sheer artificiality of writing a novel, only allowing oneself to be interested in it as an elaborate verbal structure. John Barth is a distinguished practitioner of the latter approach; he has remarked that 'if you are a novelist of a certain type of temperament, then what you really want to do is reinvent the world'. The critic Robert Scholes, who greatly admires Barth, has written :

> The old realistic novel has always assumed that a readily ascer-tainable thing called reality exists, and that we all live in it; therefore, it is the only thing to write about. But Barth says that he doesn't 'know much about Reality'. He declines the realistic gambit, refuses to accept the notion that the truth can be cap-tured just by reporting the way things are. Barth insists on an

inevitable 'discrepancy between art and the Real Thing'. (*The Fabulators*, pp. 136–7)

To recapitulate: John Bayley and John Barth represent opposed poles in the possible field of discourse about the novel; in practice most novelists and critics of the novel take up intermediate positions along the spectrum (for historical and cultural reasons most English writers will be closer to the Bayley end). Yet, for all his extremity, Barth is doing no more than develop certain implications in the traditional American way of thinking about the novel, and giving them a twentieth-century philosophical emphasis.

There is a relevant passage in Richard Poirier's *A World Elsewhere*:

> As I use the word 'environment', it means not the places named in a novel, like Chicago, let us say. Environment refers instead to the places filled in a book, filled with words that might indeed pretend to describe Chicago, but which in fact set a boundary on a wholly imaginary city in which the community of language shared by reader, characters, and author necessarily limits the possible shapes that action, persons, and language itself can assume. (1967: pp. 13–14)

I do not know whether Poirier realised it, but these words read like an expansion of a famous proposition from Wittgenstein's *Tractatus Logico-Philosophicus*: 'the limits of my language mean the limits of my world' (5.6). The mention of Wittgenstein is not fortuitous, for both Pynchon and Barth allude to, or quote from, the *Tractatus* in their novels. In chapter 9 of *V.* a German radio engineer in South West Africa called Mondaugen receives a mysterious signal, which, on being decoded, reveals Mondaugen's own name, plus a pregnant phrase in German:

> 'The remainder of the message,' Weissmann continued, 'now reads: DIEWELTISALLESWASSERFALLIST'.
> 'The world is all that the case is,' Mondaugen said. 'I've heard that somewhere before'.

The phrase is, of course, the opening proposition of the *Tractatus*; there is a joke in Mondaugen saying that he has heard it somewhere before, since the *Tractatus* was first published in 1921, and this episode takes place in the following year. The phrase recurs later in *V.*, when a strange creature called Charisma, a shapeless entity always hidden under a blanket, starts to sing:

> It is something less than heaven
> To be quoted Thesis 1.7
> Every time I make an advance;
> If the world is all that the case is
> That's a pretty discouraging basis
> On which to pursue
> Any sort of romance.
> I've got a proposition for you;
> Logical, positive and brief.
> And at least it could serve as a kind of comic relief.

We find the phrase in John Barth's early novel, *The End of the Road*, when the hero, Jacob Horner, is being harangued by a doctor about the nature of reality:

> There's no reason in the long run why Italy shouldn't be shaped like a sausage instead of a boot, but that doesn't happen to be the case. *The world is everything that is the case*, and what the case is is not a matter of logic.

And we find it again, more obliquely, in Barth's *The Sot-Weed Factor* in a conversation between Mary Mungummory and Ebenezer Cooke:

> 'Ofttimes I felt his fancy bore a clutch of worlds, all various, of which the world these books described was one –'
> 'Which, while 'twas splendid here and there,' the Laureate interrupted, 'he could not but loathe for having been *the case*.'

The 'world is everything that is the case' means that the world is what propositions are about when they are true. In the words of one commentator on the *Tractatus*:

> the principal theme of the book is the connection between language, or thought, and reality. The main thesis about this is that sentences, or their mental counterparts, are pictures of facts. Only we must not suppose that what is pictured by a proposition has to exist . . . (G. E. M. Anscombe, *An Introduction to Wittgenstein's Tractatus*, 1959: p. 19)

Not all propositions are true, of course. Why novelists like Barth and Pynchon feel interested in the *Tractatus*, presumably, is because it shows a world of language whose relation to the 'real' world, or ultimate reality, is oblique and problematical.

If Barth and Pynchon have made far less impact in England than in the United States, it is, perhaps, not just because of a lazy English distaste for literary experimentation, though this is doubtless a factor; it may also be that the English, in their conservative way, are still inclined to believe in reality as traditionally conceived, and are less readily inclined to sympathise with authors whose premise is that such reality no longer exists, or at least is inaccessible, and that the novelist must produce some new and possibly better version. One is, in fact, back with the impasse of the novel that I discussed in earlier chapters; an impasse that, on the whole, the English do not recognise, whatever Americans or Continentals may believe. As we have seen, Beckett or Robbe-Grillet deal radically with the problem: the one by collapsing all human attributes, save the voice, which continues its firm if despairing protest in a totally barren environment; the other by stripping away all attributes save the perceiving eye, which is, perhaps, another name for the camera lens.

Pynchon and Barth deal with the situation in a different way, not by abandoning the traditional attributes of the novel, but by refusing to take them seriously, exaggerating or distorting everything to the point of absurdity or beyond. As Robert Scholes remarks, 'By his exaggeration of "plottiness" in a work like *The Sot-Weed Factor*, Barth finally causes us to take his plot more lightly than we might take a less rococo arrangements of events' (*The Fabulators*, p. 173). It is not merely plot we are invited to take lightly, for humanity itself is placed at a similar discount, either being reduced to the level of comic-strip humanoids, or else subjected to the most hideous humiliations, which we are invited to observe with calm indifference. Thus, at the end of Barth's *The End of the Road* there is a scene, described in gruesome detail, in which a woman dies. from a clumsily performed abortion: this is presented with total detachment and absence of emotion. In general Barth manifests a perfect contempt for humanity, which is perhaps the penalty for desiring to construct one's own model of reality; human life, being part of the original, rejected version is inevitably swept aside. Not, of course, that one should underrate Barth's enormous literary skill, which is very prominent in *The Sot-Weed Factor*, an excessively long novel, written in an accomplished pastiche of early eighteenth-century prose, describing the adventures of Ebenezer Cooke, an English poet who becomes the Laureate of Maryland, and who is constantly encountering and losing again a protean figure called Henry Burlingame. I must confess that I found the cumulative tedium of *The Sot-Weed Factor* too much for me, and it is the only novel I discuss in this book that I have not read to the end of; nevertheless I have read enough to convince me that there is an astonishing imbalance between Barth's verbal brilliance and skill as a pasticheur, and the narrowness of his emotional range. There is an underlying crudity in the writing which can make Fielding, with whom Robert Scholes rashly compares him, seem infinitely sensitive and subtle. *Giles Goat-Boy*, Barth's most recent novel, has attained an immense reputation in America, rather similar to that of Lawrence Durrell's *Alexandria Quartet* in England in the 1960s. It is, again, a book indicating great skill and stamina on the part of the author, and an endlessly ramifying fancy, if little real imagination; reading it is rather like being imprisoned – for ever as it seems – in a vast comic strip, full of the denizens of the huge university that Barth has constructed as his alternative to the real world. The novel is, among many other things, the campus novel to end all, and may even mark the end of that interesting genre; but another reason for academic approval of *Giles Goat-Boy* may reflect the fact that it is an explicator's paradise – Martin Green has described it as the fictional equivalent of Northrop Frye's *Anatomy of Criticism* * – and full of allegorical ingenuities. Robert Scholes, who writes a detailed, rhapsodic appreciation of the novel, in fact refers to it as a new holy book for our times. For all the attempted encyclopaedism of both *The Sot-Weed Factor* and *Giles Goat-Boy*, both books are, essentially, about the diversity and unpredictability of their author's mind, as Tony Tanner has shown in a perceptive and sympathetic essay on Barth. I dislike more things in *Giles Goat-Boy* than he does : notably, its crudity of vision, its basic thinness of texture, and above all its manic repetitiveness. Nevertheless I agree with Tanner about what he calls the book's atmosphere of 'brilliant frivolity', which he compares with the *Wizard of Oz*, and with his final suggestion that 'there is a point at which the arbitrary unimpeded sport of sheer mind damages rather than nourishes a novel, and that in *Giles Goat-Boy* John Barth sails, determinedly, clear past it'.† Yet it is possible to see *Giles Goat-Boy* in a more sinister light. For all the parallels in the book between the universe and the university, which are stressed *ad nauseum* and beyond, there is another parallel, less obvious but equally significant, that

* See *Innovations*, ed. Bergonzi, p. 179 n.
† 'The Hoax That Joke Bilked', in *Partisan Review*, Winter 1967.

seems to me worth pointing out. For much of the time I am reminded less of a campus than of a camp: Mr Barth seems to have
erected and to preside calmly over the dreadful enclosed system of
l'univers concentrationnaire, and to exhibit a sensibility that I can
only describe as aesthetic totalitarianism.

What is, perhaps, generally characteristic of the writers of the
comic-apocalyptic school is a degree of deliberate coolness that
can very readily turn into an inhuman coldness. It is this that distinguishes them from writers such as Nathanael West and Ralph
Ellison, who are also preoccupied with the absurdity of the universe,
but who have an equally strong grasp on human values. The distinction is apparent in tone, even where the subject matter is similar.
Thus, there is a recurrent preoccupation with deformity in West's
writing, which is horrifyingly apparent in one of the pitiful letters
sent to Miss Lonelyhearts, like the one from the girl born without
a nose: 'I sit and look at myself all day and cry. I have a big hole in
the middle of my face that scares people even myself so I cant
blame the boys for not wanting to take me out.' For West such
things are one more outrage inflicted on a suffering humanity. For
Thomas Pynchon, on the other hand, they are a matter for comic
relief:

> Collected for her in the anteroom that day were a rogues' gallery
> of malformed. A bald woman without ears contemplated the
> gold imp-clock, skin flush and shiny from temples to occiput.
> Beside her sat a younger girl, whose skull was fissured such that
> three separate peaks, paraboloid in shape, protruded above the
> hair, which continued down either side of a densely acned face
> like a skipper's beard.

And so on for a whole paragraph of fastidious prose, which presents
these specimens of unfortunate humanity like the creatures in some
sick comic.

Again, in Invisible Man, there is an episode in which the hero is
incarcerated in the hospital of the paint factory where he has been
working, and is subjected to some form of electrical therapy by two
fiendish doctors. Ellison draws freely on the situations of sensational
science fiction:

> Now a man sitting with his back to me, manipulating dials on a
> panel. I wanted to call him, but the Fifth Symphony rhythm
> racked me, and he seemed too serene and too far away. Bright
> metal bars were between us and when I strained my neck around
> I discovered that I was not lying on an operating table but in a

kind of glass and nickel box, the lid of which was propped open. Why was I here?

Yet, for all the elaboration of farcical horror, we never forget that the victim is a real victim, and we share his successive sensations of fear, pain and outrage; all of them forming yet one more episode in the long series of humiliations he has undergone since his boyhood. This particular episode is a product, one presumes, of Ellison's imagination; but some of the earlier scenes, as when the young narrator is one of a group of negro boys who are forced by the white citizens of his native Southern town to stare at a naked blonde and then box each other blindfold, read like transcripts from a hideous reality. In Barth and Pynchon there are scenes similar to the one in Ellison's factory hospital; but there is no comparable concern for the victim's feelings. The tone is predictably cold, and the only apparent response is a certain cool relish at the monstrous absurdity of what is going on. In fact, much of the most admired American fiction of the last ten years seems to spring from a radically desensitised response to life.

Richard Poirier has remarked that 'in the works of Thomas Pynchon human beings drift into the category of the inanimate'. Certainly V., which is a highly impressive imaginative construction, is a monument to the possibilities of dehumanisation. If I prefer Pynchon to Barth, it is because he has a far lighter touch, and lacks Barth's obsessive repetitiveness; both V. and The Crying of Lot 49 are pervaded by a chilly gaiety, of a sort one does not find in Barth. Yet there are evident similarities between these writers, in the way that they project impossibly elaborate versions of reality. Both of them are given to the large-scale rewriting of actual history, as in The Sot-Weed Factor, and in V., where we find episodes set in Egypt at the time of the Fashoda incident, in Paris just before the First World War, in Malta shortly after it, then in South-West Africa, and again in Malta on the eve of the Suez invasion, all interspersed with scenes set in the America of the 1950s. In The Crying of Lot 49, which is a much shorter book, there is even more history, of a highly circumstantial kind: the book's unbelievably elaborate plot is about an underground postal service called Tristero, supposedly founded in the Low Countries in the late sixteenth century, which has persisted in a shadowy way over the centuries in Europe, and is active in California at the present time (if, of course, it has ever existed, and is not a hoax by the dead tycoon Pierce Invararity). This concern with rewriting, in an immensely detailed and plausible way, the history of both the recent and the remote past, and the constant probing of the relation between fiction and reality, seems to me to owe a good deal to the writings of Jorge Luis Borges.

V., like the *Sot-Weed Factor*, is a quest-novel, a form that allows for almost endless episodic performances. Certainly Pynchon seems to have indulged in a great deal of freewheeling improvisation in the early part of his novel, especially in the scenes dealing with Benny Profane, an amiable layabout looking for work in New York, and his friends, who are known as the Whole Sick Crew. Some of these episodes, such as the one in which Benny joins a squad whose duty is to find and shoot the alligators infesting the New York sewers, achieve a fine wild comedy. The tight plotting comes in the other, and increasingly dominant, part of the novel; it describes the attempts of a middle-aged Englishman, Hubert Stencil, to find a mysterious creature called V., who had once attracted his father. V. is probably a woman who first appears in Egypt in 1898 as Victoria Wren; in later manifestations in Malta and South-West Africa she is known as Veronica Manganese and Vera Meroving, and she is probably but not certainly killed in an air raid on Malta during the Second World War. But other lesser manifestations associated with 'V.' are a rat called Veronica, the state of Venezuela, an imaginary country called Vheissu, a bar in New York called the V-note, the German weapons known as V.1 and V.2, and the city of Valetta in Malta. Pynchon combines the intricacy of his plotting with a symbolist openness to all possible elements suggested by the. letter 'V', thereby greatly adding to the confusing quality of his book. Having established a tight structure based on the quest for 'V', to which every subsidiary manifestation of 'V'-ness can be linked in a paranoid way, Pynchon is then at liberty to intersperse it with long episodes drawn from obscure tracts of modern history that have no visible connection with the central quest; such as the attempt at an uprising by Venezuelan exiles in Florence in 1899, or the grisly account of German atrocities in South-West Africa in the early 1900s, where the cruelty is described in a predictably cool and detached manner. (There is also in V. a curious subsidiary interest in British imperialism, ranging from the Goon Show heroics of Captain Hugh Godolphin in the late nineties to its final disastrous fling at Suez in 1956.) For all the painstaking circumstantial skill with which these episodes are presented, they remain curiously intangible, like a flickering magic-lantern show; recalling, in the end, not the variousness and solidity of history, but the infinite inventiveness of the mind of Thomas Pynchon (and the large amount of research that must have been put into them).

Where I find *V.* most interesting, and at the same time most disturbing, is in the thorough way in which it shows the possibilities of dehumanisation, of people being transformed into something else. One sees it in chapter 1, with Benny Profane's vision of his own eventual dismemberment: 'if he kept going down that street, not only his ass but also his arms, legs, sponge brain and clock of a heart must be left behind to litter the pavement, be scattered among manhole covers'. (This vision has been prefigured in the dismantlement of Lemuel Pitkin at the end of West's *A Cool Million*.) A little later in *V.* we are introduced to Fergus Mixolydian, reputedly the laziest living being in New York, who has a special switch to turn his television set off, worked by electrodes fixed to his arm, which operates when he falls asleep: 'Fergus thus became an extension of the TV set.' In the Egyptian episode an Englishman called Bongo-Shaftesbury describes himself as an electro-mechanical doll, and shows Victoria Wren a switch in his arm from which wires run into his brain. There are many more examples in *V.* of Pynchon's fascination with the symbiosis of the mechanical and the organic; it is evident even in the figurative language of casual description: 'Three jailbait, all lipstick and shiny-machined breast- and buttock-surfaces, stood in front of the wheel of Fortune, twitching and hollow-eyed.'

But the most striking and extended examples occur when Benny Profane has a spell as nightwatchman at an institute called Anthroresearch Associates, guarding two humanoid entities, SHROUD (Synthetic Human, Radiation Output Determined) and SHOCK (Synthetic Human Object, Casualty Kinematics). Here is Pynchon's description of SHROUD, where the bizarre imaginings of the science-fiction writer link up with the achieved technological marvels habitually displayed in the Sunday colour-supplements:

> Its skin was cellulose acetate butyrate, a plastic transparent not only to light but also to X-rays, gamma rays and neutrons. Its skeleton had once been that of a living human; now the bones were decontaminated and the long ones and spinal column hollowed inside to receive radiation dosimenters. SHROUD was five feet nine inches tall – the fiftieth percentile of Air Force Stan-

dards. The lungs, sex organs, kidneys, thyroid, liver, spleen and other internal organs were hollow and made of the same clear plastic as the body shell. These could be filled with aqueous solutions which absorbed the same amount of radiation as the tissue they represented.

SHOCK is an equally fantastic manikin, used for testing the effect of car accidents on the human organism: 'Inside were a blood reservoir in the thorax, a blood pump in the midsection and a nickel-cadium battery power supply in the abdomen.' The numbness one feels on reading Pynchon's brilliant descriptions of these objects arises, I think, precisely because one is unable to dismiss them as wild satirical exaggeration: to return to a point I made previously: with such passages one has no assurance that American reality (or, more properly, Western technological progress) has not caught up with or surpassed even the most extravagant fictional inventions of this kind. Later, Profane reflects:

> Someday, please God, there would be an all-electric woman. Maybe her name would be Violet. Any problems with her, you could look it up in the maintenance manual. Module concept: fingers' weight, heart's temperature, mouth's size out of tolerance? Remove and replace, was all.*

V. herself, the central entity of the novel, is shown to have more and more artificial parts incorporated into her as the novel develops – in a way that recalls but goes beyond Swift's 'A Beautiful Young Nymph Going to Bed' – including an artificial eye containing a clock. In Stencil's final version of V. he sees her as entirely 'an inanimate object of desire': 'skin radiant with the bloom of some new plastic; both eyes glass but now containing photoelectric cells, connected by silver electrodes to optic nerves of purest copper wire . . .' R. W. B. Lewis (*Trials of the Word*, 1965: p. 231) suggestively relates V. to Gudrun in Lawrence's *Women in Love*, who is described as 'a new Daphne, turning not into a tree but a machine'. Certainly *Women in Love* is full of apocalyptic motifs, which have been discussed at length in a fine essay by Frank Kermode ('D. H. Lawrence and the Apocalyptic Types', in *Continuities*, 1968); but Mr Lewis, I think, overstates the resemblances.

---

* Much of this was anticipated by Marshall McLuhan in the title-essay of *The Mechanical Bride*, first published in 1951.

Lawrence regarded the mechanisation of humanity with rage and despair, whilst Pynchon sees it as a subject for cool, amused contemplation.

My admiration for *V.*, though reluctant for the reasons I have indicated, is, in the last analysis, genuine. But one cannot feel at all happy about the impetus which it and Barth's books have given to countless inferior essays in the absurdist vein by aspiring American novelists; writers who ten years ago would have written efficient, realistic campus novels, are now plunging into the comic-apocalyptic manner, which is of course temptingly easy to adopt, if one has verbal skill and inventiveness and not much experience of life. Like Barth, Pynchon is interested in exploding the traditional 'well-made' novel, by taking its conventions to the pitch of impossible elaboration. *V.*, and still more *The Crying of Lot 49*, might be described as extended puns on the different senses of the word 'plot'. The latter novel may indeed be, as Paul West implies, a penetrating portrait of society (at least, of contemporary Californian society), but it is also a literary-critical novel about what it means for a novel to have a plot. Pynchon sees a traditional literary plot as something which, if it existed in the real world, would impose incredible correspondences, coincidences, parallels, and convergences on experience, in a way that one would normally regard as paranoid. This is clear from a striking passage in *Lot 49*, where Oedipa Maas wanders at night through the streets of San Francisco, seeing everywhere the posthorn emblem of the underground postal service, Tristero, by which she is increasingly obsessed. At the end of this novel Pynchon's self-contained verbal universe moves closer and closer to the nightmare reality of America. The final pages have a more genuine emotional power than anything else in Pynchon's books, showing Oedipa Maas's culminating sense of desolation as she attends a stamp auction waiting for fresh evidence of the reality of Tristero. The tone becomes, in fact, strangely uncool, with an emotion that seems – in Eliot's phrase about *Hamlet* – in excess of the facts; since the 'facts' have always been both circumstantial and absurd. In this sequence Oedipa sees herself imprisoned in the ramifications of a 'plot' that shows no signs of converging to resolution in the traditional way, 'like walking among matrices of a great digital computer, the zeroes and ones twinned above, hanging like balanced mobiles right and left, ahead, thick, maybe endless'. The computer plays a significant part in absurdist fiction, like the

Smedley IV, in Blatty's *John Goldfarb, Please Come Home!*: 'It sat squat and arrogant, conversing with itself and thinking quicksilver thoughts. *"I love me, I love me . . ."* it pulsed serenely, over and over again.' (Computers also occur in an entertaining British novel, Michael Frayn's *The Tin Men*.) But by far the most prominent computer in fiction is in *Giles Goat-Boy*, where the giant computer WESAC not only dominates the action of the book, but actually writes it. The implication seems clear: if good old-fashioned 'plottiness' is what one wants, then the computer can be programmed to provide it more effectively than any merely human author. Here we see the ultimate triumph of dehumanisation.

The authors I have so far discussed in this chapter do, it must be admitted, possess an intellectual power, a verbal skill and a degree of ingenuity that one does not find in most of their English contemporaries. They approach the problems of writing fiction with an intense, probing consciousness, and their solutions are both very modern and very much in the traditions of American fiction, stressing the fantastic, the fabulous, the allegorical, and inventing their own 'world', in a self-contained verbal environment. They also show the novel opening itself to the non-literary elements of the comic-strip, the thriller and science fiction (though this need not seem such a radical step if one recalls Leslie Fiedler's dictum that the novel was the original form of Pop Art). Yet the cost has been high: in the hands of these writers the novel has increasingly abandoned richness for ingenuity, and has taken on a brittle, deliberately flat quality, where most of the traditional human preoccupations and emotions are conspicuous by their absence. It may be argued, of course, that they are doing no more than reflect what Podhoretz calls the 'incredible nature' of American reality; but if this is so, then it is done without comment and without apparent distancing, in ways that correspond to what Marcuse has called the 'one-dimensional' consciousness.

There are, of course, other forces at work in American fiction, notably in the writing of Saul Bellow. Readers who regard the absurdist novelists with bemusement or distaste may well turn with relief to the greater human centrality of Bellow. As, indeed, does R. W. B. Lewis who admires them: at the end of his essay, 'Days of Wrath and Laughter' (*Trials of the Word*), he refers to 'symptoms of an impatient counterimpulse, a restive disclaimer of the apocalyptic temper' (p. 234), and quotes from one of the innumerable unposted letters of Moses Herzog: 'Safe, comfortable people playing at crisis, alienation, apocalypse and desperation, make me sick.' Herzog wants to get away from the Waste Land mentality, and complains that 'we love apocalypses too much and crisis ethics and florid extremism with all its thrilling language'. Herzog's point is certainly relevant to the culture of the West, with its current orthodoxy of extremism and desperation, so acutely analysed by Lionel Trilling in *Beyond Culture*. More than with most other American novelists, Bellow's attitudes to literature are likely to appeal to an English reader. He has said, 'I think that the development of realism in the nineteenth century is still the major event of modern literature' (*Writers at Work: Third Series*, 1967: p. 180). The adverb is significant, and shows how different Bellow's position is from that of the continental or American avant-gardists. He identified himself with Herzog's distaste for the extreme manifestations of the elegiac or apocalyptic mood in modern literature, and observes: 'I think a good deal of *Herzog* can be explained simply by the implicit assumption that existence, quite apart from any of our judgments, has value, that existence is worthful.' One can regard this sentiment as more acceptable than the inhuman assumptions of the absurdist school, and yet remain unconvinced about the extent to which it is backed up in *Herzog*. It is, after all, a very enclosed, crepuscular novel, the thoughts and associations of Moses Herzog as he sits in his half-derelict house in the woods of western Massachusetts:

Tenants of the house,
Thoughts of a dry brain in a dry season.

The book's opening sentence is: 'If I am out of my mind, it's all right with me, thought Moses Herzog.' In the novel there is a good deal of incident, some of it comic, some pathetic, some absurd; there are also, of course, the famous letters, which carry an interesting collection of reflections, but which, considered as ideas, are very externally applied to the main outlines of the story. In so far as *Herzog* is a striking, and sometimes moving, revelation of character in an old-fashioned way, then it can be regarded as a traditional novel; but in so far as one never moves far away from the confined and basically self-approbating consciousness of the hero, then it is a characteristically modern one, and perhaps an example of what Moravia describes as the 'essay-novel'. At the end of the novel,

Moses Herzog's remoteness, in time as well as space, from the larger world is emphasised:

> No one came here. He had only gentle, dotty old neighbours, Jukes and Kallikaks, rocking themselves to death on their porches, watching television, the nineteenth century quietly dying in this remote green hole. Well, this was his own, his hearth; these were *his* birches, catalpas, horse chestnuts. His rotten dreams of peace.

Like nature, culture abhors a vacuum, and if the novel of character and affirmation in the worth of life is – despite Bellow's inclinations – something of a rarity in America (above, that is to say, the level of Midcult appreciation, to which *Herzog* patently owed a large measure of its success, though to say this is not to make any direct criticism of the novel), then the extravagances of comic-apocalyptic fiction, offering elaborate alternatives to reality, have arisen to fill the gap. In England, traditional attitudes are still far more alive; yet here, too, there is a noticeable strain of apocalypticism in the contemporary novel, even though it is of a less self-confident and assertive kind than the work of the American authors I have discussed.

V Looking Backward

> Imagination = nostalgia for the past, the absent; it is the
> liquid solution in which art develops the snapshots of
> reality.   CYRIL CONNOLLY, *The Unquiet Grave*

I

A NOTICEABLE development in English fiction during the last
twenty years has been the tendency for established writers to
embark on long fictional explorations of the recent past in extended
works, running into several volumes. I am thinking of such novelists
as Evelyn Waugh, Anthony Powell, C. P. Snow, Henry Williamson,
Lawrence Durrell and Philip Toynbee, who have all written works
which, whether overtly autobiographical or only obliquely so, are
largely focused on the period between 1920 and 1950 (Henry
Williamson's *Chronicle of Ancient Sunlight*, being the work of an
older man, goes back a good deal further). Two of these works,
Evelyn Waugh's *Sword of Honour* and Anthony Powell's still in-
complete *roman fleuve The Music of Time*, seem to me the major
achievements of post-war English fiction.

In his early comic novels Evelyn Waugh offered some interesting
anticipations of the American comic-apocalyptic, or black comic,
manner; indeed, the world war at the end of *Vile Bodies* is a choice
example of a global fictional apocalypse, and I have already referred
to the way in which *A Handful of Dust* seems to recall Nathanael
West. Yet this same novel, published in 1934, is also of interest in
containing the first representation of a myth that was increasingly
to dominate Waugh's fiction. Waugh was, of course, an intensely
English writer, with a willed dedication to the traditional pieties of
English life: the country house, the aristocracy, the monarchy.
Towards the end of his life he came to act out more and more the
public role of a lovable English eccentric; the nihilistic satire of his
early books, which was largely aimed at the upper classes, had been
long since abondoned. As a Roman Catholic, however, Waugh was
somewhat cut off from the main currents of English tradition,
though he had no sympathy with the Irish–Italian cultural forms
of popular Catholicism in England. As a result he became increasingly involved with an intense private cult of the English
Catholic aristocracy, of the handful of Catholic families who had

kept the faith quietly alive in England from the Reformation onwards until the renascence of Catholicism in the nineteenth century. The myth of the English Christian gentleman who is an
inevitable victim of the modern world came increasingly to dominate Waugh's responses; yet one of the qualities that, I think, made
him a major novelist was an unexpected degree of detachment, an
ability not to surrender wholly to the demands of his personal
myth, no matter how exigent. This is apparent in one of his finest
novels, *The Ordeal of Gilbert Pinfold*, where the unfortunate Mr
Pinfold, although clearly the vehicle for many of Waugh's pre-
judices and ways of looking at the world, is never wholly identified with; there is a saving detachment, an ability to place and judge
his own foibles which points to the depth of Waugh's vision.

In the figure of Tony Last, hero of *A Handful of Dust*, we see the
first tentative outlines of the myth; it was extravagantly magnified
in *Brideshead Revisited*, where the aristocracy, and particularly the
Catholic aristocracy, are presented as the custodians of traditional
values in a world increasingly threatened by the barbarians, who
are personified in the uncouth young wartime officer, Hooper. Here,
in Frank Kermode's words, 'the great houses of England become by
an easy transition types of the Catholic city' (*Puzzles and
Epiphanies*, 1962: p. 171). The point is made explicit at several
crucial moments in *Brideshead*, when we are reminded of a lamen-
tation in the traditional liturgy of Holy Week, *Quomodo sedet
sola civitas* – 'How doth the city sit solitary that was full of people'
– which echoes the decline of Brideshead Castle and the values it
enshrined. *Brideshead Revisited* first established Waugh as a
'Catholic novelist', although many readers (Catholic as much as
others) found themselves disinclined to accept his confident association of Catholicism and the aristocratic virtues, the identification of House and City. Conor Cruise O'Brien has referred in his
book *Maria Cross* to 'Mr Waugh's private religion, on which he has
superimposed Catholicism, much as newly converted pagans are
said to superimpose a Christian nomenclature on their ancient
cults of trees and thunder' (1953: p. 130).

The essential method of *A Handful of Dust* does not greatly
differ from the early farces, *Decline and Fall* and *Vile Bodies*: the
characters are puppets or two-dimensional figures rather than fully-
rounded characters. This is wholly true of John Beaver and Brenda
Last, and largely true of Tony Last. There is, perhaps, slightly more

to him to engage our sympathies, but he remains the stylised embodiment of a number of predictable gestures. Nevertheless the impact of this book is quite different from that of its two pre-decessors. The farce is very evident and is cruel as ever, in a Berg-sonian way. But it co-exists with an intense pathos that would be tragic if the characters involved had a sufficient degree of humanity to support tragedy. In presenting their inability to do so, Waugh is making a sharp though implicit comment on the empty world of the Lasts and the Beavers. The title of *A Handful of Dust* comes, of course, from *The Waste Land*, and in both Eliot's poem and Waugh's novel the characters have a similar inability to feel deeply. At the end of the novel farce turns into horror, as we leave Tony Last imprisoned for ever in the South American jungle reading Dickens to the recluse, Mr Todd. *A Handful of Dust* can be defined, like some of Wyndham Lewis's novels, as a farce in Bergsonian terms : we laugh at people, or objects resembling people, colliding like things. But we are disconcerted by the sudden realisation that these seemingly mechanical semblances of humanity are really persons, or very nearly so. Tony Last embodies the pathos of the wooden puppet that suddenly weeps real tears.

The mixture of farce and seriousness in *A Handful of Dust* gives the book its peculiar strength. It is a combination which recurs in *Sword of Honour*, but is missing from *Brideshead Revisited*, to the detriment of that work. If Tony Last lacks the depth and various-ness of a major fictional character, he has, instead, the broad, simple outlines of a hero of myth. As his perhaps too obviously symbolic name implies, he is the ultimate survivor of a former age and scheme of values, whom nobody understands, least of all his wife, Brenda. He is too good for the world he is born into, and a pre-destined victim, a scapegoat who must be cast out to a living death in the wilderness. Like most of Waugh's heroes – with the notable exception of Basil Seal – he is also slightly stupid. If he is the last wistful inheritor of a noble tradition, he is also singularly lacking in a feeling for reality; and, as Kermode has noted, Waugh is hard on such characters.

Hetton Abbey, the country seat to which Tony Last is so attached, is less intrinsically impressive than Brideshead or Broome. In the words of the local guide-book: 'This, formerly one of the notable houses of the county, was entirely rebuilt in 1864 in the

Gothic style and is now devoid of interest.' Nevertheless Tony preserves a passionate devotion to it :

> But there was not a glazed or encaustic tile that was not dear to Tony's heart. In some ways, he knew, it was not convenient to run, but what big house was? It was not altogether amenable to modern ideas of comfort; he had many small improvements in mind, which would be put into effect as soon as the death duties were paid off. But the general aspect and atmosphere of the place; the line of its battlements against the sky; the central clock tower where quarterly chimes disturbed all but the heaviest sleepers; the ecclesiastical gloom of the great hall, its ceiling groined and painted in diapers of red and gold, supported on shafts of polished granite with vine-wreathed capitals, half-lit by day through lancet windows of armorial stained glass, at night by a vast gasolier of brass and wrought iron, wired now and fitted with twenty electric bulbs; the blasts of hot air that rose suddenly at one's feet, through grills of cast-iron trefoils from the antiquated heating apparatus below; the cavernous chill of the more remote corridors where, economizing in coke, he had had the pipes shut off; the dining-hall with its hammer-beam roof and pitch-pine minstrels' gallery; the bedrooms with their brass bedsteads, each with a frieze of Gothic text, each named from Malory, Yseult, Elaine, Mordred and Merlin, Gawaine and Bedivere, Lancelot, Perceval, Tristram, Galahad, his own dressing-room, Morgan le Fay, and Brenda's Guinevere, where the bed stood on a dais, the walls hung with tapestry, the fireplace like a tomb of the thirteenth century, from whose bay window one could count, on days of exceptional clearness, the spires of six churches – all these things with which he had grown up were a source of constant delight and exultation to Tony; things of tender memory and proud possession.

In this description of the Victorian Gothic splendours of Hetton, we are made aware of the intensity of Tony's affections, but we also see that the objects to which they are directed are slightly preposterous. His bogus Pre-Raphaelite world cuts him off from the wider past, just as his conventional Anglicanism cuts him off from true religion; when Tony's son has been killed in a hunting accident the local vicar attempts to solace him, but Tony complains, 'I only wanted to see him about arrangements. He tried to be comforting. It was very painful . . . after all the last thing one wants to talk about at a time like this is religion.'

Tony Last offers only a dim foreshadowing of Guy Crouchback, who is Waugh's fully developed picture of the Christian gentleman, the doomed victim. But there are some direct anticipations. One of

them is in the romantic harking-back to the attitudes of the nursery
and the schoolroom which, as O'Brien has remarked, runs through
several of Waugh's novels: one thinks of Sebastian Flyte's teddy-
bear, and the way in which Brideshead Castle is quietly presided
over by the old nurse Nanny Hawkins, like a tutelary deity in a
remote upper room. Tony preserves quite unashamedly in his bed-
room various treasures of boyhood: 'the framed picture of a dreadnought (a coloured supplement from *Chums*), all its guns spouting
flame and smoke; a photographic group of his private school; a
cabinet called "the museum", filled with the fruits of a dozen
desultory hobbies, eggs, butterflies, fossils, coins'. In *Sword of
Honour*, Guy Crouchback, when he hears the phrase, 'tomorrow you
meet the men you will lead in battle', is reminded of a hero of boyhood adventure stories called Captain Truslove, whose exploits had
fascinated him at his preparatory school during the First World War.*

Again, in *A Handful of Dust*, Tony Last hears from Dr Messinger of
a fabulous city in the Brazilian hinterland, and he agrees to join
Messinger's expedition in search of it. Tony soon translates this
City into familiar terms:

> He had a clear picture of it in his mind. It was Gothic in charac-
> ter, all vanes and pinnacles, gargoyles, battlements, groining and
> tracery, pavilions and terraces, a transfigured Hetton, pennons
> and banners floating on the sweet breeze, everything luminous
> and translucent; a coral citadel crowning a green hill-top sown
> with daisies, among groves and streams; a tapestry landscape
> filled with heraldic and fabulous animals and symmetrical, dis-
> proportionate blossom.

This is an aesthetic fantasy rather than the Catholic City of *Brideshead* or *Helena*; but it is indeed 'a transfigured Hetton', and seems
medieval and therefore Catholic – reminiscent perhaps of the Green
Knight's castle when Sir Gawaine first encounters it – unlike the
Victorian Gothic of the actual Hetton.

Catholicism does not appear in Waugh's fiction until *Brideshead*,
but in 1935 he published his life of the Jesuit martyr Edmund
Campion, which made apparent his own religious commitments,
and showed that he was capable of a very different kind of writing
from the farcical novels which had established his reputation. In

---

* This reference occurs only in the text of *Men at Arms*, as published
in 1952; it was removed in the course of Waugh's revisions for the one-
volume edition of *Sword of Honour*.

the perspective of Waugh's later work, *Edmund Campion* is interesting because it shows, for the first time, his interest in the recusant families whom he was to commemorate in his novels, like Lady Marchmain's family in *Brideshead* and the Crouchbacks in *Sword of Honour*, one of whom, Blessed Gervase Crouchback, had, like Campion, been martyred under Elizabeth.

The Campion biography, combined with the hints of gravity in *A Handful of Dust*, might have suggested that Waugh would one day attempt a novel of high seriousness. Nevertheless, when such a novel finally appeared, in the form of *Brideshead Revisited*, many readers were disconcerted, and Waugh has remarked that it 'lost me such esteem as I once enjoyed among my contemporaries'. This lush, nostalgic story of an aristocratic Catholic family between the wars, seen through the eyes of an all too obviously fascinated hanger-on, who is the intimate friend of one member and who becomes the lover of another, was too much for many readers, even those who had most enjoyed the comic novels. And Catholicism pervaded the whole work, culminating in the death-bed repentance of the long-estranged Lord Marchmain. In his preface to the revised edition of *Brideshead*, Waugh remarked that though he makes no apology for the theme of the book, 'the operation of divine grace on a group of diverse but closely connected characters', he was not altogether happy with its form, but saw no way of radically transforming it. The cuts and revisions that Waugh made for the revised version are interesting but not extensive. Waugh explained that the book was written during the early months of 1944:

> It was a bleak period of present privation and threatening disaster – the period of soya beans and Basic English – and in consequence the book is infused with a kind of gluttony, for food and wine, for the splendours of the recent past, and for rhetorical and ornamental language, which now with a full stomach I find distasteful. I have modified the grosser passages but have not obliterated them because they are an essential part of the book.

Thus the glamorous impression that Anthony Blanche makes on Charles Ryder in Oxford is somewhat toned down, and the embarrassing prose poem in praise of Burgundy that occurs during Ryder's dinner with Rex Mottram is sharply reduced.

One of the most interesting changes concerns the crucial paragraph in which Julia, on an ocean liner, first becomes Charles's mistress. In its original version the passage read as follows:

So at sunset I took formal possession of her as her lover. It was no time for the sweets of luxury; they would come, in their season, with the swallow and the lime flowers. Now on the rough water, as I was made free of her narrow loins and, it seemed now, in assuaging that fierce appetite, cast a burden which I had borne all my life, toiled under, not knowing its nature – while the waves still broke and thundered on the prow, the act of possession was a symbol, a rite of ancient origin and solemn meaning.

This is an over-written passage, but no more so than many others. It shows that, for Charles, becoming Julia's lover was not just a personal transaction, but had a ritualistic, even a religious significance – 'the act of possession was a symbol, a rite of ancient origin and solemn meaning'. He is not merely taking possession of Julia as a woman, but is becoming carnally incorporated into the magic circle of Brideshead, a kind of earthly beatitude. Waugh realised the vulnerable implications of all this, although the revision is not a great improvement:

It was no time for the sweets of luxury; they could come, in their season, with the swallow and the lime flowers. Now on the rough water there was a formality to be observed, no more. It was as though a deed of conveyance of her narrow loins had been drawn and sealed. I was making my first entry as the freeholder of a property I would enjoy and develop at leisure.

The tone is now more restrained; and instead of a 'rite of ancient origin' we have the taking legal possession of a property. Yet in its larger context the implications of this relatively more mundane imagery are curious and surely unfortunate. For there is a point, a little later in the novel, when it seems that Charles, from having taken possession of Julia, is about to take possession of Brideshead itself: Charles and Julia are being divorced from their respective partners and intend to marry as soon as they can; while the dying Lord Marchmain, disgusted by his son Brideshead's unfortunate marriage, is bequeathing the property to Julia. In the event, things work out differently; when her father dies Julia returns to the practice of her religion and does not marry Charles. Nevertheless Waugh's revision of this paragraph still suggests that for Charles Julia could never be just a woman he was in love with. She inevitably stood for much more – for Brideshead Castle and all its treasure, both material and spiritual. Waugh's revisions, if one examines them, have the effect of drawing attention to the weak points in the narrative, showing where the author felt a certain need to tamper with the story. It is, on the whole, questionable whether the novel has gained very much from the revision. But Waugh's preface does revealingly suggest that we are to read *Brideshead Revisited* 'as a souvenir of the Second War rather than of the twenties or of the thirties, with which it ostensibly deals'. This, and the previous observation about the work being a product of the 'present privations and the threatening disaster of wartime', though made with disarming modesty, must inevitably alter our view of *Brideshead*.

It becomes, in short, much less of a sober chronicle of grace and adultery and aristocratic folly between the wars, and much more an almost uncontrolled fantasy, where Waugh indulges himself with a potent personal myth. *Sword of Honour* offers appropriate illumination on this point. Consider the account of Major Ludovic's novel, *The Death Wish*, written at much the same time as *Brideshead*:

> It was a very gorgeous, almost gaudy, tale of romance and high drama . . . Had he known it, half a dozen other English writers, averting themselves sickly from privations of war and apprehensions of the social consequences of the peace, were even then severally and secretly, unknown to one another . . . composing or preparing to compose books which would turn from the drab alleys of the thirties into the odorous gardens of a recent past transformed and illuminated by disordered memory and imagination.

Evidently Major Ludovic and Evelyn Waugh were writing much the same kind of book. Significant, too, is the phrase 'transformed and illuminated by disordered memory and imagination'. *Brideshead Revisited*, one recalls, is subtitled, 'The Sacred and Profane Memories of Captain Charles Ryder'. The whole Marchmain saga is related through the memories, certainly drenched with nostalgia and quite possibly disordered, of Charles Ryder. And Ryder is, unfortunately, one of Waugh's least interesting characters: weak, sentimental, snobbish. Even such a devoted admirer of Waugh's work as Mr F. J. Stopp refers in his book on Waugh to 'a streak of maudlin sentimentality about Charles'. Certainly the story suffers from being filtered through the sadly limited consciousness of Ryder; the events can scarcely transcend the personality of their narrator. (What, I have sometimes thought, if Ryder were a liar as well as a sentimentalist; supposing he had made it all up, as part of a huge wish-fulfilment fantasy, had scarcely even known the March-mains, perhaps merely admired Sebastian at a distance in Oxford?) And, for much of the time, Waugh seems closely identified with his narrator. But not entirely so; part of the conscience of the book is embodied in the engaging but astringent personality of Anthony Blanche, who gives Charles solemn warnings against falling a victim to the fatal charm of the Marchmains, warnings which Charles inevitably disregards.

As Conor Cruise O'Brien has pointed out, in *Brideshead* Waugh was attempting an elaborate Proustian recreation of time past for which his talents were fundamentally ill-suited. The book's elaborate metaphorical structure is superimposed rather than integral, and the absence of Waugh's comic genius is a grave weak-ness. Nevertheless the novel is efficiently planned and constructed, the characters, though often distorted by Ryder's view of them, are convincing – and, in Julia, Waugh has invented an attractive female character of, for him, unusual depth. And in the early Oxford chapters the magic that Charles found there, and the glamour of the young Sebastian, is effectively conveyed. (Though for an index of the way in which time and circumstance have blurred and softened Waugh's vision one need only compare the Oxford of *Brideshead* with the Oxford of the opening chapter of *Decline and Fall*.)

In *Brideshead Revisited* the tendency to myth-making, first evident in *A Handful of Dust*, becomes total and all-embracing. And reading *Brideshead* we have to think of the word 'myth' not only in its larger positive sense, but also, such are Ryder's insufficiencies, in the everyday pejorative sense of 'illusion'. At one point Ryder confesses his inability to live in a world without illusions:

> 'I have left behind illusion,' I said to myself. 'Henceforth I live in a world of three dimensions – with the aid of my five senses.'
> I have since learned that there is no such world, but then, as the car turned out of sight of the house, I thought it took no finding, but lay all about me at the end of the avenue.

Nevertheless the fact that Waugh thought that a world of three-dimensional reality, seen without myth or illusion, *is* possible, was apparent in his next serious novel, *Helena*. This is an odd and unsatisfactory book, which shows a different aspect of Waugh's universe from *Brideshead*; if that work had been orientated toward myth, *Helena* shows a concern for naked unadorned reality. The

Empress Helena, searching in old age for the True Cross, is concerned above all with establishing the historical reality of Christianity. Christ lived and died in a particular place, at a particular time, and the cross on which he died was simply two pieces of ordinary wood. Helena insists on the ordinariness of the Cross during her search, in the face of the pious sages who claim that it was made of every species of wood so that all the vegetable world could participate in the act of redemption; or that it was composed equally of cypress, cedar, boxwood and pine, with appropriate symbolic associations; or that it was made of aspen, which is why that tree now continually shivers with shame. To all these ingenious speculations Helena, with anti-mythical zest, replies 'Nonsense' or 'Rot'. Similarly, she resists the attempts of her son, Constantine, to mythologise the truths of Christianity. We can compare the extreme selectivity of the Catholic City in *Brideshead* with Helena's desire to extend the City far beyond the Roman Empire to take in all mankind. In *Helena* Waugh was writing of matters remote from his customary fictional interests, and perhaps for that reason he was able to assert an anti-mythical attitude with remarkable clarity. It sounded a new note in his work, and in *Sword of Honour* the struggle between myth and 'three-dimensional reality' is carried through to its conclusion.

It is instructive to approach the first part of *Sword of Honour* – originally published as *Men at Arms* – via *Put Out More Flags* (1942) which also deals with the Phony War of 1939–40. It is one of Waugh's funniest novels, in which we take leave of the denizens of his early fiction, Sir Alastair Digby-Vane-Trumpington and Basil Seal. For a time no-one takes the war seriously; Basil, who wants to be one of the hard-faced men who did well out of the war, stays in the country involved in various profitable rackets, while Alastair joins up as a ranker because he cannot bear to meet the temporary officers – though presumably the era of Hooper was still some way ahead. After the fall of France, however, both Basil and Alastair take commissions in a branch of the army that is being formed for special service. Alastair describes it in these words :

> 'They're getting up special parties for raiding. They go across to France and creep up behind Germans and cut their throats in the dark.' He was very excited, turning a page in his life, as, more than twenty years ago lying on his stomach before the fire, with

a bound volume of *Chums*, he used to turn over to the next instalment of the serial.

We are in familiar territory, the world of schoolboy heroics; it looks back to Tony Last, whose framed picture of a dreadnought had been taken from a colour-supplement of that same magazine, *Chums*; and forward to Guy Crouchback and his memories of Captain Truslove.

As the novel closes, Basil and Alastair are about to embark on unspecified romantic adventures; the Phony War is over and England is inspirited by the Churchillian Renaissance. Sir Joseph Mainwaring, who has been wrong about everything so far, remarks, 'There's a new spirit abroad. I see it on every side.' And the author comments in the last line of the novel, 'And, poor booby, he was bang right.'

In *Sword of Honour* the Commando group that Alastair refers to so enthusiastically is described in much greater detail. It is known as HOO – Hazardous Offensive Operations – and though it provides plenty of grim comedy, we find little of the schoolboy heroics of Alastair's eager description. Indeed, one of the most remarkable things about the Crouchback trilogy is that though the work of an author of extremely conservative opinions it is one of the most deeply satirical accounts of military life on record. Guy Crouchback's military career is totally inglorious, if for no fault of his own.

The military operations recorded are either failures, like the raid on Dakar or the evacuations from Crete; or else they are put on solely for propaganda purposes, like Trimmer's ludicrous raid on the coast of Occupied France, or the attack on the Croatian blockhouse in the final section. The comic parts of the book are dominated by two figures who, though wonderful fictional creations, offer between them as gross a caricature of the ideal of the officer and gentleman as one could imagine – Apthorpe and Ludovic. Those who do seem to embody this ideal betray it, voluntarily or involuntarily. By the end of the novel, what had started as a clear-cut fight against Evil has become hopelessly enmeshed in rival fanaticisms.

At the beginning of *Sword of Honour* we are introduced to Guy Crouchback, the mild, melancholy Catholic gentleman who has lived in Italy ever since his wife left him several years before. He has elements of Tony Last about him, as well as a touch of Charles

Ryder and the Marchmain ethos. With the Russo-German pact in 1939 Guy finds many issues crystallised, and he returns to England eager for a place in the fight:

> But now, splendidly, everything had become clear. The enemy at last was plain in view, huge and hateful, all disguise cast off. It was the Modern Age in arms. Whatever the outcome there was a place for him in that battle.

Before leaving Italy he takes a significant step back into the past, like Ortega y Gasset's ancient Roman. He kneels in the local church and prays at the effigy of an English knight, Sir Roger of Waybroke, who had been shipwrecked on the way to the Second Crusade: ' "Sir Roger, pray for me," he said, "and for our endangered kingdom." '

Charles Ryder too, we remember, had looked back into the past, though in a rather more pretentious way; he had complained that 'Hooper was no romantic. He had not as a child ridden with Rupert's horse or sat among the camp fires at Xanthus-side.' In his early days as an officer Crouchback has similar visions. But, unlike Ryder, he changes and learns.

In the person of Guy Crouchback, Waugh offers us his fullest and most sympathetic delineation of the ideal of the Gentleman, the embodiment of the Gothic dream, a gallant officer who would be, if he could, a twentieth-century reincarnation of Roger of Waybroke. *Sword of Honour* shows us first his disillusionment, and then the total defeat of his ideal by the forces of modern totalitarianism. Waugh traces the various stages in his disillusionment with subtlety and ingenious irony; there are many traps for the unwary reader. During the Cretan campaign Corporal-Major Ludovic notes in his diary: 'Captain Crouchback is pleased because General Miltiades is a gentleman. He would like to believe that the war is being fought by such. But all gentlemen are now very old.' (This passage disappears in the 1965 text.) Later, Ludovic, as the author of *The Death Wish*, is to become an arch myth-maker; but here he is doing no more than record what Guy has to recognise as the truth.

Guy has already heard the same thing, in more hectoring terms, from Ian Killbannock, the journalist-peer turned Government propagandist:

> 'You'll see pages about the Commandos in the papers soon. But not about your racket, Guy. They just won't do, you know.

Delightful fellows, heroes too, I daresay, but the Wrong Period. Last-war stuff, Guy. Went out with Rupert Brooke.'

'You find us poetic?'

'No,' said Ian, stopping in his path and turning to face Guy in the darkness. 'Perhaps not poetic, exactly, but Upper Class. Hopelessly Upper Class. You're the "Fine Flower of the Nation". You can't deny it and *it won't do.*'

The probable response, by a reader familiar with Waugh's personal myth would be to assume that Killbannock is a boor, that the ideals he is attacking are nevertheless admirable, and that the phrase 'Fine Flower of the Nation' remains valid despite his contempt. We think of the gay adventurers at the end of *Put Out More Flags*, and of the solemn visions of Charles Ryder, remembering perhaps his account of the three brothers of Lady Marchmain, killed in the First World War : 'garlanded victims, devoted to the sacrifice. These men must die to make a world for Hooper.' And a little later we find Crouchback doing precisely this, thinking about Ivor Claire, in language that would have been wholly appropriate to Charles Ryder :

> Guy remembered Claire as he first saw him in the Roman spring in the afternoon sunlight amid the embosoming cypresses of the Borghese Gardens, putting his horse faultlessly over the jumps, concentrated as a man in prayer. Ivor Claire, Guy thought, was the fine flower of them all. He was quintessential England, the man Hitler had not taken into account.

Yet Guy is wrong. In the Cretan campaign Ivor Claire deserts in the face of the enemy. Guy's error has far-reaching implications. If the quintessential gentleman is not to be trusted, then the whole scheme of values that has so far pervaded Waugh's serious fiction falls to the ground. An Ivor Claire is not necessarily better than a Hooper or a Trimmer, and the hero-worshipping of a Charles Ryder looks altogether suspect.

Guy's disillusionment is completed in the final stages of the war, when he is serving on a mission with the Yugoslav partisans. The splendid vision with which he started the war is wholly obscured. 'This isn't soldiering as I was taught it,' remarks a British officer when forced to acquiesce in the liquidation of a Yugoslav royalist. Guy is heavily involved in the prevalent betrayals, even if inadvertently. In Yugoslavia he learns, finally, the meaning of total war. Towards the end of the book he is addressed by a Hungarian woman, a Jewish refugee, in these terms :

'Is there any place that is free from evil? It is too simple to say that only the Nazis wanted war. These communists wanted it too. It was the only way in which they could come to power. Many of my people wanted it, to be revenged on the Germans, to hasten the creation of the national state. It seems to me there was a will to war, a death wish, everywhere. Even good men thought their private honour would be satisfied by war. They could assert their manhood by killing and being killed. They would accept hardships in recompense for having been selfish and lazy. Danger justified privilege. I knew Italians – not very many perhaps – who felt this. Were there none in England?'

'God forgive me,' said Guy. 'I was one of them.'

At this point Guy's self-knowledge is complete, and the dominating myth of much of Waugh's work is deflated. Reality is too terrible and too various to be accounted for by any simple myth, any easy pattern of heroics, no matter how splendid. Already we have seen Guy's devout and humble father exhibiting the realistic Christianity of a Helena rather than the mythologised version of the Marchmains. The romantic ideal of the gentleman, of the fine flower of the nation, may indeed have undergone an unconditional surrender. But there are other values. At the end of the novel we find Guy married to the earthy and tractor-driving Domenica Plessington, who has borne him two sons.* But the heir to Broome and to the venerable name of Crouchback is in fact the son of Trimmer, who was in all respects the antithesis of the gentlemanly ideal. This is, on the face of it, one of Waugh's most savagely sardonic ironies of situation. Yet, as old Mr Crouchback would surely have observed, even a Trimmer has a soul to be saved, and his child is being brought up in the Faith; has become an inhabitant of the City in Helena's sense rather than the Marchmains'. Significantly, Waugh wrote no more extended fiction after *Sword of Honour*. With complete honesty he accepted the collapse of the myth that had sustained a sizeable segment of his fiction, but it was hardly to be expected that he could have gone on writing happily in the absence of it. The total pattern of Waugh's work reveals a consciousness that is indeed dedicated to looking backward, to reliving the past and trying to preserve its values, and which ultimately is unable to resist the pressures of modernity, although it never willingly surrenders to them. (At the end of his life Waugh

---

* Waugh changed his mind about these sons: in the 1965 text Guy and Domenica are described as childless.

found that even the Catholic Church was failing him; in his preface to *Sword of Honour*, written in 1964, Waugh sourly described it as 'an obituary of the Roman Catholic Church in England as it had existed for many centuries. All the rites and most of the opinions described here are already obsolete.') *Sword of Honour* is a fine blend of the strongest qualities in Waugh's work: farce, social comedy and a real sense of the importance of tradition all conveyed in his impeccably incisive prose. It is the finest novel by an Englishman to have come out of the Second World War, to which it bears much the same relation as does Ford Madox Ford's *Parade's End* to the First World War. There are remarkable resemblances between the two works: both deal with a hero who is a natural victim or scapegoat, in a world of collapsing values, though Waugh preserves a more naturally ebullient tone throughout.

II

Anthony Powell's *roman fleuve*, *The Music of Time*, has some affinity with Waugh's work: in particular the three volumes dealing with the Second World War, *The Valley of Bones*, *The Soldier's Art* and *The Military Philosophers* invite comparison with *Sword of Honour*. Comparisons with Waugh have, in fact, been made ever since Powell started writing in the early thirties, and they are usually to Powell's disadvantage. This is unfortunate; to speak for myself, I admire both writers immensely, and while seeing similarities in their material and narrative manner, I am more and more conscious of their essential differences. It is certainly true that Powell's *Afternoon Men*, published in 1931, can be bracketed with *Decline and Fall* as one of the few outstanding first novels to be published in England between the wars. Both Powell and Waugh are satirically interested in the London circles, partly fashionable, partly artistic, that had been more cheerfully described and exposed in the early novels of Aldous Huxley. Yet, of the two, Waugh is more cruel, hysterical and gay. *Afternoon Men* is pitched in a uniformly minor key; it is a comic masterpiece which avoids extravagance, and achieves its effects by a relentlessly laconic wit and a stylised manner that looks like artlessness. The danger is that apparent flatness can be mistaken for the real thing, and *Afternoon Men* has never had the recognition it deserves.

In this novel Powell first established the fictional territory that he continues to occupy nearly forty years later: it is a world where

members of the aristocracy, often slightly eccentric or seedy and
never of the first brilliance, associate with writers, artists or
musicians, and other, less clearly talented, inhabitants of bohemia.
As Walter Allen has said, it can be geographically located at the
point where Mayfair meets Soho. In the later volumes of *The Music
of Time* this world has been reinforced by businessmen and – during
the war years – by soldiers, but it has never lost its basic flavour.
Apart from its intrinsic merits, *Afternoon Men* shows the essence
of Powell's fictional method. There is, in the first place, his reliance
on style as a mode of mediating experience; this is not to say that
he has sought after poetic effects or aesthetic concentration; but
Powell has relied, far more than most contemporary English
novelists, on the establishment of his own peculiar verbal environment, as have the American writers discussed in the previous chapter. The process can be well illustrated from the opening pages of
Afternoon Men, where the syntax conveys the sense of experience
fragmented into countless disparate units, with only the most
tenuous connection between them (the scene is an afternoon drinking club) :

> Atwater did not answer. He read a newspaper that someone
> had left on the table. He read the comic strip and later the column
> headed 'Titled Woman in Motor Tragedy'. He was a weedy-
> looking young man with straw-coloured hair and rather long
> legs, who had failed twice for the Foreign Office. He sometimes
> wore tortoiseshell-rimmed spectacles to correct a slight squint,
> and through influence he had recently got a job in a museum.
> His father was a retired civil servant who lived in Essex, where
> he and his wife kept a chicken farm.
> 'How long has this place been open?' said Pringle.
> 'Not long. Everybody comes here.'
> 'Do they?'
> 'Mostly.'

There may be a debt to Hemingway here, but there is also a certain
air of *Sweeney Agonistes* about *Afternoon Men*. The short sentences
and laconic understatement are characteristic of this novel and
Powell's next, *Venusberg*, and they have often been contrasted with
the style of *The Music of Time*, which, though equally mannered,
is elaborate, leisurely, and – in the opinion of unsympathetic readers
– long-winded. Yet each style is functional and equally well adapted
to convey a particular reading of experience. Another key aspect of
Afternoon Men is Powell's preoccupation with anecdote, of a kind
illustrated by this brief exchange from the opening pages :

'William has had a letter from Undershaft. He's in New York,
living with an Annamite and playing the piano.'
  'Is he making any money?'
  'Doing very well, he says.'

The Music of Time is, in essence, a vast intricate collection of
anecodotes, some of them as brief and cryptic as this reference to
Undershaft (although in such cases the story may well be elaborated
in later volumes), others of them very prolonged and circumstantial,
like Nicholas Jenkins's childhood memory of the dramatic episode
one Sunday in the summer of 1914, concerning his father's cook,
Albert, and a female servant called Billson, which takes up the first
seventy pages of *The Kindly Ones*. This superb piece of writing,
one of the great achievements of the whole sequence, also contains
within itself hints of small-scale anecdotes:

> 'Bertha Conyers has such an amusing way of putting things,'
> my mother would say. 'But I really don't believe all her stories,
> especially the one about Mrs Asquith and the man who asked her
> if she danced the tango.'

Powell's novels of the 1930s that followed *Afternoon Men* suggest
a lively talent, and a fair degree of inventiveness, but not much
staying power. One of them, however, *From a View to a Death*,
points to something more: it is a bleak book, about a vulgar, social-
climbing young artist, Zouch, who invades a world of declining
county families. Although a comic novel, *From a View to a Death*
is pervaded with a curious atmosphere of lassitude and frustration,
and in the death of Zouch it touches on the tragic. In so far as it
portrays a segment of society in greater depth than Powell's other
early novels it looks forward to *The Music of Time*.

During the 1940s Powell published no more novels, but he wrote a
life of John Aubrey and edited a selection from Aubrey's *Brief Lives*.
The interest in Aubrey is extremely relevant to Powell's later fiction,
where the anecdotal method and the unfailing fascination with the
oddities of human behaviour and character reveal a cast of mind
very much akin to Aubrey. In fact Powell has referred to Aubrey's
'presentation of life as a picture crowded with odd figures, occupy-
ing themselves in unexpected and inexplicable pursuits', words,
which, as Alan Brownjohn has remarked, could very well be applied
to *The Music of Time*; another critic, Arthur Mizener, has said, 'the
heart of Powell's work is his *Brief Lives*'. After his work on Aubrey,

Powell turned again to the writing of fiction, in the spirit that he described to an interviewer a few years ago:

> After the war when I came out of the army and returned to the writing of novels, I decided that the thing to do was to produce a really large work about all the things I was interested in – the whole of one's life, in fact – for I have no talent for inventing plots of a dramatic kind in a comparatively small space – 80,000 words. (*Twentieth Century*, July 1961)

So far, nine out of a projected twelve volumes of *The Music of Time* have appeared, sufficient to give one some idea both of the extent of Powell's achievement and of its limitations. Since the work is one continuous novel, Powell's custom of publishing a fresh volume every two years, although there may be sound economic reasons for it, does not serve him particularly well. The separate volumes are by now quite unintelligible without a good knowledge of the previous volumes, which novel reviewers do not necessarily possess, and the large-scale dimensions of Powell's unfolding narrative are often lost sight of. In fact, in its larger structure, *The Music of Time* is built up out of groups of trilogies, each of them covering a different phrase in the life of the narrator, Nicholas Jenkins. The first trilogy, comprising *A Question of Upbringing*, *A Buyer's Market* and *The Acceptance World*, covers the formative years of Jenkins's adolescence and young manhood: we see him first, in the year 1921, at his public school, we follow him to Oxford, and then into the fashionable or bohemian London of the late twenties, to a variety of parties and a steadily widening circle of acquaintances, culminating in his first serious love affair, with Jean Duport. The second trilogy, comprising *At Lady Molly's*, *Casanova's Chinese Restaurant* and *The Kindly Ones*, shows us Jenkins's life in the thirties, a period of consolidation, in which he gets married and begins to establish a modest literary reputation, against a background that looks increasingly sombre, marked by such events as the suicide of the music critic Maclintick, and the death of Jenkins's Uncle Giles. Fascism is dominating Europe, the Spanish Civil War casts its shadow over English life, and at the end of *The Kindly Ones* England is at war again, an event prefigured by the author's memory of the summer of 1914 presented at the beginning of the volume. The third trilogy, which is made up of *The Valley of Bones*, *The Soldiers' Art* and *The Military Philosophers*, covers the six years of war and the narrator's military service, first as a rather over-age subaltern with a

Welsh regiment stationed in Northern Ireland, then as an officer
with the Intelligence Corps in London, engaged on liaison duties
with the allied armies. In this part of the sequence Jenkins continues
to make fresh acquaintances, though at nothing like the rate of his
early manhood; and because of the war several of his oldest friends
disappear. Lady Molly Jeavons, Jenkins's sister-in-law Priscilla and
her husband, Chips Lovell, are killed in the bombing of London.
Charles Stringham dies as a prisoner of the Japanese and Peter
Templer is killed in mysterious circumstances on a secret mission in
German-occupied Europe. On the other hand Widmerpool continues to rise in the world. Jenkins becomes a father, and we leave
him after the Victory Service in St Paul's in 1945, preparing to return
to civilian life. *The Music of Time* would, I think seem a much more
coherent work if it could be published in these constituent trilogies,
instead of in separate short volumes which claim to be what they
are not, self-contained novels. (The first trilogy has in fact appeared
in one volume.)

The bald summary I have just given will not convey anything of
the flavour of *The Music of Time*; particularly its multiplicity and
intricacy of anecdote, and its immense range of characters, major
and minor, which must run into about two hundred names. The
appeal of Powell's work is of a suspiciously simple kind: it is, above
all, to a love of gossip, to an intense though uncommitted curiosity
about humanity, and to a general fascination with characters, and
more especially with 'characters' in the sense of eccentrics and
oddities. It is possible for sophisticated but addicted readers of
The Music of Time to become caught up in the antics and interrelations (particularly the sexual alliances and severances) of
Powell's characters, just as if, in the time-honoured phrase, 'they
were real people'. This, one imagines, is precisely how innumerable
Victorian readers responded to the work of their great contemporaries: it is not an approach likely to appeal to the practitioners
of the continental or American *avant-garde*, with their conviction
that a concern with 'character' denotes allegiance to a vanished
phase of the novel, or of civilization, or both. Nor, for that matter,
to Marxist critics, suspicious of too much interest in character as a
product of competitive bourgeois individualism. A whole-hearted
absorption in Powell's work denotes that, whether one likes it or
not, one is an adherent of what I have called the 'ideology of being

English' : to refer again to a relevant remark by Lionel Trilling : 'one of the things which makes for substantiality of character in the novel is precisely the notation of manners, that is to say, of class traits modified by personality'. This is peculiarly relevant to Powell, as is the gloss that Trilling elsewhere gives to his use of the word 'manners' :

> What I understand by manners, then, is a culture's hum and buzz of implication. I mean the whole evanescent context in which its explicit statements are made. It is that part of a culture which is made up of half-uttered or unuttered or unutterable expressions of value. (*The Liberal Imagination*, p. 206)

Powell is exceedingly conscious of this 'hum and buzz', and part of the pleasure of reading him comes from seeing made explicit what previously has only been implicit and unexpressed in one's own consciousness. He is, in fact, a superb mimic; and, arguably, such a high degree of mimicry – which we find in other English novelists also – is a danger as well as an accomplishment. One is uncertain how far Powell can appeal outside his own culture; although American critics like Arthur Mizener have written appreciatively about Powell, it may be that Edmund Wilson is more representative of American opinion : 'I don't see why you make so much fuss about him. He's just entertaining enough to read in bed late at night in summer' (*The Bit Between My Teeth*, p. 536).

The basic truth about English society – or at least about the English professional, upper-middle and upper classes – that Powell writes about is that in a loose sense everyone knows everyone else. It is still, in contrast to America, both a physically compact and a remarkably cohesive society, and was certainly a good deal more so in the twenties and thirties. Oxford, Cambridge, the major public schools, all have connections with the principal London foci of intellectual, professional and business life. A surprising number of English people know each other, or at least know of each other, and links are preserved between disparate circles by a network of friends or relations, or friends of friends. (This state of affairs is, of course, what outsiders bitterly and rightly denounce as the 'old-boy network'.) Although *The Music of Time* is full of chance meetings and the discovery of coincidental links between previously unrelated people, none of them seems to strain credulity, since they are typical of the strata of English life Powell has made his own, where novelistic possibilities lie all around. Not that the possibilities can be realised without some degree of determination and struggle; as Nicholas Jenkins remarks in *The Acceptance World*, apropos of his own novel-writing activities:

> Intricacies of social life make English habits unyielding to simplification, while understatement and irony – in which all classes of this island converse – upset the normal emphasis of reported speech.

In his fascinated awareness of these intricacies, his constant sense of the gap between aspiration and achievement, and between appearance and reality, Powell is in the mainstream of English social comedy, where our perception of the world requires a perpetual mild, ironic readjustment. Jane Austen lies not excessively far behind *The Music of Time*. Another American critic, James Hall, has written usefully about the 'polite surprise' that Jenkins is always displaying at some fresh manifestation of absurdity or unpredictability in his surroundings; for Powell, he writes, life

> is a series of small shocks to be met with slightly raised eyebrows and the instantaneous question of how it all fits. Above everything else, Nick wants to know within a safe margin of error where he is at any given moment. ('The Uses of Polite Surprise: Anthony Powell', in *Essays in Criticism*, April 1962)

This realisation helps to explain the mannered, reflective style that so many people seem to find a stumbling block; as Alan Brownjohn, in his essay 'The Social Comedy of Anthony Powell', has remarked, 'Quite often the writing is groping and tentative, a very graceful and disciplined thinking aloud about people and circumstances' (*Gemini*, Summer 1957). James Hall has further remarked, in words which are certainly true of my own experience:

> When I first read Powell, I thought a successful novel could not be written in sentences like these, but presently the style seemed so accurate a projector for the slow-motion re-run of the past that I no longer noticed it at all.

Hall's phrase about Jenkins's need to know 'where he is at any given moment' is, I think, crucial. Although Powell offers us a plenitude of character comparable to one of the great Victorians, he knows that, unlike theirs, Jenkins's world is not at all solid or stable; we are constantly aware of its inherent fragility and of the uncertainty of Jenkins's relation to it. Hence Powell's use of style – admittedly a tentacular, groping, leisurely style, in contrast to the brisk manner of the early fiction – as a means of preserving his nar-

rator's poise and equilibrium. I am reminded of the comparable
verbal complexity of some of William Empson's early poems, which
is also directed at maintaining a somewhat desperate equilibrium.
Another critic of Powell, my friend and colleague K. W. Gransden,
who dislikes *The Music of Time*, has accurately pinpointed the
function of verbal style in the sequence, even while disapproving
of it; he writes that Powell is 'chronicling not so much events as
the subtle ironies these might suggest to someone who had studied
all the dossiers exhaustively. It is at times as if the style had become
a kind of enormous secret joke . . .' (*Encounter*, December 1966).
Powell has a long way to go before constructing the self-contained
verbal environment of a writer like John Barth, but it is true that
in his work style plays an active role in helping Jenkins – and the
reader – to make sense of his past experience. Jenkins is, of course,
an exceedingly detached narrator, most of whose energy goes into
the continual fine adjustment of his responses: if he is more than
the mere camera-eye of Isherwood's early stories, while being
equally observant, he is less involved than a moralising, even slightly
hysterical, narrator, like Evelyn Waugh's Charles Ryder. It is certainly true that Jenkins's gaze is always directed outwards, and he
tells us remarkably little about his engagement and marriage to
Isobel Tolland, although, in contrast to most of the other marriages
in the book, it seems to be a happy one. Yet the omission seems
deliberate rather than inadvertent, as if Jenkins were well aware of
the limitations of his verbal resources. He writes in *Casanova's
Chinese Restaurant*:

> A future marriage, or a past one, may be investigated and ex-
> plained in terms of writing by one of its parties, but it is doubtful
> whether an existing marriage can ever be described directly in the
> first person and convey a sense of reality. Even those writers who
> suggest some of the substance of married life best, stylise heavily,
> losing the subtlety of the relationship at the price of a few
> accurately recorded, but isolated, aspects. To think at all objec-
> tively about one's own marriage is impossible, while a balanced
> view of other people's marriage is almost equally hard to achieve
> with so much information available, so little to be believed.
> Objectivity is not, of course, everything in writing; but even
> casting objectivity aside, the difficulties of presenting marriage
> are inordinate. Its forms are at once so varied, yet so constant,
> providing a kaleidoscope, the colours of which are always chang-
> ing. The moods of a love affair, the contradictions of friendship,
> the jealousy of business partners, the fellow feeling of opposed

commanders in total war, these are all in their way to be charted. Marriage, partaking of such – and a thousand more – dual antagonisms and participations, finally defies definition.

Wovon man nicht sprechen kann . . . in fact. This is an important statement, not merely about Jenkins's attitude to his narrative, and Powell's to novel-writing, but as a reminder of the inherent limitations of the novel as a literary form, even when it is most avowedly open to 'life' or 'the world'. Marriage, as a permanent and central aspect of human experience, is not readily susceptible of effective fictional treatment, while adultery is, even though statistically less frequent. Thus, even the most overtly realistic novel is to some extent about its own inherited conventions, a notion updated and simplified by Marshall McLuhan as 'the medium is the message'.

John Bayley, who clings to an idea of the novel as a form totally open to lived reality, indeed flowing into and merging with it, in a way that he sees as supremely – and perhaps uniquely – achieved in Tolstoy, has written interestingly about the narrative methods of Waugh and Powell:

> Few novelists evade some sort of concealment and composition with the reader when they are describing a social order. Evelyn Waugh's narrator in *Brideshead Revisited*, for instance, gives no sign of recognising how immensely important to him is the social life he describes to us, and what obsessional anxieties it causes him. Self-knowledge is withheld from us and therefore suspended in us; and a kind of death, which Tolstoy is pitiless in revealing, occurs in a society whose members are unable to examine their pretensions to be what they are. It is the society of *The Death of Ivan Ilyich*. Another kind of narrative evasion, effective and adroit but none the less serving also to equivocate the relation between author and reader, can be found in Anthony Powell's series *The Music of Time*. These narrators are excused any open effort at self-knowledge, and we are excused it with them, by a literary arrangement that in its unspoken intent to avoid difficulty resembles a social one. What we are offered instead is a dubious kind of detachment, a front seat at the social show.
>
> Both authors probably inherit this transaction from the great example of Proust, whose whole vast social structure exists ultimately only to give his narrator a point and a past. By remembering it all he disassociates himself from it, and this puts us outside it at two removes, which in a sense is where we want to be. We are outside Proust, who is himself outside the world of his novel. With Tolstoy this cannot happen. (*Tolstoy and the Novel*, pp. 57–8)

I will not at this point repeat objections to what seems to me the extreme partiality, always asserted and never properly argued for, of Bayley's critical position; I will, however, repeat that if I were going to use the phrase 'a dubious kind of detachment' I would be far more inclined to apply it to Barth or Pynchon or Terry Southern than to Waugh or Powell. In fact Bayley's strictures seem to me applicable to *Brideshead Revisited*, but not to *The Music of Time*. The simple difference is that Powell's novel is, after all, a comedy, and the very essence of the comic is detachment, which need not be an inhuman detachment; in such works the reader is entitled to expect a 'front seat at the social show'. The same thing is surely true of Proust, at least if one regards a good deal of *A la recherche du temps perdu* as being much more comic than many commentators like to allow for; but it is no part of my present intention to defend Proust against John Bayley's disapproval.

Yet to have Powell mentioned in the same context as Waugh and Proust is helpful at this point in the discussion, since it is precisely these two novelists who are most often compared to Powell. Compared with Waugh, Powell is not a mythologiser, and there is nothing in his fiction comparable to the recurring image of the doomed gentleman that I have tried to trace in Waugh's novels. Although Powell is acutely interested in the past, he does not lament it; change and even decay are seen as inevitable and something to be endured with as good a grace as possible, since, whatever happens, life goes on. There are certainly traces of nostalgia in Jenkins's make-up, usually called up by paintings or buildings, but he never allows them to dominate him.* His habitual stance, as I have remarked, is not that of the judge or moralist, nor of the *laudator temporis acti*, but that of a cool but kindly anthropological observer. Because of his lack of mythic or obsessive preoccupations, Powell's fiction is less clearly patterned or structured than Waugh's. Both novelists, of course, owe a debt to Proust: it was evident in the chapter headings of *A Handful of Dust*, like 'Du Côté de Chez Beaver', and in the elaborate exercises in nostalgia in *Brideshead*. Superficially *The Music of Time* seems even more indebted: in its title, its verbal organisation and the kind of life it describes. Indeed there might be a case for calling Powell's novel a deliberate 'imita-

---

* For a pleasant account of Powell's interest in painting, see Mark Glazebrook, 'The Artist in Powell', in *London Magazine*, November 1967.

tion' of *A la recherche*. Yet the crucial difference has been well stated by James Hall :

> The structure of the novel resembles Proust's formidable *recherche* of time lost primarily in its inclusive detail.; Nick has none of Marcel's form-by-association. He tells a chronological story, shifting to different locales and characters but not backward and forward in time. Time moves onward as persistently in Nick's story as in Arnold Bennett, and the changes it brings, rather than the possibility of reliving lost experience, interest him. (*Essays in Criticism*, April 1962)

Since Mr Hall wrote, Powell has made a notable venture into moving backward in time, in the juxtaposition of the events of 1914 and those of 1939 in *The Kindly Ones*. Nevertheless this analysis remains largely accurate; Powell's view of time is conservative, and unlike Sterne or Proust or Robbe-Grillet he does not see it as imposing intractable problems on the writer of fiction. As Hall suggests, Powell – or Jenkins – is interested in the past not so much to 'recapture' or 'relive' it, but simply to understand it, which is a very much cooler enterprise.

One of the best remarks about *The Music of Time* has been made by Arthur Mizener, who has called it the work of 'an enormously intelligent but completely untheoretical mind' ('A Dance to the Music of Time', in *Kenyon Review*, Winter 1957). It is true that Powell has never felt the need for the abstract sustaining principles resorted to by other writers of long fiction : history for Tolstoy, time for Proust and tradition for Waugh. His reliance on anecdote rather than theme can produce a random, even disorientating effect. Yet to be untheoretical and anecdotal is very much part of what I call the English ideology, and *The Music of Time* is not wholly free from the feelings about culture and history that are so much more dominant in Ford and Waugh. Powell's novel is a great work of social comedy in a central English tradition, but it also conveys the cumulative sense of a shabby and dispirited society; one's delight in his characters is, from time to time, tempered by a feeling akin to Matthew Arnold's outburst at the Shelley circle : 'What a set!' In the first two trilogies Powell is writing about a world still suffering from the physically and morally traumatic effects of the First World War, and in a quiet and unembittered way he is continuing the anatomy of a society in decline embarked on by Ford in *Parade's End*. Yet one must avoid seeing *The Music of Time* in too portentous terms; as I have said, it is essentially a comedy, and Powell has always been sceptical about myths of catastrophe.

Walter Allen has commented on the total blankness that Powell's characters display on the subject of religion, and although politics plays a noticeable role in the volumes set in the thirties, Powell sees it exclusively as the source of singular or aberrant behaviour, put on specially for those who have 'a front seat at the social show'. In *The Acceptance World* a young German communist called Werner Guggenbühl harangues a fashionable gathering about the revolutionary theatre, in a way that provides a marvellous exhibition of Powell's powers of mimicry and at the same time shows his capacity for defusing any form of potentially disturbing theoretical utterance:

> 'We have done with old theatre of bourgeoisie and capitalists. Here is *Volksbühnen* – for actor that is worker like industrial worker – actor that is machine of machines.'
> 'Isn't it too thrilling?' said Mrs Andriadis. 'You know the October Revolution was the real turning point in the history of the Theatre.'
> 'Oh, I'm sure it was,' said Anne Stepney. 'I've read a lot about the Moscow Art Theatre.'
> Guggenbühl made a hissing sound with his lips, expressing considerable contempt.
> 'Moscow Art Theatre is just to tolerate,' he said, 'but what of biomechanics, of *Trümmer-Kunst*, has it? Then Shakespeare's *Ein Sommernachtsraum* or Toller's *Masse-Mensch will* you take? The modern ethico-social play I think you do not like. Hauptmann, Kaiser, plays to Rosa Luxemburg and Karl Liebknecht, yes. The new corporate life. The socially conscious form. Drama as highest of arts we Germans know. No more entertainment, please. *Lebensstimmung* it is. But it is workers untouched by middle class that will make spontaneous. Of Moscow Art Theatre you speak. So there was founded at Revolution both Theatre and Art Soviet, millions, billions of roubles set aside by Moscow Soviet of Soldier Deputies. Hundreds, thousands of persons. Actors, singers, clowns, dancers, musicians, craftsmen, designers, mechanics, electricians, scene-shifters, all kinds of manual workers, all trained, yes, and supplying themselves to make. Two years to have one perfect single production – if needed so, three, four, five, ten years. At other time, fifty plays on fifty successive nights. It is not be getting money, no.

Yet although Powell shows himself indifferent to overt forms of ideology and myth, his fiction is not without convictions about the world. Their nature has been suggested by Arthur Mizener who, as an American, is perhaps more able than English critics to see fictional characters as embodiments of ideas or general attitudes. He has pointed to the contrast between Kenneth Widmerpool and Charles Stringham as 'a major contrast of twentieth century natures'.

Widmerpool is, of course, known to anyone who has read any part of *The Music of Time*; he is, as it were, a living proof that it is still possible for a contemporary novelist to create a great fictional character in a traditional way. We first meet him in the opening chapter of *A Question of Upbringing*: Jenkins is returning from a walk at dusk in winter when Widmerpool lumbers past, an ungainly boy in sweater and running shoes, returning from a solitary run. He was already notorious at the school as an oddity, and an unusual overcoat he had once owned had become a legend; but, says Jenkins, it was at that point that 'Widmerpool, fairly heavily built, thick lips and metal-rimmed spectacles giving his face as usual an aggrieved expression, first took coherent form in my mind'. He is to go on moving in and out of Jenkins's life for the next quarter of a century, an unattractive but magnetic and even captivating personality. We see him showered with sugar by Barbara Goring at the Huntercombes' dance, and delivering an incomprehensible lecture on international economics at an Old Boys' dinner; he rises in the business world, and during the brief reign of Edward VIII hints that he is moving in very exalted circles. About this time he becomes improbably engaged to the sophisticated divorcee, Mildred Haycock, although she soon breaks it off after they have spent a night together. During the Second World War Widmerpool rises steadily in the military hierarchy, indulging in incessant and ruthless intrigue. At the end of the war he is a full colonel and is finally married, to Charles Stringham's niece, Pamela Flitton, a beautiful, promiscuous and savagely bad-tempered girl.

For Powell, Widmerpool represents in an unusually pure form the power of the will: he is insensitive, pompous, socially inept and monstrously selfish; yet he possesses an almost demonic energy and an unstoppable urge to succeed. At intervals Jenkins reflects with reluctant admiration on Widmerpool's prowess, as when he instantly summons a taxi at a moment of crisis: 'A cab seemed to rise out of the earth at that moment. Perhaps all action, even summoning a taxi when none is there, is basically a matter of the will.' A fascination with the will is the closest Powell comes to a consistent philosophical motif in *The Music of Time*; there are various

other figures who embody it, though in a less intense form, like
Erridge, or, to give him his full title, Lord ('Alf') Warminster, and
the tough left-wing literary critic J. G. Quiggin, although in the
later volumes Quiggin's powers seem to be declining. In *The Valley
of Bones* Captain Rowland Gwatkin would like to possess this
quality but fails to achieve it, quite ignominiously; his place is
taken as Jenkins's company commander by a younger and more
ruthless compatriot, Idwal Kedward. And towards the end of *The
Military Philosophers*, a new note creeps into Jenkins's narrative
as he describes in frankly admiring tones his meeting with a celebrated British Field-Marshal (unnamed but clearly recognisable) :

> the Field Marshal's outward personality offered what was per-
> haps even less usual, will-power, not so much natural, as developed
> to altogether exceptional lengths. No doubt there had been a
> generous basic endowment, but of not the essentially magnetic
> quality. In short, the will here might even be more effective from
> being less dramatic. It was an immense, wiry, calculated, insis-
> tent hardness, rather than a force like champagne bursting from
> the bottle.

Against Widmerpool and the forces he represents is set, initially,
Charles Stringham, a young man of sensibility, wit and charm. Here
is how he is presented in *A Question of Upbringing*, shortly after
Jenkins's encounter with Widmerpool (one sees Powell's characteristic use of art-historical images) :

> He was tall and dark, and looked like one of those stiff, sad young
> men in ruffs, whose long legs take up so much room in sixteenth-
> century portraits : or perhaps a younger – and far slighter –
> version of Veronese's Alexander receiving the children of Darius
> after the Battle of Issus : with the same high forehead and sugges-
> tion of hair thinning a bit at the temples. His features certainly
> seemed to belong to that epoch of painting : the faces in Eliza-
> bethan miniatures, lively, obstinate, generous, not very happy,
> and quite relentless. He was an excellent mimic, and although he
> suffered from prolonged fits of melancholy, he talked a lot when
> one of these splenetic fits was not upon him : and ragged with
> extraordinary violence when excited.

In the early stages of the novel the elegant Stringham seems an immeasurably superior person to the gross and pompous Widmerpool.
But by degrees their relative positions change, as Stringham is
undermined by his own weaknesses, becoming an alcoholic' and
having to be looked after by a former governess, Miss Weedon;
while Widmerpool continues inexorably to exert his iron will. The

crucial change in their relationship comes in *The Acceptance World*, where Jenkins and Widmerpool take the drunken Stringham home, and Widmerpool succeeds in getting him into bed by sheer physical force. Thereafter Stringham's fortunes decline sharply: in *The Soldier's Art* he serves as a humble but apparently contented private soldier, until Widmerpool, now a major, arranges a transfer for Stringham, which means he is sent to the Far East, where he dies as a prisoner of the Japanese. Arthur Mizener has suggested that Powell sees the twentieth century as 'a world nearly transformed by Widmerpools though still haunted by Stringhams'. This was a reasonable, even perceptive comment to make after four volumes of the sequence had appeared, though it tends to make Powell sound too consciously elegiac a writer, in the manner of Waugh. Now that so much more of the whole work is available, it seems inadequate: by now Jenkins seems ready to write off the Stringhams entirely, and to make the best he can of a future dominated by the Widmerpools.

Most commentators on *The Music of Time*, including the present writer in an earlier essay, have taken their cue from the elaborate description of a Poussin at the beginning of *A Question of Upbringing*, where the image of a stately dance is introduced:

> The image of Time brought thoughts of mortality: of human beings, facing outward like the Seasons, moving hand in hand in intricate measure: stepping slowly, methodically, sometimes a trifle awkwardly, in evolutions that take recognisable shape: or breaking into seemingly meaningless gyrations, while partners disappear only to reappear again, once more giving pattern to the spectacle: unable to control the melody, unable, perhaps, to control the steps of the dance.

The image of the dance seemed wholly appropriate for the earlier volumes, certainly for the first trilogy, which has actually been re-issued under the collective title of *A Dance to the Music of Time*, and possibly for the second. Yet, with nine volumes available, I have become increasingly doubtful about its adequacy to provide a structure for the whole work. The dance, as understood in the iconography of modern art and literature, implies a freedom from time, change and contingency. The dancer, as Frank Kermode has shown in *Romantic Image*, is an emblem of the symbolist aesthetic monad, set apart from the flux and transcience of ordinary living. Or, in different terms, the dancer is *homo ludens*, carefree and timeless. These terms were appropriate to the earlier volumes, where Nicholas was concerned with discovering the pleasures of an intricate and expanding world. But at the end of the third trilogy Nicholas has become inescapably aware of the pressures of history and mortality. Two of his oldest friends, Stringham and Templer, are dead, and Templer, before he died, seems to have driven his wife mad. Widmerpool's love of power and taste for intrigue is displaying an increasingly ugly side; and, in the larger world, Jenkins becomes aware that modern war means not only death and destruction, but endless deceit and betrayal. His work as liaison officer with the Polish army in London involves him in the bitter discovery that the Russians had murdered thousands of Polish officers at Katyn; Widmerpool's comment on this news is a singularly cold-blooded piece of *Realpolitik*. Guy Crouchback made similar discoveries about the world, and responded in the way that we have seen. Jenkins, the cool observer of a comic order, seems unable to respond at all to the private and public tragedies that represent the intrusion of time and history into the closed world of the dance. Unless, of course, the apparent refusal or inability to respond covers something deeper and incommunicable; in Empson's words:

It is this deep blankness is the real thing strange.
The more things happen to you the more you can't
Tell or remember even what they were.

The ultimate question is, how far can *The Music of Time* continue as the great comic work that it has, so far, essentially been. And then, how can it end? The dance is less elaborate and assured, and the surviving dancers are beoming visibly older and infirmer. For all his distanced discipleship of Proust, one doubts if Powell has the capacity for the triumphant recapitulation of a *Temps retrouvé*. His sceptical, empirical, untheoretical vision does not seem capable of a final, large-scale resolution. With this conviction, one regards the whole work at the three-quarter point with gratitude for what Powell has given us, and a certain muted disquiet about its future. The final volumes are likely to be increasingly overshadowed by what Kermode has called 'the sense of an ending', a sense which is not, I think, reconcilable with the freedom from change and mortality that we inevitably associate with the dance.

III

Any discussion of *The Music of Time* inevitably invites comparison with C. P. Snow's rival — and longer-established — enterprise,

Strangers and Brothers, which, at the time of writing, has reached
ten volumes as against Powell's nine. Both authors are indebted to
Proust, and in each work a first-person narrator carries the story
through several decades of twentieth-century English life, intro-
ducing a large and varied array of characters; beyond this, one can
see no further similarities. *Strangers and Brothers* has many admirers
– more, perhaps, than *The Music of Time* – and it does investigate
whole areas of contemporary experience that other novelists are
either disinclined or unequipped to deal with. Snow is uniquely
concerned with the public life, with power struggles and politics,
whether in a small, enclosed society, or in the state itself, and part
of the interest of his sequence is in watching his narrator, Lewis
Eliot, move, with immense deftness, onwards and upwards through
one area of society after another. We start with Eliot as a young
man in a provincial town in the twenties, then follow him to the
Inns of Court in London, to the senior common-room of a Cambridge
college, and into an ever-widening circle of acquaintances, taking in
aristocratic life in a country house, big business and the intimate
friendship of a wealthy Anglo-Jewish family. During the Second
World War Eliot joins the civil service, and we see through his eyes
the inner workings of an atomic research establishment. In recent
years Eliot has been awarded a knighthood and has become the
friend and confidant of cabinet ministers; now he seems to have
given up public life and is devoting his time to writing. Snow himself has been involved in more kinds of occupation than most
writers; first as a scientist, then as an administrator in the civil service
and in business; and briefly as a junior minister in the Wilson government. Nor has he denied his own identification with Lewis Eliot: 'I
would have thought that in depth Lewis Eliot is myself. In a good
many of his situations, a good many of his external appearances
he is not me, but in any serious and interesting sense he is.' * This
admission gives a certain piquancy to the unfailing approbation
with which Eliot is regarded by his creator.

Snow is well known for having argued that the scientists are
more fitting guardians of humanistic tradition than the most admired
literary figures of the twentieth century, whom he sees as implicitly

* 'Lewis Eliot is myself.' C. P. Snow, quoted by Rubin Rabinovitz in
The Reaction against Experiment in the English Novel 1950–1960 (New
York, 1967) p. 155.

or explicitly helping the advance of totalitarianism. For Snow, the scientists 'have the future in their bones', while the men of letters are distinguished by a vain adherence to vanished values and attitudes. Yet on considering Snow himself as a literary figure one is struck by the immense disparity between what he says and what he does. In fact Snow's belief in the humanistic, melioristic, progressive qualities of scientific culture has become blended in the most singular way with the salient assumptions of the English ideology. Snow has complained in his Rede lecture, *The Two Cultures and the Scientific Revolution*, that modern literature has shown no sign of absorbing the achievements of twentieth-century science, beyond a certain amount of trivial and inaccurate allusion. Yet it could be argued that the art and literature of the Modern Movement reflect the deeply changed concept of reality that has been indicated, in its own way, by twentieth-century science. Cubist painting and *Ulysses* and *The Waste Land*, whatever else they may be, can be seen as products of a post-Newtonian model of the universe. Marshall McLuhan has shown ways in which the characteristic discontinuities and associations of symbolist literature anticipated the patterns and responses imposed by an age of electronics, and has seen the *avant-garde* artists as antennae picking up impending changes as yet imperceptible to the ordinary man; thus having, in their own way, 'the future in their bones'. (For all the vulnerable and wayward elements in his work, which English critics have been very quick to seize on, McLuhan, who was for several years director of the Centre for Culture and Technology at Toronto, has done more than anyone to suggest ways of bridging the gap between the scientific and literary cultures, but I am not aware that Snow has taken any great interest in his work.)

Snow has never, in fact, shown any openness to the idea that changes in science and changes in art and literature may both be part of the same *Weltanschauung*, nor, indeed, that literature may depend on any causes other than the mere whim of the writer. He has at least arguable grounds for condemning the ideological opinions of Pound and Eliot and Yeats – his attack has been enlarged on in a notably poor book, *The Reactionaries*, by John R. Harrison – although he has never tried to show the connection between ideology and literary form. Yet he has also attacked, on literary grounds, writers whom one could certainly not accuse of political

wickedness, such as Joyce and Virginia Woolf and Dorothy Richardson, for what he sees as the disintegratory effect of their fiction.
Snow intensely dislikes their adherence to the stream of consciousness, their reduction, as he sees it, of fiction to a record of disjointed
momentary sensations, which he dismisses as a passing fad of the
twenties and thirties. His own novels, and those of writers who
think like him, such as Pamela Hansford Johnson and William
Cooper, are intended to mark a decisive break with such pernicious
trends and to return to the mainstream of nineteenth-century English realism. (There is a convenient summary of Snow's critical
ideas in Rubin Rabinovitz's *The Reaction against Experiment in the
English Novel 1950–1960*.) The position is certainly familiar, for it
echoes the rejection of Modernism by other contemporary English
writers, such as Philip Larkin and Robert Conquest. Yet in Snow's
case it is peculiarly paradoxical, for it implies that whereas in
science change is inevitable, in literature it is undesirable, thus
separating the two cultures with a vengeance. Snow may, in principle, adhere to a view of the world that is scientific and anti-
traditional, but in his fiction he embodies it in a medium that ignores
any changes made after the end of the nineteenth century. Snow is,
admittedly, an avowed admirer of Proust, but he clearly reads him
in a way that ignores him as a literary innovator, and pushes him
back, as it were, into the nineteenth-century realistic tradition :
Snow's reading of Proust is different from that of John Bayley, and
different, too, from Anthony Powell's. As we have seen, Saul Bellow
is another novelist who adheres, in principle, to the conventions of
nineteenth-century realism; but in *Herzog* he subjects those conventions to an ironical and undermining treatment that is far beyond
the scope of Snow. There is a conspicuous gap between those American or continental novelists who assert that the changed nature of
our sense of reality in the twentieth century has made the traditional novel of character, narrative and action no longer viable; and
Snow's assertion that it remains perennially valid. For all his knowledge of men and affairs, of society and history, it is questionable
whether Snow could grasp the sense of the American or continental
claim. Robbe-Grillet, I imagine, would apply to Snow the strictures
he has already made on certain 'committed' social-realist novels :

> Their literary form, which is often pre-1848, makes them the
> most reactionary of bourgeois novels : their real meaning, which
> becomes perfectly clear as one reads them, and the values they

stand for, are precisely identical to those of our capitalist nine-teenth century . . . (*Snapshots and Towards a New Novel*, p. 72)

In respect of his own fiction, Snow appears to deny that there can be any relation between literary form and ideology, although he is quick to detect and condemn such connections in the work of the writers of the early twentieth-century Modern Movement. In prac-tice, whatever his overt beliefs, Snow is the most deeply backward-looking and nostalgic of living English novelists, forcing his civil servants and businessmen and scientists into a Trollopian mode that is maintained without the faintest hint of conscious pastiche. I should, however, add that one critic of Snow's work, Stephen Wall, has objected to the association of Snow with Trollope: 'C. P. Snow is sometimes said to be the new Trollope: if only he were. If only he had Trollope's curiosity, his empathy, his realistic assessment of his own talent' (*London Magazine*, April 1964). Perhaps one needs to stress that there is a crucial difference between, say, John Barth's *conscious* imitation of Defoe in *The Sot-Weed Factor*, and Snow's presumably *unconscious* imitation of Trollope throughout *Strangers and Brothers*. Of course, if it could be proved that Snow was really writing a work of prolonged *pastiche* of a kind akin to Barth's, one's reading of his sequence would have to become spectacularly different. But that is not likely. In fact Snow's indifference to any conscious concern with literary technique, and to the question of what is and is not possible to a novelist trying seriously to practise his art in the middle of the twentieth century, is very much part of the English ideology, which regards writing novels as something one just *does*, like breathing or walking, without any need for conscious thought. Indeed the whole burden of Snow's attitude to his craft suggests that too much concern with language and construction is actively undesirable, since it may lead the novelist away from the everyday intercourse of decent, rational men into a realm of un-healthy aestheticism. Lionel Trilling has an engaging little fable, which to my eyes reads more sourly than I think Trilling intends, about the way in which Snow might have been launched on his fictional career. He imagines a group of members of a London club – described with all the charming externality that Trilling usually brings to his references to English life – who are arguing about whether or not the novel is dead. Finally, one of them, Mr Snow, responds to a challenge and undertakes to prove that the novel is not dead by writing one himself.

'Will you lay a wager on it?' said the other. 'Will you bet? . . .'
and he named a sum the loss of which would bring Mr Snow to
ruin and the Marshalsea. One of the barristers said, 'Let it pass,
Snow.' And the BBC official said, 'You'd be a fool to take him
up.' For it was not as if Mr Snow were a literary man – he was a
scientist, a physicist of solid reputation. But Mr Snow did not
heed these friendly warnings. 'Done', he said quietly, and his face,
as he put a match to his pipe, was every bit as imperturbable as
Phileas Fogg's. (*A Gathering of Fugitives*, 1957: p. 127)

The implication is that Mr Snow, not possessing elaborate literary
gifts but secure in the possession of a strong sense of social fact,
manages to bring it off and wins the bet. The ten volumes of
Strangers and Brothers that have so far appeared undoubtedly con-
tribute to the contemporary novel as an ongoing sociological activity : what is far from being the case is that they add anything to
the power of the novel to grasp and transform our experience.
Snow's gifts, in short, are quite inadequate, and are employed with
a striking unawareness of their inadequacy, to meet the ambitious
demands of his fictional enterprise.

Snow himself has made it clear that although *Strangers and
Brothers* is meant to convey a wide range of insights into modern
English society, the focus and central interest of the work lies in
Eliot himself. In a note to *The Conscience of the Rich* he remarks
that the inner design of the sequence 'consists of a resonance
between what Lewis Eliot sees and what he feels. Some of the more
important emotional themes he observes through others' experience,
and then finds them enter into his own.' There is an immediate difficulty here in that Snow's use of language is so flat and inexpres-
sive, so tied to a norm of shrewd worldly observation, that he has
great difficulty in making it convey any detectable nuances of feeling on Eliot's part at all. As an instance of this thematic resonance,
Snow refers to possessive love, which appears in *The Conscience of
the Rich* in Mr March's attitude to his son, and which reappears in
The New Men with Eliot's relation to his brother, Martin, and again
in *Homecomings* in his relations with Margaret. One may legitimately doubt how far this intention is enacted in *Strangers and
Brothers*; yet Snow's statement does show that he regards the whole
sequence as a carefully planned whole : that it fails, in practice, to
convey anything like such an impression is partly due to Snow's
excessive reliance on the convention of the first-person narrator. One
does not need to share all Henry James's objections to 'that damned

autobiographical form' to realise that its use involves the novelist in considerable problems. In general, first-person narration falls into two kinds. In one, the narrator is no more than a detached observer who records the events taking place around him and keeps his own personality as unobtrusive as possible: a good example is the 'camera eye' of Isherwood's early stories. In the other kind, the narrator is actively involved in the story, often as the central character, and what he undergoes and records and recollects *is* the essential fictional experience: here, of course, Proust is the great exemplar. In Powell's *The Music of Time* Nicholas Jenkins is a narrator of the second type who has elements of the first; he never pretends to omniscience, is prepared to admit the limitations of his observations, which are not self-authenticating, and yet throughout the story tries hard and intelligently to make sense of what he has seen. Recent critics of fiction have become increasingly concerned with the problems raised by 'unreliable' or 'deluded' narrators, as in works like Henry James's *The Aspern Papers* or Ford Madox Ford's *The Good Soldier* (and *Brideshead Revisited* might be a suitable candidate for discussion in these terms). On the whole, these subtle questions do not arise in reading *Strangers and Brothers*, although a number of cruder ones do. With the 'camera eye' mode of narration the narrator has to see and record everything important that happens: if he is writing about a small and enclosed world this need not present any difficulties, but the wider and more varied the society he moves through, the greater the danger of manifest contrivance on the author's part in order to have his narrator in the right place at the right time. With the other or 'Proustian' method, which I shall call the 'autobiographic' mode, there are dangers of another kind, particularly that the narrator will be unable naturally and convincingly to relate his own deepest emotional experiences; in such cases a note of embarrassment or strain often intrudes. For me this is often the case in Proust and *a fortiori* in Snow. (Powell solves, or eludes, this question by not allowing Nicholas Jenkins to talk about such matters.) In *Strangers and Brothers* Snow employs both methods in different volumes: in *Time of Hope* and *Homecomings* Eliot is mostly concerned with his personal story, which he picks up again in *The Sleep of Reason*; in the other volumes the stress is mainly on Eliot as the vigilant onlooker, the observer of the lives and behaviour of others.

In *Time of Hope* and *The Masters* Snow largely avoids the inherent dangers of first-person narrative, though for very different reasons. *Time of Hope*, which came out in 1948, was the third novel in the sequence to be published, but it takes first place chronologically, for it deals with Lewis Eliot's boyhood, youth and early manhood. We begin with Lewis as a small boy in a Midland town just before the outbreak of the First World War, and end with him as a young barrister in London, unhappily married to Sheila Knight. The opening chapters of this novel, describing the boy's ambiguous relations with his possessive and ambitious mother, have an imaginative quality and emotional force which is very rare in Snow's fiction, and which in places recalls the Lawrence of *Sons and Lovers*. There is an authenticity of feeling in these chapters which make one realise, by contrast, the thinness and shallowness of much of the rest of *Strangers and Brothers*. In the later chapters we follow Eliot through his early struggles and successes, culminating in his intense, hopeless love for Sheila Knight. It is true that we do not completely participate in Eliot's feelings, and this is hardly surprising. For a first-person narrator to convey convincingly the quality of an overpowering sexual love is rare. Snow's attempt to do so results in passages that are not merely banal, but embarrassingly bad:

> No rest from the torments, the insane reminders, of each moment when her body had allured me; so that standing in the street, looking at her window, I was maddened by sensual reveries.

Nevertheless something comes across of the object of Eliot's love: the elusive personality of Shelia Knight, neurotic, destructive, pitiable, and yet oddly engaging, is somehow caught and realised. She is almost the only one of Snow's female characters of whom this can be said; she is certainly far more completely present than Eliot's second wife, Margaret, who appears in *Homecomings*.

In the other novels, apart from the most recent, *The Sleep of Reason*, Eliot is not at the centre of affairs but is, to a greater or lesser extent, an observer of other people. And here Snow falls foul of the danger that the 'camera eye' method of narration will make the story-teller seem excessively inquisitive, even something of an eavesdropper and *voyeur*. Though Eliot's personality remains in many respects elusive, one carries away the impression – which can hardly be congruent with Snow's intentions – that he is an indefatigible recipient of other people's confidences, and the kind of person who is given to listening quietly and intently to private conversations. One tends to find passages like this: 'I got up to go. "No, please stay, Lewis," he said, "I want you to hear this. . . ."' It is a somewhat transparent device, and it is particularly obtrusive in *The Conscience of the Rich*, where we have to believe that Eliot, a Gentile and something of a social outsider, is so completely accepted by an aristocratic and clannish Jewish family that he is able to be present at their most intimate family discussions.* There is one scene in this novel where Eliot just happens to be in the room of the elderly politician Sir Philip March at the precise moment when March receives a letter of dismissal from the Prime Minister. This *could* happen, one readily agrees, but few of us have the good fortune to be so persistently in the right place at the right time as Lewis Eliot. Again, in *The New Men*, one can believe that Eliot, as a wartime civil servant, is actively concerned with an atomic research project, but when we also find that his brother, Martin, is one of the scientists engaged on the project, so that Eliot has personal as well as official knowledge of what is going on, one becomes a little incredulous.

In some of the novels Eliot is not so much concerned with a succession of events as with telling the story of some particular personality who is close to him. This, for instance, is the basis of *The Light and the Dark*, a work which I can only regard as a conspicuous failure. The central figure is Roy Calvert, Eliot's closest friend, a brilliant scholar and a wildly attractive personality with a tragic manic-depressive side to his nature. He is constantly before our eyes, and we are *told* a great deal about him. Nevertheless he remains totally unrealised as a character: we simply do not feel that he was such a remarkable man as Snow wants us to believe. In this failure of realisation the limitations of Snow's narrative style are an important factor. Here, for instance, is his initial description of Calvert:

> He was over middle height, slightly built but strong; and each physical action was so full of ease and grace that he had only to

---

* Snow himself has written: 'When I was very poor and very young, I was taken up by one of the rich patrician Anglo-Jewish families. It was a startling experience. I was a Gentile, and I had never seen the inside of a Jewish family before. This was my first contact with the easy, interconnected world of the English ruling class.' It is, however, part of the burden of fiction to have to be more plausible than life itself. (Quoted in Rabinovitz, *Reaction*, p. 153)

enter a room for eyes to follow him. . . . His eyes were glinting a clear hard transparent hazel yellow, and his whole expression was mischievous and gay. . . . In repose, his face became sad and grave, and in a moment the brilliant high spirits could be swept away and he would look years older, more handsome, more finely shaped. And once or twice already I had seen his face, not sad, but stricken and haunted by a wild melancholy, inexplicably stricken it seemed for so young a man.

This reduces Calvert to a set of stock epithets from a women's magazine serial; in the rest of the novel, although he is presented with considerable elaboration, he never becomes more alive than this account might suggest. It is instructive to compare this passage with Anthony Powell's description of Charles Stringham that I quoted earlier in this chapter; by all accounts the two young men are supposed to be similar types. Snow's inferiority as a literary artist is strikingly revealed in such a comparison.

Strangers and Brothers – the novel which gives its name to the whole sequence – is another work where the action is focused on a supposedly powerful and unusual personality. Here, George Passant emerges more fully as a character than Calvert, and within limits one can accept him for what he is: a solicitor's clerk in the provincial town where Eliot grew up, who is unusually able and intelligent, idealistic and at the same time somewhat boorish, with strong physical passions. Yet the whole intention of the novel is that we should see Passant as more than just this. We also have to believe that he was a man of such charm and personal magnetism that he could command the devotion and allegiance of a large circle of young people. And this is asking us to believe rather more than we are actually given: one is never shown just what it is in George Passant's character that makes him such a commanding person.

It is, then, to *The Masters* that we must turn if we wish to see Snow at his most effective in using Eliot as an observer. This story of Cambridge college politics has become deservedly popular, and has been accurately described by Lionel Trilling as 'a paradigm of the political life'. In one way it suffers from a similar fault to *The Light and the Dark* in that though Jago, the favoured candidate for the mastership of Eliot and his party, is frequently described as a man of admirable and unusual personal gifts, these are in no way made real to the reader. Yet in *The Masters* this is not a major disability, since the real interest is centred not in Jago but in the cross-currents of intrigue and bargaining that surround him in the small, jealous

world of the senior common-room. We are not concerned with
exploring a single personality in depth, but with the interrelations
between a group of characters, none of whom need be so fully
realised. The peculiar structure of *The Masters* means that Snow's
weaknesses are less apparent than usual, while at the same time his
strength can be fully displayed. Thus, since Eliot is one of the dons
most actively concerned in the election, he takes an integral part in
all the conversations which he reports: here he is in no sense an
eavesdropper. Again, the subject of sexual love, which Snow usually
has trouble with, is largely absent from the novel (Roy Calvert's
affair with Joan Royce, which plays an important part in *The Light
and the Dark*, is only marginal in *The Masters*). Most of the time we
are in a wholly masculine society given over to intrigue and a particular struggle for power. And it is in writing of intrigue and power-
struggles that Snow excels. The other novels are most alive when
dealing with similar subjects: as for instance in the trial of George
Passant in *Strangers and Brothers*, the manœuvres concerning the
communist newsletter in *The Conscience of the Rich*, the unmask-
ing of the spy Sawbridge in *The New Men*, the high-level arguments
about defence policy in *The Corridors of Power*, and in the trial of
the two female murderers in *The Sleep of Reason*. Again, in *The
Masters*, Snow has scope for his own particular kind of characterisation; usually unsuccessful in depicting attractive young men or
women, he can draw effective sketches of middle-aged or elderly
men, especially if they have tendencies to eccentricity. In *The
Masters* there are the two elderly dons, Despard-Smith and Gay;
and elsewhere in the sequence there are such men as Mr March,
Martineau, Bevill, Austin Davidson, Lewis Eliot's own father, and,
most vividly presented, perhaps, of all, the shady but amiable
barrister Herbert Getliffe.

In *The Affair* Snow returned with some success to the setting
and to some of the same characters as *The Masters*. Whereas the
earlier novel had been dominated by a clash between two kinds of
personality, with ideological and thematic elements only implicit,
The Affair is a meditation on justice and the way it works in a
small, tightly integrated society. Snow seems to have constructed
his story with some deliberate reference to the Dreyfus case in
mind: Donald Howard, a young scientist, is deprived of his fellow-
ship at a Cambridge college for what looks like a clear-cut case of
scientific fraud, and, since he is generally unpopular, most people in

the college are happy to regard the incident as closed. But a piece of evidence turns up which makes it look as if Howard might, in fact, be as innocent as he claims. The senior common-room is then divided between the decent men who want justice to be done at all costs, and the other decent men who want to avoid any further disturbance to the life of the college. The only exception to the general decency is the victim, Howard, who is indeed a thoroughly objectionable young man. Eliot's brother, Martin, joins the pro-Howard faction, and Eliot himself is brought in as a legal adviser. In the end justice is done to Howard, though only in a strictly technical sense, and no-one ends up with much sense of satisfaction. 'Sensible men usually reach sensible conclusions', remarks Crawford, the Master (whose election had been the subject of *The Masters*), after the final decision, and Eliot receives this ambiguous remark in silence. Although it is an accomplished narrative, *The Affair* under-lines the insufficiencies of Snow's customary view of existence: sensible men, in public office and with a good deal of pragmatic experience of the way the world is run, may, indeed, in the end reach sensible conclusions. Increasingly, though, Eliot seems to sense that there are other and deeper values in life than theirs, but re-mains unable to formulate what they may be.

A significant element in *The Masters* is Snow's use of motifs which occur throughout the sequence, and which provide some of the few imaginative links between the separate volumes. There are two recurrent images: the snug, enclosed room, usually with a bright fire burning in the grate and the curtains drawn; and the complemen-tary image of lighted windows seen from outside. At the beginning of *The Masters* Eliot is reading by a huge fire in his room; it is a bitter January night but he is in 'a cosy island in front of the fireplace'. (The word 'cosy' recurs in similar passages elsewhere: 'The reading lamp shone on the backs of my books, on the white shelves; the room was cosy and confined, the double curtains drawn', *Home-comings*; '. . . the evening was a cosy one. Out of doors, the country-side was freezing', *The New Men*.) When we first meet Eliot, at the beginning of *Strangers and Brothers*, he is associated with a similar image: 'The fire in our habitual public-house spurted and fell. It was a comfortable fire of early autumn, and I basked beside it, not caring how long I waited.' The motif occurs naturally in *The Masters*, since so many of the discussions take place in front of bright fires in curtained college rooms, and gives a degree of imaginative unity to the book. Here and there in the sequence the image of the cosy, enclosed room takes on a positively uterine quality, underlining the potentially regressive elements in Eliot's personality :

> It was strangely warming to be sitting there, in that safe room, as the noise grew. It was like lying in front of the fire as a child, while the wind moaned and the rain thrashed against the windows. It gave just the same pulse of rich, exalted comfort. (*The Light and the Dark*)

The opposed image, of the lighted window seen from outside, occurs more often. It was first apparent in *Time of Hope*, when the young Eliot spent long painful hours looking up at the lights of Sheila's house. As he grows older it is used to emphasise the glamour of life in London: 'On the way down St James's Street, the windows of the clubs glowing comfortably warm through the deepening fog . . .' (*The Light and the Dark*). 'The clouds were low, it was dark early; through the trees one could see the lights of the tall houses in Bayswater Road' (Ibid.). 'It was a hot brilliant summer, and sometimes I used to walk past those houses, whose lights shone out while the sky was still bright' (*The Conscience of the Rich*). It is not difficult to associate these recurrent images with the personality of Eliot: the 'lighted windows' motif can be taken as standing for his sense of himself as an outsider, looking aspiringly at the symbols of power, riches and sexual success. At one point in *The New Men* he seems to project these feelings onto a younger man, the scientist Luke :

> Perhaps he would never lose his sense of being deprived, of being left out of the party – of being outside in the road, of seeing the lights of houses, homes of voluptuous delight denied to him. (ch. IX)

(In a phrase like 'homes of voluptuous delight', the writing sinks to one of its characteristic depths.) In *The Sleep of Reason* Eliot, now middle-aged, knighted and by most standards a considerable worldly success, uses such an image once more, making explicit its associations :

> Was that why, as I stood outside the Residence and saw the bright drawing-room, blinds not drawn, standard-light by the window, I felt a pang, as though I were an outsider? It seemed so for an instant: and yet, in cold blood, I should have known it was not true. I was still capable of walking any street, seeing a lighted window, and feeling that same pang, which was made up

of curiosity, envy and desire: in that sense, one doesn't age: one can still envy a hearth-glow, even if one is returning to a happy home: it isn't a social chance, but something a good deal deeper, that can at untameable moments, make one feel for ever youthful, and, as far as that goes, for ever in the street outside.

Such observations tell one something about the personality of the mature Eliot. In *Time of Hope* Sheila says to the young Eliot, 'You're not as nice as people think you are', but one is inclined to reflect that one has very little idea how nice or nasty Eliot in fact is. Snow regards him with unlimited approbation, which the reader is urged to share; Eliot seems to have considerable charm, since so many people like him, and to be trustworthy, since so many confide in him. At the same time, he is obsessed with power; as he remarks in *Homecomings*, 'I had kept an interest in success and power which was, to my friends, forbiddingly intense', and he can act with extreme ruthlessness, as when he destroys Sheila's love affair with Hugh Smith, and breaks up Margaret's marriage to Geoffrey Hollis. All these characteristics could exist in the same individual, admittedly, but he would be, to say the least of it, a complex personality who would need very careful realisation to appear convincing. And such realisation is beyond Snow's powers as a novelist: Eliot remains a fragmentary collection of attributes.

This fragmentation is, I think, at the heart of *Strangers and Brothers*, and is inherent in the manner in which Snow has chosen to unfold the sequence. It proceeds by a method of simultaneous rather than successive progression. That is to say, two or three novels may cover the same period of time, and in each of them Eliot will be concerned with a different set of events. Thus, by cross-referring between *The Light and the Dark*, *The New Men* and *Homecomings*, one can work out that in the autumn of 1941 Eliot was falling in love with Margaret Davidson, involved in his official capacity with the atomic project at Barford, and deeply concerned about the marriage of his friend Roy Calvert. Were Eliot really presented to us as a whole man, then these separate strands of experience would be co-existing in his consciousness and sensibility, modifying each other and converging to form new patterns. Instead of which they are presented in separate watertight compartments. Although Snow may have been prompted in his fictional project by the laudable intention of showing the unreality of our customary rigid separation between the personal and the social, in practice he has only made the distinction seem more absolute. Stephen Wall has produced an apt quotation from *Howards End* to describe the fragmented presentation of Lewis Eliot; in Forster's novel the Wilcoxes 'did not make the mistake of handling human affairs in the bulk, but disposed of them item by item, sharply'.

It may be that the Wilcoxes of our society, the people who actually run the world, have not had an adequate innings in English fiction, and that Snow has tried to do something to give them their due. But in practice *Strangers and Brothers* shows that whatever practical virtues the Wilcoxes may possess they lack the sensibility to inform a long work of fiction. In his stress on pragmatic worldly wisdom, and his fascination with a world of manipulation and operation, Snow has come close to providing a fictional embodiment of what Marcuse calls 'one-dimensional man', where the very terms of reference preclude the possibility of transcendence. These strictures apply with much less force to the most recent volume in the sequence, *The Sleep of Reason*, where some new elements seem, very late in the day, to have entered into Lewis Eliot's understanding. Much of the book is taken up, it is true, with familiar and mechanically efficient committee-room stuff; Eliot serves on the court of a new university, and mounting pressure is put on the vice-chancellor to resign. But, more interestingly, Eliot is made to encounter death in a fuller way than at any point previously in the sequence. His own father dies, and a child is murdered. A lesbian couple are charged with the murder, and eventually convicted after a long and very fully described trial scene. Lewis finds himself emotionally and practically involved with the case, since one of the accused is the niece of his old friend George Passant. Snow's treatment of this crime clearly owes a good deal to the Moors Murder case (which was written up by his wife, Pamela Hansford Johnson), and Eliot, who has undergone lesser tribulations, such as being threatened with the loss of the sight of one eye, responds to this atrocious event as though it were a unique revelation of human cruelty and irrationality. Here, for the first time in Snow's fiction, we find not tragedy, but some faint realisation of the meaning of tragedy. The insufficiencies of a world of sensible men and practical solutions are exposed, and Snow at last seems ready to enact with some degree of imaginative conviction the sentiment that he dutifully set down in the pages of the Rede Lecture: 'but those triumphs of life we make for ourselves while the edge of the road is black: each of us dies alone'. What is good in *The Sleep of Reason* is not enough to redeem the whole novel, which is more than usually shapeless, and Snow's linguistic resources are still inadequate to meet his emotional demands. Yet the new sense of self-knowledge, and indeed, self-doubt, that Eliot acquires in this book represents a significant development in the sequence, and one which is likely to make us see the preceding volumes in a different, though scarcely more flattering, light.

VI Between Nostalgia and Nightmare

> If the scientists have the future in their bones, then the
> traditional culture responds by wishing the future did not
> exist.
>
> C. P. SNOW, *The Two Cultures and the*
> *Scientific Revolution*

I

I F many of the most accomplished novels of the past twenty years
bear out Paul West's charge that the English are very much in love
with their own society, they also hint at attitudes that go beyond
simple infatuation with a familiar environment: one can also detect
an intermittent fascination with the past, and a variety of fears
about the future. There is not, perhaps, anything particularly
English about such a set of attitudes: critics such as Leslie Fiedler
and R. W. B. Lewis have shown how American fiction tends to
alternate between nostalgia for a vanished childhood or Eden and
visions of the kind of collective disaster we call apocalypse. Indeed
in the life of every individual there may be constant archetypal
alternations between regressive longings and eschatological fears.
But the attitudes I am interested in are reinforced by, and take a
particular quality from, the English cultural crisis that I discussed
in my third chapter. A book such as Frank Kermode's *The Sense of*
an Ending has shown ways in which the very nature of fictional
form may involve apocalyptic implications, and in a brilliant essay
in his book *Continuities*, Kermode has shown the dense apocalyptic
elements in such a crucial English novel as *Women in Love*. Since
the Second World War many novels have contained images of
collective catastrophe, whether in conventional literary terms or as
science fiction, dwelling on the horrors of totalitarianism, a Third
World War and nuclear devastation. Perhaps the most celebrated
of these books, by an English author, has been George Orwell's
Nineteen Eighty-Four, 'the strongest possible wish that the future
should not exist', as C. P. Snow has called it. A great deal of space
has already been devoted to discussions of this novel – more perhaps
than its somewhat limited literary qualities deserve – and I do not

need to add to it here. One need merely note in passing the book's remarkable insight into the varieties of contemporary totalitarianism, whether exercised by direct political control, or forms of media or thought control: in so far as western democratic societies have become increasingly totalitarian it is largely by the latter devices. (Although – as Brian Wicker has pointed out in *Culture and Theology*, 1966: pp. 151–69 – one of Orwell's most publicised notions, 'newspeak', shows considerable philosophical and linguistic *naïveté*.) At the same time *Nineteen Eighty-Four* is very much a product of a particular time and place: England during the desperate shabbiness of the final phase of the Second World War, when the true nature of Soviet totalitarianism was becoming apparent through the official rhetoric glorifying the wartime alliance. It is a book about life after the apocalypse has happened; at the same time it is shot through with wistful nostalgic recollections of life before the disaster. One finds very much the same pattern in an earlier novel of Orwell's, written and published just before the Second World War, *Coming Up for Air*. Here the impending disaster is war itself; in the person of his dissatisfied suburban hero – a radically disillusioned version of the Wellsian 'little man' – Orwell projects all his own distaste for contemporary society. In the words of the blurb of the Penguin edition: 'War overshadows every chapter. The fear of it forces George Bowling, a very ordinary suburban Englishman of forty-five, to go back in his mind to that other "before-the-war" – to the peace of his childhood in a small country town.' But his physical return to Lower Binfield merely completes his disillusionment, and the book ends with a direct anticipation of *Nineteen Eighty-Four*. 'The old life in Lower Binfield, the war and the after-war, Hitler, Stalin, bombs, machine-guns, food-queues, rubber truncheons – it was fading out, all fading out.' *Coming Up for Air* shows, in a remarkably lucid, even diagrammatic, form the alternation between nostalgia and catastrophe that has been evident in the work of later English novelists.

The desire to escape the present by looking back to the era before the First World War seems to be a remarkably constant element in the contemporary English imagination. In the fifties it was manifested in such things as the personal style of Harold Macmillan and the cult of the teddy-boy; more recently there has been the taste for *art nouveau* and the Pop Art uses of the trappings of Kiplingesque patriotism. One has seen a remarkable revival of interest in Galsworthy, sparked off by an interminable television serialisation of *The Forsyte Saga*. Among living writers John Osborne offers a clear example of this tendency to look back to a vanished era : Colonel Redfern, the only sympathetic character in *Look Back in Anger*, exemplifies it, and so, at a lower social level, does Archie Rice in *The Entertainer*: both are anachronistic Edwardian survivals. Some novelists have attempted an imaginative reconstruction of Edwardian life, such as William Cooper in *Disquiet and Peace* or Christine Brooke-Rose in *The Dear Deceit*, and others have introduced episodes from that era into their fiction : I am thinking, for instance, of the early chapters of C. P. Snow's *Time of Hope* and the retrospective opening section of Anthony Powell's *The Kindly Ones*, or the splendid account of the Wild West Exhibition in 1912 that opens Angus Wilson's *No Laughing Matter*. Again, there are the several volumes of Henry Williamson's *A Chronicle of Ancient Sunlight* that describe the Edwardian London childhood of Phillip Madison, although they have never achieved the popularity one might expect in such a climate of taste.

Of the novelists who have emerged since 1945, Angus Wilson particularly embodies this English cultural preoccupation, while, at the same time, infusing it with his own highly personal predelictions or even obsessions. He is both a writer of middle-brow appeal and true literary seriousness, a fact which enables him to elude confident critical placing. Without doubt Wilson is a writer of unusually fine intelligence, wide reading and great sensitivity. Yet for him, as for many of his contemporaries, writing is just a question of writing, of saying what one wants to say, without theoretical worrying. He has been applauded for his pragmatic approach by John Bayley: 'The common reader probably clings to novelists who appear unaware that a loss of confidence in their old-fashioned power of creation has taken place – in England, Anthony Powell or Angus Wilson' (*Essays in Criticism*, April 1968). (It is, of course, in England that such unawareness is easiest to sustain.) I do not, in fact, think that John Bayley's point is true of Anthony Powell, since, in my reading, many of the stylistic strategems of *The Music of Time* are precisely attempts to cope with such a loss of confidence; but in respect of Angus Wilson his point is well taken. A similar observation has been made, though from an opposed critical stance, by a novelist of experimental inclinations, B. S. Johnson :

It's silly to pretend that one can solve the problems of writing in the middle twentieth century with the methods of Henry James, and even less with the methods of Dickens. One thinks of a very good writer like Angus Wilson who, I think, is a marvellous observer of twentieth century *mores*, and I'm sure social historians in the future will look to Angus Wilson and say, 'Yes, that's what it must have been like to live then.' But the actual methods he uses are those of Dickens, which seem to me to conflict with what he's writing about, a conflict, in fact, between form and content. (BBC recording, 1967 : 'Novelists of the Sixties')

Broadly speaking, Wilson's attitude to his craft is similar to Snow's, although he does not share Snow's ideological opposition to the achievements of the Modern Movement. At least, if Wilson once disapproved of Virginia Woolf, he now admires her very much (Rabinovitz, *Reaction*, p. 67). His first three novels, *Hemlock and After*, *Anglo-Saxon Attitudes* and *The Middle Age of Mrs Eliot* – published between 1952 and 1958 – are very English in their nonchalance about form, in their precise social mimicry, and in the nature of their moral preoccupations. Despite a sense of what James called 'felt life' and, in the first two, a Dickensian range of characters, the thematic elements in these novels are obtrusive. One is constantly invited to ponder questions of responsibility and guilt, the familiar Wilcox–Schlegel opposition between the public life of busy achievement and the private life of spiritual cultivation, and the dilemmas inherent in truly understanding the motives for one's actions. Whereas for Baudelaire true progress lay in diminishing the traces of original sin, for many English novelists it lies in diminishing the traces of self-deception, in steadfastly eradicating the original Emma Woodhouse from one's soul. Wilson is a distinguished practitioner in this tradition, whose brightest luminary is George Eliot: the novel is seen as the vehicle for a particular liberal ideology, where characters are secure in their freedom to refine on their motives, truly to understand each other, and, above all, themselves. *Nosce teipsum* is the beginning of all true wisdom, and one wholeheartedly admires the achievements of a tradition so splendidly dedicated to the cause of moral clarity. Yet with a mid-twentieth-century representative of this tradition such as Wilson, one's admiration is tempered with a sense that the questions so searchingly gone into for the nth time in this or that novel are beginning to look trivial, both intrinsically and in the larger context of the history of our times. It is in the centripetal nature of its preoccupations that English culture can look parochial and irrelevant to outsiders. For writers who have known, and often still live in, a world where torture and deportation, the arbitrary exercise of unlimited power and the familiarity of casual violence are a part of daily experience, the dilemmas of the English liberal are likely to seem a little fine drawn. The experiences that have gone into the fiction of Camus or Pasternak or Günter Grass are of such a different order to those reflected by someone like Angus Wilson that a critical comparison is difficult. Wilson is aware of these disparities, and in *The Middle Age of Mrs Eliot* he makes an interesting effort to cope with them : Meg Eliot, the archetypal liberal heroine, whose forebears can be found in Forster and George Eliot and Jane Austen, is good-looking, sensitive, intelligent without being clever, and modestly complacent. Yet she loses her handsome, devoted, successful husband in a bit of casual political violence at the airport of an Asian country they are visiting, and the rest of the novel shows her valiant attempt to make something of her life in widowhood and poverty.

Certainly, within clearly defined limits, *The Middle Age of Mrs Eliot* is an admirable novel, which shows, among other things, that Wilson is better at creating memorable female characters than male ones. I am much less convinced of the enduring qualities of his first two novels; their plots seem creakingly contrived, and I cannot work up anything like the degree of interest in the dilemmas of the self-flagellating Bernard Sands or the spiritually sluggish Gerald Middleton that Wilson so urgently invites. Nevertheless *Anglo-Saxon Attitudes* does offer the relaxed interest provided by a busily crowded fictional canvas – with part of his mind it seems that Wilson has always wanted to *dépasser The Forsyte Saga* – and it shows his fascination with the years just before 1914. The whole elaborate plot of his novel depends on an event in the year 1912 when a pagan fertility idol is introduced into the tomb of an Anglo-Saxon bishop. The hoax, which reverberates through the novel (and is clearly a fictional version of the Piltdown Man scandal), was perpetrated by a friend of the young Gerald Middleton called Gilbert Stokesay. Although he was killed in the First World War, Stokesay persists in Gerald's memories as one of the central characters of the story : a reactionary poet and essayist of the cast of T. E. Hulme and Wyndham Lewis, a disciple of Nietzsche and a sadist. Although, as a good liberal, Wilson deplores such types, he is evidently interested in them; one finds them again in *The Old Men at the Zoo* and a short story called 'More Friend Than Lodger'. There had been one or two Edwardian echoes of a sinister kind in *Hemlock and After*: the corrupter of children, Hubert Rose, affects Ewardian speech and appearance, and Sherman Winter and his degenerate friends misbehave in the bedrooms of Varden Hall because 'it was somehow, they felt, Edwardian'. In both novels, and again in *The Middle Age of Mrs Eliot*, there is plenty of evidence that Wilson's liberal imagination is deeply affected by recurring images of violence and cruelty, in ways that both point to deep-seated private obsessions and reflect the public violence of our times. C. B. Cox has accurately remarked of Wilson's first three novels:

> There is an ambiguous relationship between the vivid dramatic action and the intellectual analysis, almost as if Wilson feels that nightmare is truth, and the reconstructions of his art, like social poses, are only coverings for a reality which is inescapably horrible. (*The Free Spirit*, 1963: p. 152)

The sense of nightmare, apparent in the first three books in isolated incidents and recurring images, provided the central material of Wilson's fourth novel, *The Old Men at the Zoo*, a venture into prophetic fantasy. After rereading it, I feel that I dismissed it in much too summary a fashion when discussing Wilson's work a few years ago.* It undoubtedly has major faults. The first part of the book, which deals with the petty intrigues of the directors of the London Zoo, reads rather like a wooden and slow-moving imitation of Snow; the prevalent animal symbolism makes its point, but is too heavily handled.

In later chapters, however, the book becomes imaginatively alive. In the situation that Wilson describes the England of 1970 is militarily threatened by an alliance of European powers; the impending war lends an apocalyptic note to the story, but the atmosphere is hardly suggestive of the outbreak of the Third World War as usually imagined in such fantasies, or even of the advent of the Second World War; rather it seems to recall the summer of 1914, and in the idea of an alliance of European powers threatening Britain it looks back to the alarmist stories of imaginary wars and invasions of Britain that appeared in abundance between 1870 and

---

* *New York Review of Books*, 23 February 1965.

1914, and which have been discussed in detail in I. F. Clarke's *Voices Prophesying War*. How far the distaste for a unified Europe presented in his story is part of Wilson's own view of life is not clear: as a proponent of the English ideology he has gone on record as objecting to anything that smacks of continental metaphysics. John Holloway has quoted Wilson's remark at the International Writers' Conference at Leningrad in 1963:

> Until yesterday I think that most of the English delegates listened with surprise to the unfamiliar, and for us sterile, disputations expressed in a distorted metaphysical jargon. However, yesterday we heard addresses which were expressed in the simple, direct tone which we are used to. (*Listener*, 19 January 1967)

In *The Old Men at the Zoo* the only committed pro-European is a vulgar fascist demagogue called Blanshard-White who talks of 'throwing off the puritan legacy' and getting closer 'to the rich vein of Mediterranean brutality on which our European legacy so much depends'; he plans to revive the gladiatorial shows of Ancient Rome by putting on public combats between political prisoners and the animals of the Zoo. Blanshard-White offers a simplified version of the attitudes of Montherlant or Maurras, or rather of the kind of deracinated Englishman who might be expected to admire them. Blanshard-White is only a minor character and a sketchily rendered one at that, yet he does seem to embody some puzzling phobia in Wilson's imagination, where repulsion is mingled with a degree of secret fascination. In this aspect *The Old Men at the Zoo* echoes, in a more sinister way, the gallophobia of Kingsley Amis's *I Like It Here*. In so far as its infra-plot touches on recent history, one notes that *The Old Men at the Zoo* was published in 1961, the year when Britain first applied to join the Common Market (an attempt which was to be twice rejected by the French).

In this novel Wilson tries to show his narrator, Simon Carter, struggling with larger moral dilemmas than have previously concerned the characters of Wilson's novels. That is to say, politics impinges on private life in a somewhat un-English way. Carter, the secretary of the Zoo, who is both an animal-lover and an efficient administrator tries to carry on with his work as best he can after England has been defeated by the Europeans. In doing so he embodies the classical dilemma of the public servant in a period of defeat and oppression: should one try to keep society going and risk being labelled a collaborator, or should one keep up a possibly

vain and even disastrous resistance? By temperament Carter inclines towards the first course, but finally the excesses of pro-
Europeans like Blanshard-White are too much for him and he tries
to escape from London, only to be thrown into a concentration
camp, from which he is rescued, at the end of the novel, by an
incredible, fairy-tale 'Liberation'.

Where *The Old Men at the Zoo* seems to me to achieve its maxi-
mum imaginative intensity is in the remarkable chapter called 'A
Good Old, Rare Old, Armageddon'. Here the new director of the
Zoo, Sir Bobby Falcon, a rakish old gentleman, who looks like a
figure in a whisky advertisement, and who has a passionate love of
everything Victorian, is putting on a special exhibition called a
British Day; at the same time the outbreak of war is imminent, and
the Zoo is bombed (with small, old-fashioned bombs) before the
exhibition can be officially opened. In this chapter Wilson achieves a
striking juxtaposition of insular nostalgia and apocalyptic nightmare. The British Day, as Falcon conceives it, looks back to the
Festival of Britain in 1951, but it also anticipates the camp
patriotism of the Sunday colour-supplements :

> On that clear, moonlit night, the extraordinary theatricality of
> the Zoo's new decor merged happily into the starry background.
> We wandered round looking happily at the great massed beds of
> auriculas and tulips and wallflowers that spelt 'God Save the
> Queen', and 'Norman, and Saxon and Dane are We', and the foun-
> tains playing in coloured jets. Here at the entrance to what was
> being shown as the Old Victorian Zoo were to be the recitations
> and the tableaux and later a show of fireworks with two set pieces
> – a British lion and an Indian elephant. The Old Zoo looked par-
> ticularly charming with all the Decimus Burton Houses picked
> out with very subtle lighting (Jane's work), with a chalet for
> the old woman who was to sell fresh cows' milk and bags of
> buns, and booths for the peanut man and coconut shies, with
> goat chaises, and a wondrous bear pit. Beyond the Old Zoo, the
> Lemur House, its modern lines disguised with ferns and hot-
> house plants, had been converted into a *chef d'œuvre à la* Paxton;
> and in this great glass palace, to Matthew's delight, were to be
> housed birds from every corner of the earth that was now or
> ever had been British. For, of course, it was only by cheating and
> taking in history, that a British Day could cast its net wide
> enough. From this show centre of the Old Zoo, the aviaries and
> the gardens, five separate roads led off each to a separate con-
> tinent – to Stanley's Africa, to Botany Bay, to a Hudson Bay fur
> station, to the jungle of the British Raj, and, a little incommen-

surately (but by a determined whim of Bobby's) to the Apes of
the Rock.

In this colourful assembly, patriotism is reduced to childlike re-
gressiveness; but the splendours of the British Day are soon dimmed.
The bombs fall, and we see our last of Falcon in a posture of calculatedly absurd symbolism :

> There above us on the top of the bronze lion that crowned the
> Lion House was Sir Robert Falcon, doubled up with pain, but
> still wildly shouting, blown on high by some freak of blast,
> whole though bruised and shaken.

The Old Men at the Zoo seems to have performed a kind of blood-
letting for Wilson's imagination, as though it enabled him to face,
and for the time being at least subdue, his own inner fantasies. His
next novel, Late Call, is, by contrast, a work of considerable serenity and relative freedom from obsessions, although the serenity
is tempered by spiritual bleakness. In contrast to Wilson's earlier
novels, one might call it 'positive' or 'affirmative', although one
should, perhaps, preserve a cautionary memory of Bernard Sands,
the novelist hero of Hemlock and After, who read with sardonic
enjoyment the eager though uncomprehending reviews that described one of his books as a 'refreshing, if unexpected, source of
renewed hope and affirmation in living' and 'a sadly needed
testimony to the endurance of the human spirit'. 'And all this,
Bernard reflected with amusement. proceeded from an irrational
preoccupation with evil that was probably the result of nervous
anxiety.' Wilson has not lost his own sense of evil, but whereas
in the earlier books it had shown itself in intense marginal fantasies, like the grotesque procuress Mrs Curry in Hemlock and
After or the corrupt Irish youth Larry O'Rourke in Anglo-Saxon
Attitudes, or the innumerable scenes of brutality and mutilation
in The Old Men at the Zoo, in Late Call it is integrated with Wilson's
principal strength as a novelist, his infallible sense of social fact.
Late Call explores the spiritual desolation of life in a New Town in
the Midlands, where the gimmickry of affluence has become a way
of life rather than an aid to living.

The heroine of Late Call, Sylvia Calvert, is a woman in her
sixties, who has retired after a lifetime spent managing small,
unfashionable hotels. Accompanied by her sponging idler of a
husband – one of Wilson's most crisply drawn characters – who
cares only for playing cards and reliving the days when he was a

temporary officer in the First World War, she goes to live in the New Town of Carshall with her recently widowed son, Harold. He is a progressive headmaster and educational theorist, a writer of profitable books with titles such as *The Blokes at the Back of the Class* and an active citizen of Carshall and believer in the ideal of the New Town. Harold flaunts his filial feelings and warmly welcomes his parents to his handsomely equipped modern house. Why, and how, the Calverts cannot live with Harold and his three teenage children is the story that Wilson goes on to tell.

Sylvia Calvert has some affinities with Meg Eliot, but does not fit so easily into the literary archetype of the liberal heroine. Although basically shrewd, she has a limited intelligence and very little education; her sensibility is formed by popular biographies, light historical novels and sentimental television serials. In achieving so much with a character so far removed from what most novelists would consider an appropriate fictional consciousness, Wilson has done remarkably well. The essential point about Sylvia is that she represents a standard by which to judge the progressive pretensions of Harold and his children, and the ideals of the New Town generally; and, significantly, her own standards are based in the vanished pre-1914 world. *Late Call* opens with a beautifully written prologue called 'The Hot Summer of 1911', which shows Sylvia as a child of ten on an East Anglian farm, bullied by her boorish parents and weighed down with the responsibility of looking after a brood of younger siblings. She is at first patronised, then victimised by some middle-class summer visitors. Taken separately, this 'Prologue' reads like one of Wilson's sharpest short stories. It scarcely idealises the world in which Sylvia grows up – one is only too aware of the prevalent snobbery and insensitive treatment of children – but it shows how the values Sylvia absorbed as a child have remained with her throughout her life, and establishes the difference between her and Harold and his friends. In fact Wilson uses Sylvia's honest but often baffled consciousness to make a remarkably sharp exposure of contemporary progressive attitudes. *Late Call* is, in essence, a highly conservative book, although it puts forward no propositions, and does not seem unfairminded in its descriptions of British life in the 1960s. Wilson aims some accurate satire at what one might call the *Observer*-ethos, with its naïve love of gadgets, doctrinaire progressiveness, would-be-exotic eating habits, cultural status-seeking and neurotic concern to be with-it. There is a nice illustration when

Harold explains to his mother the workings of a new electric cooker: 'With this heatview you've got a double check – this marker is going up and down the whole time, it's just as if you had your beloved gas flame.' It is on such things, or Harold's eagerness about them, that his relationship with his mother starts to founder.

On Easter Sunday Sylvia is taken to church – though the church is more like a meeting hall – to hear a sermon by the local vicar, who is much admired in the New Town for his up-to-date ideas: 'Last Easter he gave a sermon on the eleven plus.' But he is ill, and the replacement, an elderly Scot, preaches a traditional sermon, with Calvinist overtones, about Grace. Harold is deeply scandalised by such obscurantism, but Sylvia has been touched by the sermon, and addresses a word of thanks to the old man. In Wilson's earlier books religion was regarded as, at best, an evasion of human responsibility; but in *Late Call* Sylvia's response seems to suggest that it might be a touchstone for various kinds of contemporary insincerity. In so far as Sylvia is the embodiment of a set of attitudes deeply at variance with the dominant assumptions of the age, then *Late Call* can be called a nostalgic work in the positive sense described by D. W. Harding:

> It can be said in general that complete absence of nostalgia in a modern writer is suspect, suggesting complacent fellowship with the main commercial group, or seclusion with an academic group, or life among the cliques, or too little questioning and testing of the tradition. (*Scrutiny*, May 1932)

It is, I think, better written and less diffuse than Wilson's earlier novels; if it is, at the same time, more thematically limited, it is arguably his most achieved work of fictional art.

Several critics have, however, reserved their highest praise for Wilson's most recent novel, *No Laughing Matter*. This is his longest and most ambitious book so far, in which he returns to the crowded canvas and broad temporal sweep of *Anglo-Saxon Attitudes*, tracing the fortunes of a not very ordinary English upper-middle-class family called Matthews from 1912 to the present day. Wilson uses the Matthews family as a focus for his fictional attempt on the Condition of England question: he might have taken as his epigraph George Orwell's remark: 'A family with the wrong members in control – that, perhaps, is as near as one can get to describing England in a phrase.' We first encounter them – William and Clara, known to their family as Billy Pop and the Countess – together with their six vivacious and articulate children, a globe-trotting maiden aunt and a comic cockney servant when they are visiting the Wild West Exhibition at West Kensington in 1912. The handsome, bland William is a literary gent in the casual Edwardian fashion; his principal work is a study of cricket in English literature. Clara is darkly beautiful, witty, vain and consumingly egotistical. We never see the Matthews family in such an agreeable light again; the opening chapter, which describes their visit to the exhibition in fascinating and meticulously researched detail, is a brilliant performance by Wilson, showing once more the extent of his imaginative attachment to the pre-1914 world. As the children grow up we observe the decline of their seemingly radiant parents into debt, infidelity and increasing seediness, and the growth of implacable hostility between parents and children. *No Laughing Matter* is a defiantly traditional generations-novel, with a bustling variety of characters and a great deal of exuberant interplay between them. At the same time Wilson's prose is richer and more relaxed than in his early novels, and his language is able to embody a wider spectrum of feeling and to draw on a greater variety of technical devices. Indeed, several of the chapters take the form of playlets imitating the successive theatrical styles of the past fifty years; a nice example of Wilson's mimetic talents and one that, on the whole, comes off. The novel contains many brilliant episodes, yet the successes remain local and remind one that Wilson began his literary career as a short story writer, and has always had difficulty in responding adequately to the structural demands of the full-scale novel, greatly drawn to it though he is. Increasingly in *No Laughing Matter* one feels that Wilson has not been able to muster sufficient imaginative energy to animate the whole of his ample design, and there is a palpable weariness in the last part of the book, as compared with its brilliant opening.

Undoubtedly the novel represents a continuing desire on Wilson's part to take in history and the public world, as opposed to the largely private concerns of the first three books. The obsessions have largely disappeared, or at least been mastered, and replaced by an attempt at a calmly comprehensive panoramic vision. The Matthews family are more than just a collection of latter-day Forsytes; their changing situation does in some sense identify them with England, 'the family with the wrong members in control', from the seemingly elegant Pop and Countess of 1912, already nurturing the seeds of dissolution, down to their great-grandchildren, students at a New University in 1967. And for all their liveliness, they cannot sustain such a representative role. There is plenty of history in *No Laughing Matter*, at least as brilliant particularised description, like the account of a fascist march in Bermondsey in the thirties, but not much sense of history. Wilson's gifts are fully in evidence in this novel, and so are his limitations. His intuitions and his power of mimicry are as keen as ever: he can instantly reveal the subtle tensions in a complex family relationship, or the unexpected contortions of a consciousness suddenly brought against a new level of reality. He is, above all, a novelist of manners and not at all of ideas, and ideas are what *No Laughing Matter* conspicuously lacks; not, of course, as conversational tags or fashionable allusions, but as a significant dimension in the narrative. Despite Wilson's admirable wish to include history in this novel, it does not transcend the personal.

II

A writer who has established a comparable reputation to Angus Wilson's in the last fifteen years is Kingsley Amis: like Wilson's, his fiction is marked by an acute comic sense, a finely responsive eye and ear for social nuance, concern about the difficulties of behaving decently, and an intermittent sense of nightmare. Admittedly these qualities, which occur in Amis's fiction in roughly the order in which I have set them down here, assume a different pattern of frequency in Wilson's work; one does not regard him primarily, as one still tends to regard Amis, as a comic novelist. Even so, to describe Amis in this way may surprise those who still think of him only as the author of *Lucky Jim* and a founding father of the Angry Young Men. But it is over fifteen years since *Lucky Jim* came out, and in that time Amis has published seven more novels, a collection of short stories and two books of poems, together with critical studies of science fiction and the writings of Ian Fleming. One thing that this sizeable *œuvre* makes clear is that the comic spirit in Amis's work has become steadily less dominant since Jim Dixon made his carefree debut. Amis admirably refused to repeat his initial success (although a quite recent novel, *I Want it Now*, does look uncomfortably like an attempt to do just that) in a way which disconcerted readers who were eager for more of the same thing, and who were disinclined to pursue the interesting mixture of comedy and seriousness in Amis's subsequent fiction. There are also those who claim that Amis is not worth anyone's serious attention, that *Lucky Jim* is at worst a crude and childish farce, and at best no more than a faded relic of the taste of the early fifties. Nevertheless *Lucky Jim* remains, for me, a comic masterpiece, the funniest English first novel since Anthony Powell's *Afternoon Men* appeared in 1931, and a work that is surpassed only by the very best of Waugh and Powell. One would like to think that it will retain its appeal, just as their early books have, even when its sociological implications, of which so much was made in the fifties, have dwindled into a historical footnote.

On its first appearance *Lucky Jim* was assumed to inherit the comic manner of the early Waugh; but some readers also related it to famous works of Edwardian comic fiction, like Wells's *Kipps* or Arnold Bennett's *The Card*. (Jerome K. Jerome's *Three Men in a Boat* is another possible antecedent.)*

This critical perspective seems to me largely correct, although it needs a certain qualification. In the remarks about fiction scattered about his reviews and other critical writings – conveniently summarised in Ruben Rabinovitz's book – Amis has shown himself to be assertively anti-modern, anti-experimental, anti-cosmopolitan, to at least the same degree as Snow or William Cooper; indeed his tastes are narrower, since he does not share Snow's admiration for Proust. Yet his way of writing fiction suggests that he has undergone, no matter how unwillingly, the influence of the Modern Movement, at least in his reliance on linguistic effect; style functions actively in Amis's comic writing, as it does in Powell's. John Gross has remarked on the way in which many of Amis's comic effects originate in his linguistic finesse rather than in the comedy of situation. Throughout his novels there is a steady preoccupation with language; we see it in characters such as Julian Ormerod in *Take a Girl Like You* or Harry Bannion in *I Like it Here*, compulsive and singular verbalisers, who are regarded by their creator with considerable affection. In *That Uncertain Feeling*, John Lewis, in the midst of his troubles, finds time to reflect on his children's speech habits : ' "Yas," she said. This lowering of the *e*-phoneme is

* One critic who pointed out the parallel was John Holloway, in *The Charted Mirror* (1960). In an essay on Amis published in the *London Magazine* for January 1964 I dismissed any possible similarities between his work and Edwardian fiction; wrongly, as I now think.

widespread, I've noticed, in childish dialect.' In *One Fat Englishman* the Danish philologist Ernest Bang keeps up a running commentary on the way the other characters talk. This concentration on verbal effects shows that Amis believes that fiction, whatever else it may be made of, is also made of words; this implicit conviction places him as a post-Joycean novelist, and distinguishes him not only from Edwardian comic writers such as Bennett or Wells or Saki, but from contemporaries such as Snow or Cooper. The stylistic dimension in Amis has been discussed at some length by David Lodge in his book *Language of Fiction*, and he gives good reasons for seeing Amis as a novelist worth serious critical attention, no matter how flawed his output might be. Although Amis writes what can be regarded as a traditional, uncomplicated narrative, he differs from the Edwardians in his degree of concentration; there are no loose, low-pressure transitional passages of the kind that one finds in Wells or Bennett, and although Jim Dixon resembles their heroes, he also exhibits an exacerbated sensitivity akin to that of Stephen Dedalus.

Even in *Lucky Jim*, which remains the most light-hearted and innocent, and certainly the funniest, of Amis's novels, there are casual references that would seem savage if it were not for the tone and the stylistic controls which preserve it: Jim dreams of stuffing Professor Welch down the lavatory, or of beating him about the head and shoulders with a bottle until he explains why he gave his sons French names; at one angry moment he is tempted to push a bead up Margaret Peel's nose. In the later novels these fantasies of hostility and aggression are more frequent and less controlled. And traces of nightmare are quite apparent in Amis's other writings. His poems, which are mostly deft, glum and *borné*, afford some relevant insights: one thinks, for instance, of 'The Box of Friends' and 'Dirty Story' from *A Case of Samples*, or 'Out-Patient' and 'Nothing to Fear' from *A Look Round the Estate*:

> it's a dead coincidence
> That sitting here, a bag of glands
> Tuned up to concert pitch, I seem to sense
> A different style of caller at my back,
> As cold as ice, but just as set on me.

The latter volume also includes 'Science Fiction', which explains Amis's own interest in that literary genre. This is one of Amis's best poems; the first stanza talks of the attraction of finding 'simpler versions of disaster', like 'a ten-clawed monster' or some other traditional horror; but the second stanza turns to contemporary apocalyptic imaginings:

> In him, perhaps, we see the general ogre
> Who rode our ancestors to nightmare,
> And in his habitat their maps of hell.
> But climates and geographies soon change,
> Spawning mutations none can quell
> With silver sword or necromancer's ring,
> Worse than their sires, of wider range,
> And much more durable.

One of Amis's own occasional ventures into science fiction, the story called 'Something Strange' is a pure exercise in nightmarish mystification.

Nostalgia, which I see as the opposite pole to nightmare, is also evident, though in a more subdued form. In *Lucky Jim* the past is regarded as a matter for suspicion: Jim Dixon has no commitment to the history he is supposed to teach, and he loathes Professor Welch's bogus attempts to revive the past by means of handicrafts and madrigal singing. Indeed, when he is forced to give a public lecture on 'Merrie England', Jim turns it into a virulent hymn of hate against all the more obvious forms of cultural nostalgia. Nevertheless Amis's attachment to a central thread of English insular nonconformism, and his distaste for cosmopolitan modernism, were sufficiently pronounced for Martin Green, in his book *A Mirror for Anglo-Saxons*, to place Amis in a select pantheon representative of the traditional English virtues, the other heroes being Lawrence, Leavis and Orwell. In so far as Amis's basic ideas about novel-writing are traditional – both as stated in his criticism and implicitly expressed in his fiction – then it is a tradition whose roots lie closer to the robustness and moral simplicity of the eighteenth century than to the high Victorian seriousness admired and to some extent imitated by Snow or Wilson. The point is made explicitly in Amis's third novel, *I Like it Here*, when Garnet Bowen, on visiting Fielding's tomb at Lisbon, falls into a vein of unexpected seriousness:

> Perhaps it was worth dying in your forties if two hundred years later you were the only non-contemporary novelist who could be read with unaffected and wholehearted interest, the only one who never had to be apologised for or excused on the grounds of changing taste. And how enviable to live in the world of his novels, where duty was plain, evil arose out of malevolence and

a starving wayfarer could be invited indoors without hesitation and without fear. Did that make it a simplified world? Perhaps, but that hardly mattered beside the existence of a moral seriousness that could be made apparent without the aid of evangelical puffing and blowing.

In *Take a Girl Like You* Amis seems to have turned to Richardson rather than Fielding for his inspiration: its plot is remarkably close to *Clarissa* in outline, and offers much the same kind of interest in a long-deferred rape. Will Patrick Standish, an engaging, rakish grammar-school master of thirty succeed in laying the delectable Jenny Bunn, a virgin infant-school teacher, just down from the backward reaches of the North of England? In the end he succeeds, but not before a very long pursuit, and only when Jenny is drunk. *Take a Girl Like You* has many entertaining passages, but it is heavily padded, and it suffers from the incoherence at its centre. Patrick Standish is shown as an agreeable and gay fellow; he may be irascible and a bit promiscuous, but this is forgiven easily, just as it is with Tom Jones. Nevertheless the final rape is *not* a good thing to have done. Patrick feels badly about it, of course, but perhaps Jenny was really to blame for hanging onto her old-fashioned ideas about sex and giving him such a rotten time. The novel circles uneasily around these unresolved dilemmas, and the result is not merely ambivalence but moral and artistic incoherence. As a character Patrick is interesting, but not in focus. He is full of fears about cancer and impotence and death, which he tries to keep at bay by thinking about sex most of the time. He regards most of the world with unrelieved hostility, particularly the ugly or the tiresome: thus when driving in the rain he gets immense satisfaction when he is 'lucky enough to send the greater part of a puddle over a sod in ragged clothes who was doing his level best to blow his nose into the gutter'. Patrick and his friend Graham concoct an elaborate fantasy directed against Jenny's landlord, Dick Thompson; they imagine that Dick is naked and they are pursuing him with syringes filled with acid or a solution of itching powder; admittedly Dick's meanness and boringness are unpleasant characteristics, yet this seems an over-compensated reaction. 'But bang's the way to get things done', writes Amis in the last line of his poem, 'Mightier than the Pen', and the lesson is applied late in *Take a Girl* when Dick is wounded by a shotgun. The world of Amis's fiction is basically Hobbesian, where mutual hostility is the normal relationship between the inhabitants. Patrick, we have to assume, is verbally aggressive, obsessed and sexually attractive; yet we never see him objectively, for the author's sympathy covers him with a protective mantle of charm. To have made him fully convincing would have required a kind of characterisation closer to Stiva Oblonsky than to Tom Jones.

Yet although *Take a Girl Like You* is an imperfect and indeed annoying novel, it remains a remarkably interesting book. It is an incisive anatomy of the England of rising affluence in the late fifties, yet it is shot through with a sense of other values which are fast disappearing. In chapter 2 there is a striking paragraph, which not only characterises Jenny but sets out some of the dominant themes of the novel. In presenting Jenny's impressions Amis shows a remarkably mimetic sense, which recalls, even if it is not intended to, the consciousness of Gertie MacDowell in *Ulysses*:

> They had been walking slowly over to the corner of the play-ground, where a church of no particular coloured stone was to be seen on the far side of the road. The sight of it depressed Jenny. There was a lot about it that reminded her of what it had been like to go out for walks with her parents when she was a child. These walks now seemed to have always taken place on cloudy Sunday evenings at about this time of the year, they had always gone through a street where, so it was said (and she could well believe it), a famous mass murderer had done his stuff, and they had always ended up at her grandma's, where in semi-darkness – the old lady had not cared much for switching on what she called the electric – Jenny had had to keep Robbie quiet while hymns of the sort that made you want to do away with yourself had been sung: *The King of Love My Shepherd Is* and *There is a Green Hill Far Away*. Over the road now an elaborately got-up notice-board advertised forthcoming attractions in gilt on black and a wayside-pulpit placard told her that there would not always be a tomorrow on which to do better than yesterday. A draught of cold air – the evenings were turning chilly about now – passed up her spine. She longed for the sight of cheerful modern colours, the cover of a new copy of *Woman's Domain*, the yellow or blue label of a record on the top twenty, somebody passing in scarlet jeans and luminous socks.

Young Jenny has left the dull and backward North, where her father is, appropriately enough, a hearse-driver, for the bright lights and gay consumer-goods of the corrupt and affluent South. She has left behind, however, not only the grime of decaying industrialism, but family pieties and evangelical religion. She sees these values –

the traditional positives of Richard Hoggart's England – as wholly negative, remembered as hymns that made you 'want to do away with yourself' and the gloom of her grandma's house, the whole picture haunted by the ghost of a famous murderer. Elsewhere in Amis's fiction, however, these values are treated in a more positive way : in *That Uncertain Feeling* they are embodied in John Lewis's admirable father, a colliery clerk; at the end of that novel John Lewis flees from the corrupt society symbolised by Mrs Gruffyd-Williams to go back to the mining town where his father lives. This retreat into a grimy pastoral is not at all convincing, but it has affinities with the conviction expressed in Raymond Williams's two novels, *Border Country* and *Second Generation*, that a proper loyalty to the traditions of the labour movement is inextricably involved with having the right attitude to one's father. (Richard Hoggart has remarked that at twenty-five the mature scholarship boy should be able to smile at his father with his whole face (*Uses of Literacy*, 1957 : p. 239).

In *Take a Girl*, however, Jenny puts all that behind her, and commits herself to a new and lively world, without a fixed sense of values : 'people down here bothered less about there being a time and a place for everything than the people at home.' On rereading, when one knows how the story will end, the novel looks like a prolonged proleptic elegy for Jenny's lost virginity, itself a symbol for traditional pieties. At one point an exasperated Patrick accuses her of harbouring nostalgic sexual fancies :

> There are two sorts of men today, those who do – you know what I mean – and those who don't. All the ones you're ever going to really like are the first sort, and all the ones those ideas of yours tell you you ought to like are the second sort. Oh, there wouldn't be any problem of temptation there. The problem would come on the wedding night. And on all the nights after that. There used to be a third sort, admitted. The sort that could, but didn't – not with the girl he was going to marry, anyway. You'd have liked him all right, though, and he wouldn't have given you any trouble trying to get you into bed before the day. The snag about him is he's dead. He died in 1914 or thereabouts. He isn't even going to turn up, Jenny, that bloke with the manners and the respect and the honour and the bunches of flowers *and* the attraction.

At the end of the novel a deflowered Jenny resignedly observes, 'Well, those old Bible-class ideas have certainly taken a knocking, haven't they?' To which Patrick replies that, given a girl like her, it was inevitable. Jenny agrees, but the novel ends with the words, 'But I can't help feeling it's rather a pity.' The ideals of provincial rectitude give a last faint flicker before being lost for ever in the swinging scene of the top twenty and somebody's scarlet jeans.

The hero of Amis's next novel, the short and sour *One Fat Englishman*, is as far on in unpleasantness from Patrick Standish as Patrick was from Jim Dixon, though he has affinities with both of them. Roger Micheldene, the fat Englishman, is a publisher searching for literary talent in the neighbourhood of an American university. He is an old-world, upper-class Englishman with a classical education: he makes no secret of the way in which he despises Americans (and, for that matter, most Englishmen). He is a snuff-taker, a frank glutton – he reflects that 'outside every fat man there was an even fatter man trying to close in' – and a fastidious connoisseur of cigars. His principal vices, in addition to greed, are lechery (frequently frustrated by circumstances) and anger. He is also a lapsed Catholic who at intervals prays in the Augustinian spirit of 'Make me chaste, Lord, but not yet'. Roger is both a snob and an oaf, with an instant line in gratuitous rudeness and no respect at all for anyone's feelings. Apart from a certain sympathy with Roger's fleshly failings, Amis's earlier nonconformist, *declassé* heroes would certainly have loathed him. And so, one assumes, does Amis: at the end of the book Roger gets everything he has been asking for in the way of retribution. And yet the same ambivalence that was apparent in the treatment of Patrick Standish is even more apparent. If Amis does not endorse Roger's odious attitudes, they are not very energetically distanced or disowned. Although Kingsley Amis, as an enthusiastic supporter of the American cause in Vietnam, would not endorse Roger's anti-Americanism, it may well be that, in Amis's present rightist stance, some of Roger's generally anti-progressive sentiments may have caught up with him.

There are a number of ways in which *One Fat Englishman* amplifies the preoccupations of the earlier novels. One of them is the natural oppugnancy between man and objects, and another, closely related, is the idea that the organisation of the universe is not random, but that man and things are in the grip of a malign but perversely intelligent force. In this respect Amis is at the opposite pole to Alain Robbe-Grillet, who posits man and objects as existing in icy mutual indifference, in a cool, neutral universe without plan or design. The difference can, I think, be neatly shown in the dif-

ferent ways in which they are both interested in the minute delineation of material objects. Here, for instance, is a paragraph from
Jealousy:

> The furnishings of this room are very simple: files and shelves
> against the walls, two chairs, the massive desk. On one corner
> of the latter stands a little mother-of-pearl inlaid frame with a
> photograph taken at the seaside, in Europe. A . . . is sitting on the
> terrace of a large café. Her chair is set at an angle to the table
> on which she is about to set down her glass.

And so on, with a detailed account of everything in the photograph,
implicitly emphasising its total detachment from the observer. We
can compare it with a passage from *Lucky Jim*. Jim Dixon is having
breakfast in his digs, and is joined by his tough, silent friend Bill
Atkinson:

> He halted contemptuously at his chair, clicking his tongue and
> sighing histrionically like one kept waiting in a shop. His dark,
> mysterious eyes ran round the walls, making leisured halts at
> each photograph, summing up adversely Miss Cutler's nephew in
> the uniform of a Pay Corps lance-corporal, Miss Cutler's cousin's
> two little girls, Miss Cutler's former employer's country house
> with a gig at the portico, Miss Cutler vehemently dressed as a
> bridesmaid in the fashions of the First World War. He was per-
> haps engaged in whittling down the huge volume of abuse evoked
> by each of these sights into four tiny toxic gouts of hatred, one
> for each photograph.

Amis, one must admit, is trying to be funny, whilst Robbe-Grillet
is not. Yet one notices at once the marvellous accuracy of social
observation that is Amis's principal strength as a novelist; how
many of us have found in similar establishments, if not precisely
those photographs, others scarcely distinguishable from them? And
Amis's characteristic verbal irony is evident in the deliberate use
of the cliché, 'dark, mysterious eyes'. But this passage also shows
that while Amis can rival Robbe-Grillet in the precise delineation
of objects, *his* objects do not exist in cold indifference to human
beings; they are, rather, actively hostile to them, triggers to set off
ever-present reserves of hatred and resentment.

As I have remarked, mutual hostility is the usual relationship
between the inhabitants of Amis's world. And things join in enthusiastically on the side of their owners, like Professor Welch's car,
where a broken spring rips open Jim's trousers, or the terrifying
geyser in Dick Thompson's bathroom which intimidates Jenny Bunn
in the opening chapter of *Take a Girl Like You*. Robbe-Grillet would,

no doubt, regard this as deplorably superstitious, and in a way he would be right. For there is something profoundly animistic about Amis's universe: it may not contain a God, but its characters are constantly in the toils of a powerful and malign governing force. Patrick Standish refers to this as 'Bastards' H.Q.', and this phrase seems to be a part of Amis's personal terminology. In *That Uncertain Feeling* John Lewis, swallowing a mouthful of tea-leaves after entertaining adulterous thoughts, reflects, 'Life, that resourceful technician, had administered a typical rebuke.' Dixon obtains a book he wants from a library 'with almost sinister promptitude'. A few pages later there is an elaborate example of this quasi-magical attitude. Jim, riding in Welch's car, sees a fat man walking with lustful intent towards two pretty girls at a pillar-box. A little later he notices a cricket match in which the batsman, another fat man, is violently hit in the stomach by a ball. Jim is 'uncertain whether this pair of *vignettes* was designed to illustrate the swiftness of divine retribution or its tendency to mistake its target'. It would be paradoxical to call Amis a religious writer; but he is undoubtedly a superstitious one.

In my chapter on American fiction I referred to the possibility of imagining the real world as though it were a novel, in which case the 'plot' of conventional fiction would seem like a 'plot' of a conspiratorial kind, full of sinister coincidences and parallels. Thomas Pynchon, as I have suggested, is interested in this possibility; and John Barth has said that 'God wasn't too bad a novelist, except he was a Realist'. Amis, too, has become increasingly interested in it. He has, for instance, a poem called 'The Huge Artifice', in which human history, seen as a novel written by God, is subjected to a long and adverse review:

> Enough of this great work has now appeared
> For sightings to be taken, the ground cleared,
> Though the main purpose – *what it's all about*
> In the thematic sense – remains in doubt.
> We can be certain even at this stage,
> That seriousness adequate to engage
> Our deepest critical concern is not
> To be found here. First : what there is of plot
> Is thin, repetitive, leaning far too much
> On casual meetings, parties, fights and such,
> With that excessive use of coincidence
> Which betrays authorial inexperience.

In *One Fat Englishman* Roger Micheldene finds himself being mani-
pulated in a quasi-fictional way by his arch-enemy, the young hipster
novelist Irving Macher, who intervenes in Roger's life like an
accredited representative of Bastards' H.Q., making things difficult
for him out of disinterested curiosity.

The preoccupation with malign purpose is fully exploited in
The Anti-Death League, which is Amis's blackest and most obsessed
novel, with few pretensions to the comic. In this novel Jim Dixon's
cheerful conviction that 'nice things are nicer than nasty ones' is
replaced by a death's head and the traditional injunction *memento
mori*. The world is irretrievably in the power of Bastards' H.Q.,
which is now starkly identified with God. The story opens with three
army officers going to visit another officer who is undergoing a cure
for alcoholism in a mental hospital. One of them, James Churchill,
is struck by a girl he sees in the grounds of the hospital, and with
whom he subsequently falls in love. Most of the action is divided
between the hospital and the near-by army camp, both institutional
settings where life is inevitably depersonalised, and in *The Anti-
Death League* Amis has written a more generalised kind of fiction,
with more clearly symbolic implications, than in any of his earlier
novels. There is still a trace of sardonic humour, and his ear remains alert to the placing details of individual speech; but Amis has
here abandoned the incisive social mimicry, the memorable responses to the specificity of a person's appearance or the look of a
room that have previously characterised his fiction. The military
establishment may, in one way, recall the army stories in *My
Enemy's Enemy*, but it is less human and more portentously sinister;
it also recalls 'Special Welfare Research Station No. 4 ' in 'Something Strange' from the same book. This anonymous establishment,
concealed by a security blanket, reflects those aspects of the real
world which already overlap with the more serious forms of science
fiction : blank, closely guarded structures, which could equally well
conceal a centre for experimenting with new and ever more fright-
ful kinds of warfare, or for the liquidation of human beings. There is
an apocalyptic passage by Marcuse which seems relevant here :

> Auschwitz continues to haunt, not the memory but the accom-
> plishments of man – the space flights; the rockets and missiles;
> the 'labyrinthine basement under the Snack Bar'; the pretty
> electronic plants, clean, hygienic and with flower beds; the poison
> gas which is not really harmful to people; the secrecy in which we

all participate. This is the setting in which the great human achievements of science, medicine, technology take place; the efforts to save and ameliorate life are the sole promise in the disaster. (*One-Dimensional Man*, 1964: p. 247)

The apocalypticism is not misplaced. Although the camp in *The Anti-Death League* seems, at first, to house nothing more alarming than a new type of atomic tactical rifle, we subsequently learn that some of the officers there are being trained for a project called operation Apollo, which is designed to meet a threatened Chinese invasion of India by spreading a particularly horrible form of plague through the Chinese army (Apollo being, in addition to his more familiar roles, the god of disease). At the end of the book we learn, in fact, that the whole scheme was an elaborate bluff, to deceive the Chinese intelligence and force them to abandon the invasion. At a superficial level *The Anti-Death League* is something of a spy story, in the morally depressed, double- and treble-crossing vein of Len Deighton and John Le Carré, with little to remind us of Amis's admiration for Ian Fleming, apart from a spot of implausible gunplay. But this level is very superficial indeed, and the thriller elements are so feebly handled as to be easily disposed of; in essence *The Anti-Death League* is a novel of ideas, and its theme is the inevitability of death. The ideas dominate the action, and tend to lead us away from the novel as 'felt life' towards the moral fable, or even the Platonic dialogue (there is a remarkable amount of slightly flat conversation in the book). This novel differs from Amis's previous books in not being told through the consciousness of one or two central characters; here we follow the fortunes of several at once: the young lieutenant, James Churchill; Catherine Casement, the girl he falls in love with; the chaplain, Ayscue; the ineffectual security officer, Brian Leonard; and the alcoholic, Max Hunter. Churchill is, however, closest to the moral centre of the narrative, and what is most noticeable about him is that he has the two-dimensional thinness of an allegorical hero; as a novelistic character he remains wholly unrealised. Until he meets Catherine, Churchill has been loyally performing his duties as a serving officer, including his part in Operation Apollo. But Catherine, who has been driven temporarily insane by a sadistic husband, and who is soon to be threatened by cancer, makes him conscious of the universal reality of arbitrary suffering and death. He revolts angrily against whatever God could have made such a world, and harries the unfortunate clergyman Ayscue with bitter questions (although Ayscue, as we are to discover, is a secret unbeliever). An anonymous anti-religious poem sent to the camp magazine, and a subversive circular inviting the formation of an 'anti-death league', show that Churchill is not alone in his sentiments.

Churchill's attacks on God are not new – for they occur, in similar terms, in the Book of Job – and as a response to the casual cruelty of the universe they are not unjustified; at least, as attacks on the detached manipulator of a purely rationalistic theology. The Christian concept of an incarnate God who himself underwent suffering and death may afford a greater insight into, though not a solution of, the mystery of suffering, although Amis has expressed his dissatisfaction with Christ in his poem 'New Approach Needed'. But such protests are themselves religious; they are meaningful only if they come from a believer, for whom reconciling belief in a good and all-powerful God with the manifest evil of the world is likely to be most agonizing – as Dostoievsky, for instance, showed. An atheist would not waste his time in railing against 'God'. In a tele-vision interview after the novel was published Amis suggested that by 'God' he intends a metaphor for 'the way things are'. To revolt against the nature of reality, and in particular the inevitability of death, is an extreme but tenable philosophical position, and one which has been explored by Camus, but the only way in which the revolt can be fully expressed is by an Empedoclean suicide. Amis does not carry the argument so far, though he perhaps approaches it when Churchill decides to have nothing more to do with the army, the supreme death-dealing mechanism, and retires to his bed in a cataleptic state, from which only Catherine can arouse him.

The other anti-death crusader, Max Hunter, is a more interesting character. As a practising homosexual and an alcoholic, he recalls the monumental self-indulgence of Roger Micheldene. When we first see him in a hospital bed he is surrounded by all the character-istic amenities of earlier Amis heroes:

He was lying back against advantageously arranged pillows within reach of various comforts: non-glossy illustrated magazines, paperback novels on the covers of which well-developed girls cringed or sneered, a comparatively hard-back work on how to win at poker, a couple of newspapers folded so as to reveal half-completed crossword puzzles, a tin jug containing a cloudy greyish fluid, packets of French cigarettes and an open box of chocolates.

Later, Max confesses: 'I've never been particularly keen on having to think about things. And on things that make you think about things. You know, like music and all that. Love's another one. I joined the Army specially to get away from them.' But, he continues, the imponderable realities of love and death have caught up with him, and shown the insufficiency of this carefree view of the world. So he, too, is in revolt against death and God. *The Anti-Death League* is enough of a moral fable for one to feel that Amis is close to the attitudes of his anti-death crusaders, so that Max Hunter's rejection of his past can be seen as a valediction to Lucky Jim. One is not, of course, certain whether Amis would endorse all the ideas expressed in the novel; as, for instance, when Churchill tells Catherine: 'If there were no such thing as death the whole human race could be happy.' The Tithonus myth is surely a potent reminder of the ills of immortality. The essential difficulty Amis faces in *The Anti-Death League* is that it is intensely concerned with the questions that lead to tragedy – death, cruelty, loss of every kind – while lacking the ontological supports – whether religious or humanistic – that can sustain the tragic view of life. And to this extent it is representative of contemporary attitudes.

Considered as an anti-theological novel of ideas, *The Anti-Death League* is provocative and intelligent, even though it may ultimately lack the courage of its philosophical convictions. It represents Amis's immersion in the nightmare that flickers at the edges of his earlier fiction. It is a brave book, for in writing it Amis surrendered a great deal of the novelistic territory in which he is most at home, and got very little in exchange; considered as a novel in the everyday sense, *The Anti-Death League* is feeble and unconvincing, and the supererogatory spy story jars against the novel's deeper preoccupations. Yet it is a work of impressive seriousness and marks a crucial point in Amis's development.*

---

* Amis's latest novel *The Green Man* is thematically a direct development from *The Anti-Death League*. There is the same obsession with death and evil, and an explicitly religious frame of reference. The book is entertaining though ambiguous in its attempt to combine the ghost story and the moral fable.

III

So far in this chapter I have discussed two distinguished novelists, whose work is usually seen as representing a traditionally English kind of moralising social comment, or social comedy, but which is, in fact, permeated by a deep strain of obsessive fear and irrationality. I do not claim any originality in discussing them in these terms; the essential point was made as long ago as 1963 by Richard Hoggart:

> So today we talk chiefly about, for instance, Angus Wilson's skill as a social satirist whereas he is at bottom, I think, a novelist of horror, horror at cruelty and perhaps at final meaninglessness. We may eventually have to make something of the same adjustment to our view of Kingsley Amis, from some touches in his last novel. (*Schools of English and Contemporary Society*, 1963: p. 4)

In the remainder of this chapter I should like to refer, more briefly, to some other English novels of the last twenty years in which the polarity that I describe, using the words loosely, but not, I hope, meaninglessly, as between nostalgia and nightmare seems to me very apparent. In the work of both conventional novelists and writers of science fiction there have been many apocalyptic visions of the Third World War, where traditional and generic versions of horror are combined with speculative scenarios about the possible nature of a nuclear conflict and its aftermath. John Wyndham's *The Chrysalids*, a harrowing story in the Wellsian tradition, about genetic mutations, is a distinguished example; one may also mention Aldous Huxley's treatment of the same topic in *Ape and Essence*, even though Huxley could scarcely be considered an English novelist at the time he wrote. The science-fiction treatment of the theme of the Third World War and after has, of course, been internationally pursued.* Among writers who are British by birth or adoption the influence of Orwell has been pronounced; and the fears engendered during the fifties by the Cold War were directly reflected in a number of novels, such as Arthur Koestler's *The Age of Longing*, Anthony West's *Another Kind* and Constantine Fitzgibbon's *When the Kissing had to Stop*.

More directly relevant to my theme are two works by authors of

---

* See for instance the later chapters of I. F. Clarke's *Voices Prophesying War*.

established reputation and conservative attitudes, whose conventional fiction is pervaded with nostalgic feelings: Evelyn Waugh's *Love Among the Ruins* and L. P. Hartley's *Facial Justice*. Both are satirical, anti-utopian treatments of an imaginary totalitarian England; both seem to reflect the influence of Orwell (and of Orwell's own models, Wells's *When the Sleeper Wakes* and Huxley's *Brave New World*), and indicate an immense distaste for the welfare state and the planned society associated with the post-war Labour Government. They are products of the same historical moment: *Love Among the Ruins* was published in 1953, and *Facial Justice*, although not published until 1960, was started in 1953. One need not spend much time on Waugh's insubstantial *novella*, which tells the story of one Miles Plastic, who is convicted for arson and sent for treatment – rather than punishment – to an agreeable rehabilitation centre, a converted mansion called Mountjoy, which he dimly regards rather as Charles Ryder had regarded Brideshead:

> Mountjoy had been planned and planted in the years of which he knew nothing; generations of skilled and patient husbandmen had weeded and dunged and pruned; generations of dilettanti had watered it with cascades and jets; generations of collectors had lugged statuary here; all, it seemed, for his enjoyment this very night under this huge moon. Miles knew nothing of such periods and processes, but he felt an incomprehensible tidal pull towards the circumjacent splendours.

Miles is pronounced cured and sent to work in the state euthanasia department where he falls in love with a ballerina called Clara who, because of a sterilisation operation that went wrong, has a handsome beard. *Love Among the Ruins* is no more than a *jeu d'esprit*, pleasantly written and with a few faint hints of Waugh's early satirical manner, but without any sense of conviction. *Facial Justice* is a more substantial and impressive book. The setting is England at some point after a Third World War; the physical aspects of the country and even the weather have been changed, and the population, clad in sackcloth, is ruled by an egalitarian dictatorship; the natural elements reflect the dominant ethos:

> In the New World there was no frost, no soft spring mornings – the war had swept them away, along with all the other changes of climate, temperature and season; they had this uniform, perpetual March, with an east wind that indeed grew keener towards evening and a grey sky which the sun never quite pierced. But the language hadn't adapted itself to the new meteorological

conditions; it was still, as ours is now, a storehouse of dead metaphors, still retained phrases like 'at daggers drawn', though no one in the New State had a dagger.

In addition to language and metaphor, the one tangible reminder of the old order is the tower of Ely Cathedral, which has unaccountably survived nuclear war and remains as a vertical contradiction to the prevalent physical and ideological flatness. In this society the dominant positive quality is 'Good E' (equality) and the opposed negative one is 'Bad E' (envy). The story hinges on the inequality of nature, which sees to it that unusually beautiful women are still born into the world, and arouse unfortunate special attraction in men and 'Bad E' in their less well-endowed sisters. Since arousing 'Bad E' is the unforgiveable social sin, great pressure is put on beautiful girls to undergo plastic surgery to make them more ordinary and less provocative. Hartley tells his gloomy story very effectively, and it seems to me to raise questions that socialists usually disregard. One may read, for instance, through the writings of Raymond Williams, whose prose seems to echo the March wind and perpetual grey skies of Hartley's New World, and find much admirable stress on equality and the ordinariness of culture, and no concern at all with the flagrantly unfair advantage that one individual can receive at birth simply by being born beautiful (intelligence, presumably, can be much improved by growing up in the right sort of environment, but beauty is wholly genetic). In this Mr Williams merely reflects the deep distrust of the aesthetic and ludic dimensions of life that characterises the contemporary left and its theorists: only Norman Mailer, a self-styled 'left conservative' and a master of language, has shown any understanding of these questions.

The writer of anti-utopias is inevitably conservative, since he hates or fears what the future may bring, while the progressive assumes that it must, by definition, be better than the present. Furthermore, all such projections originate in a given historical situation, and successive visions of the future reflect the preoccupations of the time when they were written. Thus Wells's *The Time Machine* is an intensely imaginative response to the idea that the late-nineteenth-century class system may become incorporated into the evolutionary development of the human race; while *When the Sleeper Wakes* is a cruder response to the growth of huge cities, the increasing power of the proletarian and the influence of Nietzschean ideas. Huxley's *Brave New World* reflects the advent of characteristically modern totalitarian societies, the technological development of leisure industries, and an awareness of the possibilities of genetic manipulation. *Nineteen Eighty-Four* reflects a similar concern with totalitarianism, particularly the Stalinist variety, and also indicates the intellectual and moral corruption of the latter years of the Second World War. *Facial Justice* stems from a distaste for the ideology and cultural atmosphere of post-war British socialism. All such works can be attacked as regressive and unfair, but one can scarcely argue against them; they advance no propositions, and their appeal is to the imagination and the secret fears of their readers. The only answer is to create an equally convincing projection of the future in optimistic or truly utopian terms; and this, because of the inevitable biases of the human imagination, is extraordinarily difficult, if not impossible, to accomplish: Wells's *A Modern Utopia* is no match for his earlier *The Time Machine*.

These reflections are all relevant to the remarkably talented and prolific writer whom I want, finally, to discuss in this chapter. Anthony Burgess was born in 1917, but he did not turn to novel-writing until he was nearly forty, having spent much of his life composing music and working as an education officer in Malaya. He seems to me to embody the opposition between nostalgia and nightmare in an exemplary form; he is also a passionate Joycean, and the one English novelist of his generation who has the verbal inventiveness, energy, and self-confidence that one takes for granted in American fiction. He also neatly illustrates the argument that I tried to outline in the opening chapter of this book: in one sense Burgess is a very derivative writer; his early novels, based on his experiences in Malaya, owe a good deal to the Forster of *A Passage to India*, and his anti-utopias are equally indebted to Huxley and Orwell, while the influence of Evelyn Waugh is apparent passim. Nevertheless his imagination is entirely his own, and in his best work these influences are fused into an original entity: what, above all, characterises his fiction is a unique sense of humour combined with a desolate philosophical despair that makes Burgess one of the few novelists to whose work the much-abused label 'black comedy' can reasonably be applied.

Burgess's first three published novels, which came out between 1956 and 1959, have been collected as his *Malayan Trilogy*, which in the American edition is called, more elegantly and suggestively, *The Long Day Wanes*. Compared with his later novels, this is a farily unsophisticated piece of writing, in which Burgess was evidently feeling his way into the art of fiction. The organisation is casual and episodic: a conscientious but faded British schoolmaster in Malaya, named Victor Crabbe, is the target of a variety of minor persecutions, but he remains less interesting than the rich collection of racial types which surround him, and which are presented by Burgess with rather unfocused comic exuberance. One of his underlying subjects is racialism, which Burgess sees in more complex terms than the conventional Western liberal; he shows Malaya as a melting-pot of races where, quite apart from the British, the Malays, Chinese, Tamils, Sikhs and Eurasians all express a profound contempt for each other. This may, perhaps, be one more unhappy product of the alienating structures of imperialism; but it may also happen because human groups tend, in essence, to feel like that about each other anyway; Burgess, in whose vision of life an Augustinian sense of human depravity plays a large part, inclines towards the second opinion. At the same time he extracts a great deal of abrasive comedy from these racial collisions, which is genuinely funny if not always in enlightened taste. *Malayan Trilogy* deals with a country shaken not only by these inner racial tensions, but also afflicted by active violence from the communist terrorism of the mid-fifties; at the same time it is preparing for independence, and Victor Crabbe is about to hand over his educational duties to a Malayan subordinate who actively patronises him. The trilogy takes its place in a line of descent from the accounts of the White Man's Burden produced by Conrad and Kipling in the heyday of the British Empire, and which later included *A Passage to India* as a memorable statement of the beginning of the end of the colonialist state of mind: *Malayan Trilogy*, in fact, marks the end of the line.*

After *Malayan Trilogy* Burgess published one more book with an exotic setting, *The Devil of a State*, which takes place in the mythical African kingdom of Dunia. This is the most Waugh-like of Burgess's novels, consistently entertaining, but with an accompanying sourness of tone. At the end of the novel, the hero, a battered

---

* William Golding's *The Inheritors* described the original act of colonialist exploitation: the supersession of Neanderthal man – seen by Golding as an immensely gentle and attractive creature – by the more ruthless *homo sapiens*. The whole of humanity is involved in the guilt for this crime, a fact which may prove slightly comforting to worried white liberals.

Englishman who has spent all his life in the tropics and has developed some unenviable marital complications, is subjected by his author to a fate very nearly as bad as Tony Last's at the end of *A Handful of Dust*. Burgess has no great affection for his characters, or at least he feels that they deserve what they get: at the end of *Malayan Trilogy* the dim but likeable Victor Crabbe is stubbed out as casually as a cigarette.

In both works the author's scepticism about progress and the possibility of political freedom is apparent. (In a short primer called *Language Made Plain* Burgess remarked, with Nominalist primness, 'in every serious discussion much time has to be spent in redefining common terms like "Love", "justice", "freedom" '.) Burgess's conservatism does not stem from any pattern of systematic political convictions, for its background is metaphysical and religious. Burgess, who now describes himself as a renegade Catholic, received a traditional Catholic education in Manchester: there is a vivid, horrifying account of such a school in the opening pages of his novel *Tremor of Intent*. What, above all, he seems to have acquired from his early background is the blackly Augustinian or Jansenist state of mind that was readily imparted by an old-fashioned English (and still more, Irish) Catholic upbringing. Burgess himself has remarked: 'The God my religious upbringing forced upon me was a God wholly dedicated to doing me harm . . . A big vindictive invisibility' (*The God I Want*, ed. James Mitchell, 1967: p. 57). Burgess still has ideas about God, which he goes on to develop in the dialogue from which I have quoted these words, but in practice his early conditioning has left him more convinced of the depravity of man than of the possibility of transcendent goodness. He has observed: 'any political ideology that rejects original sin and believes in moral progress ought strictly to be viewed with suspicion by Catholics' (*Urgent Copy*, 1968: p. 14). It is this Augustinian pessimism – which has literary antecedents in Baudelaire, Eliot and Graham Greene – that informs Burgess's two finest novels, *A Clockwork Orange* and *The Wanting Seed*.

In these books Burgess projects a horrifying vision of the English future, but I should like to approach them via the novel in which Burgess, after years of expatriation, first examined the contemporary English scene. This was *The Right to an Answer*, published between *Malayan Trilogy* and *The Devil of a State*, which Burgess has described as 'a study of provincial England, as seen by a man on leave from the East, with special emphasis on the decay of traditional values in an affluent society' (*The Novel Now*, 1967: p. 212). The indictment may be a familiar one, though here it is not made from a position of High Tory isolation from the common scene, but through the eyes of an unpretentious observer who has lived out of the country for a long time; this was Burgess's own situation, and *The Right to an Answer* has, as a result, a peculiar conviction that has not reappeared in his later novels. It is, undoubtedly, one of his funniest books, with a variety of crackling incidents, much verbal brilliance, and some nicely rendered characters, like the put-upon and infinitely resilient Ceylonese sociologist, Mr Raj, or the cheerful but shifty and mean pub landlord, Ted Arden, who claims to be descended from Shakespeare's mother's family, and in whose attic a long-lost quarto of *Hamlet* is discovered. (Ted's claim to family recollections of Shakespeare – 'E'd got a dose. This black one ad given it im' – was later worked up by Burgess into a whole novel, *Nothing Like the Sun*, a triumph of stylistic invention and historical recreation.) Yet the comic elements are held in tension with a feeling that modern England is a flat and dismal place, of petty lusts and feeble adulteries, drawing its values entirely from television, though faint traces of an earlier England can still be discerned:

> The Black Swan stood in a pocket of decaying village, the dirty speck round which the pearly suburb had woven itself. The village had shrunk to less than an acre. It was like a tiny reservation for aborigines. From the filthy windows imbeciles leered down at the weed-patches; cocks crowed all day; little girls of an earlier age shnockled over stained half-eaten apples; all the boys seemed to have cleft palates. Still, it seemed to me far healthier than the surrounding suburb. Who shall describe their glory, those semi-detacheds with the pebble-dash all over the blind-end walls, the tiny gates which you could step over, the god-wottery in the toy gardens?

There is more here than a nostalgic preference for the decaying remains of rural or feudal England to the affluent small-scale hell of suburbia. It also indicates Burgess's vestigial Jansenist conviction that one is closer to spiritual reality in a state of misery and deprivation. Yet Denham, the narrator of *The Right to an Answer*, for all his total disillusionment with the present-day suburban or provincial scene, still hankers after an impossible ideal of England, whose unreality is emphasised by the very words in which he describes it:

> Where then should I eventually spend my tired retirement? There was, of course, only one vague answer, a vague picture of a dead England, by the sea and yet all deeply rural, boozy and squiry, haunch-of-venison, wenchy, Hollywood's English dream.

Despite his Augustinian scepticism about all forms of worldly commitment, there is a strain of idiosyncratic, English cultural nationalism in Burgess's writings which becomes explicit from time to time, although his quasi-theological bias gives him a different approach from that of the orthodox liberal novelist. In *Language Made Plain* he admits that the apparent Americanism 'I guess' is in fact an old English form that can be found in Chaucer:

> But, like most of us, I do not really like submitting to reason: I much prefer blind prejudice. And so I stoutly condemn 'I guess' as an American importation and its use by a British writer as a betrayal of the traditions of my national group.

The Right to an Answer is Burgess's depressed anatomy of England and a rendering of what the language of Eliot has accustomed us to speak of as 'spiritual death'; in the epigraph to *Tremor of Intent* Burgess quotes from Eliot: 'The worst that can be said of most of our malefactors, from statesmen to thieves, is that they are not men enough to be damned.'

In *A Clockwork Orange* Burgess goes on to explore the kind of spiritual life that might, in fact, lead to damnation. This novel, which is, I think, Burgess's most brilliant and blackest achievement, is set in a shabby metropolis at some unspecified time in the future, where teenage gangs habitually terrorise the inhabitants. The story is told by one of them in the first person, in a superb piece of mimetic writing. This narrator is morally but not mentally stunted; he writes an alert witty narrative in a special kind of slang that incorporates a large number of words of Russian origin; one is never told the social or political events that underlie this linguistic intrusion, but it is possible that Burgess is trying to comment, in a mirror-image fashion, on the current dominance of Americanisms in colloquial English speech. The invention of this idiolect is an extraordinary achievement; it is hard to read at first, but with a little persistence it can be mastered (the American Norton Library edition contains a useful glossary); in fact, after a second reading of *A Clockwork Orange* I found myself starting to think in it. One of its functions is to keep at a certain distance the horrors that Alex, the young narrator, so cheerfully describes: to say, 'we gave this devotchka a tolchok on the litso and the krovvy came out of her rot' is less startlingly direct than, 'we gave this girl a blow on the face and the blood came out of her mouth'.

Alex is cheerful, even high-spirited in his life of crime: older citizens, particularly of a square or bourgeois disposition, are fit material for beating-up; books are to be destroyed, and girls are to be assessed by the size of their breasts, and raped where possible. In *A Clockwork Orange* none of this behaviour is ascribed, as contemporary psychologists or sociologists would have it, to a mindless protest against lack of love or cultural deprivation or the alienating structures of capitalist society. Alex makes it clear that he has chosen evil as a deliberate act of spiritual freedom in a world of sub-human conformists. Despite everything – and this is, perhaps, the most disturbing thing about Burgess's novel – Alex is engaging. His adventures are often funny, or at least his way of describing them is: whereas Amis and Wilson keep comedy and horror on separate planes in their fiction, Burgess, like Waugh, often fuses them. In some respects Alex is not at all a stereotype delinquent. He and his friends, having robbed and beaten an elderly couple in a shop, make off with the takings and then buy innumerable drinks and presents for a couple of old women in a pub, partly to secure an alibi for themselves, but also out of pure generosity. Alex spurns pop songs and is a passionate listener to classical music, which inspires him to thoughts of violence and rape, sometimes to the point of orgasm.

Alex does not, in short, reflect an exact sociological understanding of present-day youth and its problems. Burgess uses him to illustrate his own quasi-theological conviction that men do extreme evil because they choose to, and enjoy doing it, rather than because they are reluctantly or unconsciously forced to it by social conditioning. In presenting Alex, Burgess has drawn on a familiar literary tradition. Marcuse has spoken of the way in which bourgeois society

> remained an order which was overshadowed, broken, refuted by another dimension which was irreconcilably antagonistic to the order of business, indicting it and denying it. And in the literature, this other dimension is represented *not* by the religious, spiritual, moral heroes (who often sustain the established order) but rather by such disruptive characters as the artist, the prostitute, the adultress, the great criminal and outcast, the warrior, the rebel-poet, the devil, the fool – those who don't earn a living, at least

not in an orderly and normal way. (*One-Dimensional Man*, pp. 58–9)

In the language of Baudelaire or Eliot this is the opposition between the masses of the spiritually dead and null, and those who, however evil they may be, are at least alive. Balzac's Vautrin stands some way behind Alex, but his more immediate literary antecedent is Pinkie in Graham Greene's *Brighton Rock*, the articulate, lucid, cruel, young Catholic diabolist. Alex is more alive, and less improbable than Pinkie; yet he remains the embodiment of a literary idea, a late instance in the milieu of the cosh and the bicycle-chain and the gang-bang, of the romantic antinomian cultivation of evil.

Eventually Alex is caught by the police, and after being roughed up by them and imprisoned, he is selected for a new form of remedial treatment, since the prisons are now all needed for political offenders, and common criminals are to be rehabilitated and permanently 'cured'. Alex is given an intensive course of aversion-therapy; he is injected with a drug and shown films of brutality and sexual assault, accompanied by classical music. Eventually he is cured of his taste for all three, since any hint of them causes uncontrollable nausea. (The music is regarded by the authorities not as having any aesthetic or spiritual dimension, but merely as something that arouses unwelcome emotional excitement in Alex.) After the course Alex is released, a good citizen, yet a person in whom the capacity to choose has been wholly destroyed. In his account of the therapy Alex undergoes, Burgess is describing known techniques, and it is here that the novel acquires philosophical profundity: in what sense is a man who has been *forced* to be good better than a man who deliberately asserts his humanity by choosing evil? For the behaviouristic pragmatism that invents such procedures, the question is presumably meaningless; but genuine humanists will recognise its urgency, even if they cannot fully answer it. Towards the end of the novel Alex gets caught up in a political plot against the government and is exploited by the opposition (very much as Ralph Ellison's Invisible Man is used by the communists); in a final unexpected twist of circumstances, the government reverses Alex's treatment, and he ends the novel as a free individual with all his criminal impulses – and his love of music – restored. Many of Burgess's assumptions are, of course, vulnerable. The notion of 'spiritual death' is a powerful literary idea, but it is existentially specious; it is merely a way of reinforcing one's sense of the otherness of other people. Non-Augustinian Christians as well as conventional progressives will want to object to the extremity of Burgess's pessimism, as well as his basically romantic conception of evil. Nevertheless, as an embodied imaginative vision of life *A Clockwork Orange* is hard both to forget and to refute, and in its emphasis on the nature of human freedom in a totalitarian society the book has philosophical as well as literary importance. As a novel of ideas that projects a conservative and pessimistic view of human nature, *A Clockwork Orange* seems to me to have a similar quality and significance to William Golding's *Lord of the Flies*, while being more humorous and less diagrammatic. One wishes that it had achieved the same reputation.

   The Wanting Seed appeared in 1962, the same year as *A Clockwork Orange*, and is clearly the product of much the same imaginative impulse. It is a less tightly organised and gripping book, yet it is, on the other hand, more inventive. It describes a future England where urban sprawl has gone so far that Greater London extends to Lowestoft and Birmingham, and in the South to Brighton, where the government offices are now situated and where the story opens. Overpopulation has become such a menace that space and food are in increasingly short supply.* In order to keep down population, procreation is actively discouraged, homosexuality encouraged, and infanticide condoned. To rise in this society it is desirable to be a homosexual, which causes a good deal of dissembling. The hero, Tristram Foxe, is a somewhat shadowy figure, and the main interest is in Burgess's total picture of this horrifying society; Foxe is a schoolteacher, and in his history lessons Burgess finds a useful way of inculcating some key ideas. History, it seems, is cyclic, moving through three phases. The first is the Pelagian phase – or Pelphase – named after the British monk who believed in human perfectibility. This traditionally shows itself in progressive politics, liberal humanism, treatment rather than punishment for criminals; in an over-populated world it relies on contraception and homosexuality to keep down the population. In time people become dissatisfied, and society moves into an intermediate period – or Interphase – then

---

   * Burgess's treatment of this topic, though harrowing and ingenious, is less convincing than *The Space Merchants*, a brilliant piece of science fiction by Frederik Pohl and C. M. Kornbluth. Overpopulation also forms the theme of another effective work in this genre, John Brunner's *Stand on Zanzibar*.

into the Augustinian or Gusphase. Here the stress is all on human depravity and man's total inability to do anything to better his lot; discipline and punishment come back, and so do heterosexuality and fertility. The population problem is taken care of by wars, which are deliberately organised, with men and women fighting each other. Then more liberal attitudes creep back, Interphase begins again, Pelphase follows, and so on for ever. *The Wanting Seed* describes one cycle from Pelphase to Gusphase, in the course of which the inhabitants of England discover that cannibalism is an acceptable answer to the problem of food-shortage, and a strange, debased kind of Catholicism spreads in which human flesh is consecrated instead of the host.

The novel culminates with Tristram, in the army, taking part in a battle being specially staged in the interests of population control, somewhere in the west of Ireland. This, one of Burgess's most brilliant pieces of invention, turns out to be an exact replica of one of the big offensives of the First World War, with every military detail right, and the background noise of an artillery bombardment relayed from loudspeakers:

> There were still distant crashes and bumps – a twenty-four-hour performance, probably with three shifts of lance-corporal disc-jockeys – but no fire in the sky. At noon an ancient aircraft – strings, struts, an open cockpit and waving goggled aeronaut lurched over the camp and away again. 'One of ours', Mr Dollimore told his platoon. 'The gallant RFC.'

Here, as elsewhere, nostalgia for a vanished phase of history coexists with the extremity of nightmare. In writing this section Burgess must have drawn effectively on the memoirs of the 1914–18 war – which he was born in the middle of – and as a piece of fictional recreation of history it ranks with comparable passages in Thomas Pynchon's *V*.

The degree of Burgess's verbal finesse, his wit and satirical energy prevent *The Wanting Seed* from being an unrelieved display of horrors; his material has, for the most part, been transmuted into art, even though the novel tends to be over-episodic. *A Clockwork Orange* and *The Wanting Seed* are two of the most accomplished and literally thoughtful novels to have been published in England in the 1960s: however unedifying they may be to the doctrinaire liberal, they enlarge one's imagination and thrust into consciousness questions that are often and easily ignored. Burgess's peculiar and challenging value is that he speaks, urbanely enough, the same language as our dominant literary and intellectual culture, but rejects many of its basic, unexamined assumptions. His later novels, which are numerous, are frequently entertaining, though only one of them – *Nothing like the Sun* – seems to me to have achieved a distinction approaching that of the books I have discussed. Yet with a novelist so fertile of invention, one remains confident of his continued ability to surprise one.

VII Beyond Fiction?

> Shanahan at this point inserted a brown tobacco finger in
> the texture of the story and in this manner caused a lacuna
> in the palimpsest.
>
> FLANN O'BRIEN, *At Swim-Two-Birds*

A s the twentieth century moves into its final decades, it is doubtful
if the themes that have been so noticeable in English fiction during
the past twenty years will continue to prove fruitful; nor, one
imagines, will the English assumption that the novel simply *is*, as it
always has been and always will be, go on receiving such wide and
unquestioning assent. The problems raised in the first part of this
book about the continuing status of the novel as a literary form will
inevitably have to be faced. As we have seen, many American
novelists are concerned with refashioning the concept of the novel,
and although their solutions are not easily transmitted into English
terms, there is some evidence from England that during the sixties
the idea of the familiar, well-made novel was less easily taken for
granted; significantly, several novelists in their thirties have been
rethinking the basis of their own fiction.

The tradition of nineteenth-century realism, which underlies most
contemporary English fiction, depended on a degree of relative
stability in three separate areas: the idea of reality; the nature of
the fictional form; and the kind of relationship that might predictably exist between them. There is a useful illustration in Anthony
Trollope's *Autobiography*; Trollope is indulging in one of his periodic
passages of self-congratulation, and quotes some laudatory remarks
from a writer of a very different cast of mind, Nathaniel Hawthorne:

> Have you ever read the novels of Anthony Trollope? They pre-
> cisely suit my taste – solid and substantial, written on the strength
> of beef and through the inspiration of ale, and just as real as if
> some giant had hewn a great lump out of the earth and put it
> under a glass case, with all its inhabitants going about their daily
> business, and not suspecting that they were being made a show
> of. (1953: p. 125)

This is an accurate comment on the quality of Trollope's art, which
Trollope fully endorsed. There could be no more effective, if crude,
image of a transferred concreteness than the notion of hewing out a

great lump from the earth and placing it under a glass case; the image also emphasises the impersonality and detachment of the artist, seen as a giant wielding a spade. This runs counter to the common notion of Trollope – and such contemporaries as Thackeray and even George Eliot – as artistically imperfect because he involved himself too much in his own creation in the guise of an intrusive narrator. The 'intrusive narrator' raises important critical questions, to which I shall return, but as practised in major nineteenth-century fiction it does not undermine the assumed reality of the world or of the fictional form. It goes without saying that for many twentieth-century novelists and critics this assumption is no longer credible, as we have seen from the opinions of Robbe-Grillet or Moravia, Hawkes or Barth. Yet if we move, not forward from the heyday of European realism, but backward, towards the origins of the novel, we find a comparable uncertainty about the nature of the form and its power to convey reality, even if this is not accompanied by the epistemological scepticism about the nature of common experience that provides the *raison d'être* of a writer such as Robbe-Grillet. It is the great early novels, such as *Don Quixote* and *Tom Jones*, that contain a high percentage of literary-critical reflection, and which offer a running commentary on their own procedures. They reflect, admittedly, a different kind of uncertainty, that stems not from extreme sophistication or critical self-consciousness, but from simple temerity about the enterprise of writing novels. Was it morally respectable? How did the novel differ from the older modes of writing that it so evidently depended on? How much of the world could it hope to embrace? We are familiar with the way in which so many eighteenth-century novels – and similar kinds of prose narrative – keep nervously close to more familar ways of establishing verisimitude: they pretend to be travel books, or collections of letters, or faithful autobiographies, or accurate transcripts of ancient manuscripts, or even, as with Henry Mackenzie's *The Man of Feeling*, a bundle of disconnected fragments rescued from use as waste-paper. At the same time the novel as an essentially typographical form showed an exuberant enjoyment of the possibilities of the printed book, as in Swift's *Tale of a Tub*, with its satirical galaxy of prefaces, introductions and footnotes, or in the typographical fooling of Sterne.

There is also an engaging air of improvisation about the early novels. In the Dedication and Prologue to the second part of *Don*

Quixote Cervantes explains that he has gone on with his narrative since someone else had published an unauthorised continuation of Quixote's adventures. Richardson, again, substantially added to *Pamela* in response to public demand. *Tristram Shandy*, above all, is a triumphant example of the novel as pure improvisation, a narrative that is never extricated from a commentary on its own composition. In Cervantes and the eighteenth-century novelists the authorial voice and presence are so naturally part of the story that only blind critical purists could object to them. Yet as the novel developed throughout the nineteenth century, it became more self-confident, took itself more seriously, and evolved its own formal justifications. The author became less of a presence, as frankly before us as Montaigne is in his essays, and dwindled to a voice, a commentator obtruding from time to time through the chinks of an increasingly autonomous narrative, to offer reflections or speculations on the action. It was inevitable that with the advent of a consciously dramatic and impersonal form of the novel, this remnant of the authorial presence would be swept away. The principles (though not invariably the practice) of Flaubert and James, of Conrad and Ford and Joyce, banished the obtrusive narrator, and stressed the ideal of the novel as a self-contained, self-sufficient work of art, whose creator would be conspicuously absent. In the celebrated words of Joyce's Stephen Dedalus: 'The artist, like the God of the creation, remains within or behind or beyond or above his handiwork, invisible, refined out of existence, indifferent, paring his fingernails.' This concept of impersonality, memorably stated in Eliot's early essays, has ramified in innumerable ways in modern literature and criticism; there is an early version of it in the symbolist notion of the poem as an 'aesthetic monad', and a later, more rigorous version in the New Critics' stress on the formal, textural and structural properties of literature. There is a related approach which argues that all forms of literature, even down to the most seemingly subjective lyric poem, are essentially 'dramatic' modes of utterance. In general these approaches are best suited to Renaissance literature on the one hand, and to symbolist and post-symbolist literature on the other; it is notoriously difficult (though not impossible) to make them fit Romantic poetry. Of late, the impersonal, formalist approach has been somewhat declining, even among those who once upheld it: a recent, important article by Donald Davie (*Encounter*, October 1968) seeks to restore the role of personality in poetry, and looks for the re-establishment of 'sincerity' as a valid critical concept. Such shifts of emphasis are inevitable; while accepting them, one needs to salute the achievement of the New Critical and related approaches in immeasurably enlarging our understanding of poetry.

One says 'poetry' advisedly, for these methods were developed in relation to poetry and always remained most readily applicable to it. The critical approach to fiction was less fruitful. As we have seen, the ideal of the novel as impersonal, dramatic and formally self-contained, was developed by several great novelists: Henry James's collected prefaces were influential in advancing it, and so were such important secondary works as Percy Lubbock's *The Craft of Fiction*. Yet this approach, which was valid and enlightening in its own terms, and was an accurate description of a great deal of late-nineteenth- and early-twentieth-century novelistic practice, was imprudently seized on by critics and teachers, and turned into a set of rules. It hardened into the academic orthodoxy that, as I have remarked in an earlier chapter, was a source of legitimate scandal to Dan Jacobson: such are the simplifications inherent in any teaching situation.

The reaction against the dogmatic banishment of the author was inevitable, and it seems to have started independently by several different critics in the late fifties; there was Kathleen Tillotson's inaugural lecture at London University, *The Teller and the Tale*, and the late W. J. Harvey's *The Art of George Eliot*; and, most magisterially, Wayne C. Booth's *The Rhetoric of Fiction*. All these critics advanced much the same arguments: a novel is a narrative as well as an object, that is to say, it is a tale that has been told; even the most rigorously impersonal and dramatised piece of fiction was written by *someone*. Once this is recognised, one may then go on to argue that even in such fiction the author's voice will be implicitly but palpably there; and one can also argue that the author of an eighteenth- or nineteenth-century novel has every right to appear as a character in his own narrative. Booth talks of the author's 'second self' – in a phrase taken from the late-Victorian critic Edward Dowden – or the 'implied narrator'; and although his book came out as recently as 1961 it has already become remarkably influential, and not only for critics of the novel.* Yet Booth remains

---

* See, for instance, the use made of Booth by Stanley Fish in his study of *Paradise Lost, Surprised by Sin* (1967).

prudently within the canons of post-symbolist aesthetics by emphasising that the narrator, whether real or implied (and assuming that the narrator is not clearly distanced, by being 'unreliable' or otherwise limited, like the narrators of many post-Jamesian novels), is still a persona, to be identified with the author's *second self*, but not with the man himself, whose name appears on the title-page of the book. Thus, the self-containedness of the fictional artifact is preserved, though in a much more extended form than that recognised by the upholders of a narrow impersonality. Booth writes very perceptively about the part played by Fielding-as-narrator in *Tom Jones*, showing how the reader's relationship with him becomes deeper and more intimate as the book advances; but he affirms that this is not the real Fielding:

> The author has created this self as he has written the book. The book and the friend are one. 'For however short the period may be of my own performances, they will most probably outlive their own infirm author, and the weakly productions of his abusive contemporaries.' Was Fielding literally infirm as he wrote that sentence? It matters not in the least. It is not Fielding we care about, but the narrator created to speak in his name. (*The Rhetoric of Fiction*, 1961: p. 218)

Booth is persuasive here, but not convincing: the separation between the historical Henry Fielding and Fielding-as-narrator cannot be as absolute as he implies, even though the relationship between them is problematical. No reader who has finished *Tom Jones* with appropriate enjoyment can be so indifferent to the mind that has created it and the personality that informs it. After several decades of critical emphasis on 'impersonality' the market for literary biographies is as active as ever.* Part of Booth's problem may be that as a Chicago-trained genre critic he looks for, or imposes, a neat separation of kinds, and for him everything in a novel must be 'narrative'. In fact one may adapt Poe's remark about not all of a long poem being poetry, and say that not all of a novel is narrative. The directly reflective parts of *Tom Jones* are much more easily assimilated to, say, the essays of Montaigne than to the tight constructions of later fiction. Fielding as both narrator and author wishes to take the reader into his confidence, to invite his moral

---

* I have attempted a fuller discussion of this question in 'Thoughts on the Personality Explosion', in *Innovations* (1968).

support in the complex and difficult undertaking in which he is involved. Nevertheless the problem about relating the narrator to the man is not acute with Fielding, and on the whole one can leave it alone, whether or not one agrees with Booth.

Reading Sterne is a different matter. Tristram Shandy is evidently not just Sterne-as-narrator; he is a character in his own right, lovable, odd and distanced. Booth's discussion of *Tristram Shandy* is splendidly acute; he admits that much of the novel recalls Montaigne, but goes on to argue that even the essays of such a man as Montaigne are a form of fiction. The author himself never appears quite nakedly: their very literary excellence imposes a degree of verbal autonomy, and 'Montaigne' the literary persona remains distinct from the real Montaigne. The short answer to this is that the *real* Montaigne remains for ever unknowable, except to God; any attempt to render the self in verbal terms, whether in a fully literary way, or in the bleakness of a case-history or the answers to a questionnaire will involve unimaginable distortions and omissions. Yet if Montaigne sometimes tells lies about himself, the presence of a real man is unmistakable, just as it is in the discursive passages of Fielding or Sterne. There are places in *Tristram Shandy* where the persona – or literally, the mask – slips, and the author appears. A. E. Dyson (*The Crazy Fabric*, 1965: p. 40) has drawn attention to the conclusion of Book IV:

> And so, with this moral for the present, may it please your worships and your reverences, I take my leave of you till this time twelve-month, when, (unless this vile cough kills me in the mean time) I'll have another pluck at your beards, and lay open a story to the world you little dream of.

This passage is, I think, radically devalued if we do not assume that the 'vile cough' which may prevent the book being finished is, in fact, the real cough of a real man. One cannot adapt Booth here and say 'it is not Sterne we care about'; we do care, for he has made us care. I am not, of course, denying the reality of fictional personas, nor am I making any general identification of narrators and authors; what I am saying is that the distance between the actual author and his implied narrator is liable, in early novels, to fluctuate considerably, and at times to dwindle to zero. When that happens, assumptions about the impersonality of fiction and the autonomy of narrative are likely to be unhelpful.

In Cervantes and the eighteenth-century English novel the relation between the narrator who was inside the book and the author who was partly inside and partly outside was one recurring illustration of the larger question of relating the world of the novel to the macrocosmic world outside it. During the nineteenth century the relations between the writer, the book and the world seem to have stabilised. The novelist could see himself as a recorder, an observer, a collector, even, as with the case of Trollope, a giant hewing out chunks of reality. Yet he could safely remain apart from his material, secure in the knowledge that the fictional enterprise had generated enough momentum to go on running, even if, for a while, narrators continued to obtrude, and stage-managers to tell the audience what was coming next. In the nineteenth century we do not find many novels about writing novels, or authors who insist on involving themselves with their material: the end of the line was the enclosed symbolist novel of a self-contained formal perfection, the kind of book which Iris Murdoch calls 'crystalline'. The one major exception was to be found in South America: the great Brazillian novelist Machado de Assis was born in 1839 (one year before Zola, whom he detested) and was a life-long admirer of Sterne. His influence is apparent in the verbal joking, parentheses, puzzles, digressions and free treatment of time in the major novels, *Epitaph for a Small Winner* (1880) and *Dom Casmurro* (1900). Whereas Sterne had begun *Tristram Shandy* at the point of his hero's conception, Braz Cubas, the narrator of *Epitaph for a Small Winner*, starts the story after his death – 'I expired at two o'clock of a Friday afternoon in the month of August, 1869, at my lovely suburban home in Catumby' – and then works backward. A later work by Machado, *Esau and Jacob*, preserves the eighteenth-century flavour; it purports to be a novel found in the notebooks of a retired diplomat called Ayres after his death; Ayres himself appears as a character in his own narrative. Despite his leaning toward early fictional modes, Machado is anything but naïve or simple; he was a poised and sophisticated artist and a considerable psychological realist who combined Sternean digressiveness with the dry, ironical insights of Stendhal. He deserves to be better known in the English-speaking world; primarily for his intrinsic merits, which are considerable, but also for the remarkable way in which he offers a bridge between the eighteenth-century novel and the preoccupations of twentieth-century fiction, in a way that by-passes some of the central developments of nineteenth-century realism. In fact

there is a persistent modernity about Machado's writing. In his
short story 'The Looking Glass' – published in 1882 and subtitled
'Rough draft of a new theory of the human soul' – Machado anticipates the unending debate about identity and the psychology of
role-playing. It develops the idea that every individual has two
souls: the private and the public. By degrees the latter becomes
dominant; a young army lieutenant finds that his reflection in the
mirror is becoming dim and distorted, but returns to its normal
state when he stands before the glass in his uniform. Waldo Frank
has written of *Dom Casmurro*, 'At the turn of the last century, a
Brazillian writes a novel that presages Proust and Kafka.' It is certainly very unlike the rich but well-rounded creations of the European realistic tradition; Machado's narrator, Santiago, is obsessed
with the thought of his wife's possible infidelity, in a consciously
Othello-like way. He exemplifies the problem of the 'unreliable
narrator', and at the end of the novel the reader is still uncertain
whether or not Santiago is justified in his suspicions; the evidence is
never quite conclusive. The novel's deliberately inconclusive, open-
ended quality makes it seem both behind and ahead of its time; it
requires the reader's active collaboration, rather than his passive
witness, and in this respect Machado both looks back to Sterne and
forward to Kafka and Borges and the practitioners of the *nouveau
roman*.

There was one late-Victorian English novelist who also admired
Sterne and came to feel an increasing resentment about the novel of
solid character and consistent construction. This was H. G. Wells,
who, after beginning his literary career with a series of brilliant
mythopoeic scientific romances, and then going on to realistic social
comedies and portentous novels of ideas, came to feel that the novel
form, like many other things in the world, needed a good shake-up.
Not, indeed, that Wells was interested in greater aesthetic precision
or comprehensiveness; after writing several admirable works of true
fiction, he turned to books which, though looking like novels, were
dialogues, or even monologues, where the vital and urgent issues
of the day could be thoroughly ventilated and thrashed out: without the conserving power of the imagination they have now become
irredeemably dated. But as Wells told Henry James in their celebrated debate in 1915, 'I had rather be called a journalist than an
artist – that is the essence of it.'

In his *Experiment in Autobiography*, published in 1934, Wells tried to justify his ideas about fiction, and reflected on the way in which nineteenth-century assumptions no longer seemed adequate for twentieth-century novelists:

> Throughout the broad smooth flow of nineteenth-century life in Great Britain, the art of fiction floated on this same assumption of social fixity. The Novel in English was produced in an atmosphere of security for the entertainment of secure people who liked to feel established and safe for good. Its standards were established within that apparently permanent frame and the criticism of it began to be irritated and perplexed when, through a new instability, the splintering frame began to get into the picture. (1934: II. 494–5)

Wells is referring here to his own overturning of established ethical attitudes and impatience with the fixed form of the novel; in his way he was an innovator; in *The Research Magnificent* he tried, as he says, 'the device of making the ostensible writer speculate about the chief character in the story he is telling. The ostensible writer becomes a sort of enveloping character, himself in discussion with the reader.' And *The World of William Clissold*, thin and pretentious work though it is, can hardly be regarded as a piece of conventional novel-writing. In *The Undying Fire*, Wells explained, he was trying to revive the Dialogue in a fictional form: 'I was not so much expanding the novel as getting right out of it.' In his final reflections on the novel, Wells sees the form as doomed before more avowedly factual kinds of writing. Novels are less interesting than histories and biographies:

> Who would read a novel if we were permitted to write biography – all out? Here in this autobiography I am experimenting – though still very mildly, with biographical and autobiographical matter. Although it has many restraints, which are from the artistic point of view vexatious, I still find it so much more real and interesting and satisfying that I doubt if I shall ever again turn back towards the Novel. (Ibid. II. 503)

Certainly the *Experiment in Autobiography* is more real, satisfying and interesting than any of Wells's attempts at novel-writing after 1910. And in his speculations about the advent of the factual mode he was being quite accurately prophetic. As George Steiner has lately remarked: 'We are, it would seem, in a transitional stage of poetic documentation, a period in which the techniques and conventions of the novel are used for the presentation of psychological, social and scientific material' (*Language and Silence*, p. 421).

Wells's striking image of the splintering frame getting into the picture, though meant to apply to his own fictional activites, can also refer to the great Modernist innovations in twentieth-century fiction, which realigned the traditional fixed relation between the word and the world. In autobiographical fiction, like *A Portrait of the Artist as a Young Man* and *A la recherche du temps perdu*, we are forced to be aware of the relation, intimate yet severely distanced, between 'Marcel' and Proust, and Stephen Dedalus and James Joyce. At the end of each work the hero prepares, in a ritualistic way, to undertake a great task, which is to be none other than writing the novel we have just completed: here the art-reality pattern is, as it were, turned inside out. Even those elements in *Ulysses* which have long been regarded as wholly naturalistic, offering an impeccable guide and gazetteer of the city of Dublin in the year 1904, have been shown by Robert Martin Adams (*Surface and Symbol*, 1962) to contain many wilful inaccuracies and arbitrary discontinuities, deliberately introduced by Joyce, it seems, to disrupt the fictional illusion. The most radical instance of this disorientation and disturbance of fixed notions about the nature of fiction is to be found in Gide's *The Coiners*, which must be the most thorough example of a novel about writing a novel since *Tristram Shandy*: it is a brilliant but, I think, frigid performance, with the stress very much on the performance; for all Gide's dexterous manipulation of different levels of reality, the finished work remains an excessively enclosed artifact. Some editions of this novel contain, as an appendix, the extracts from Gide's journals that concern the composition of *The Coiners*: it is then an interesting question to' decide if these passages become part of the novel by more than merely bibliographical assimilation; if they do, then in these editions the novel becomes more interestingly open to the actual and the existential. More recently we have had Nabokov's equally brilliant though less solemn game with the conventions of the novel in *Pale Fire*. Borges is another major writer much concerned with probing, or exposing by asserting, the fictional illusion. Several of his short stories offer a combination of detective fiction and fictitious literary investigation – presaged, perhaps, by Henry James in 'The Figure in the Carpet'. In 'The Library of Babel' the universe is imagined as a vast, even infinite library where the whole of reality is contained in the books on the shelves. I have suggested that Borges may have influenced Pynchon, and this influence may extend to Barth, though

I much prefer Borges's library to Barth's campus as a model of the universe. In another of Borges's stories, 'Pierre Menard, Author of Don Quixote', a twentieth-century French author learns Spanish and undertakes the gigantic task of writing *Don Quixote* again in exactly the same words. This story, as well as being an entertaining piece of fiction, is a splendid critical inquiry into the questions I am discussing here. Borges remarks: 'The texts of Cervantes and that of Menard are verbally identical, but the second is almost infinitely richer.' He shows that two identical passages take on very different meanings if one assumes that one was written in the seventeenth century and one in the twentieth.* The story ends with the suggestion that there can be an endless source of literary satisfaction in reading celebrated books as if they were written by quite different – and improbable – authors: 'Would not the attributing of *The Imitation of Christ* to Louis Ferdinand Céline or James Joyce be a sufficient renovation of its tenuous spiritual counsels?' A similar, if less extreme, assumption lies behind the prominence of parody, pastiche, imitation, and the unexpected switching of contexts (as in collage) that we find in all forms of twentieth-century art, and not merely in literature. In another story by Borges, 'Tlön, Uqbar, Orbis Tertius', some puzzling entries in a certain volume of an encyclopaedia lead by degrees to the discovery of a new, separate, self-contained world; here we have an effective comment on the monadism at the heart of symbolist aesthetics.

The fiction which explores the relation between art and life, rather than takes it for granted, is open to the criticism of being self-absorbed and perhaps trivial, and of stemming from a pathological uncertainty about the nature of reality, instead of, as in the eighteenth century, from a simple degree of wariness towards the form of the novel. Certainly I have no desire to praise such fiction merely for its novelty, but it may offer possible pointers out of the impasse of the novel that I have tried to describe. However wide the debt to Sterne may be, it is true that in this century such fiction has appeared more often on the Continent and in the United States and South America than in Britain. Again this need not be surprising; I have tried to indicate the extraordinary conservatism of English cultural life and the tenacious survival of nineteenth-century

---

* There is a parallel inquiry in Leonard B. Meyer's essay, 'Forgery and the Anthropology of Art', in *Music, the Arts and Ideas* (Chicago, 1967).

literary forms, despite the early iconoclasm of someone like Wells. Yet in the last decade or so, the critical movement away from impersonality and dramatised fictional autonomy has been interestingly matched by developments in the practice of English fiction, not all in themselves particularly meritorious, but with nonetheless significant implications.

At Swim-Two-Birds by the late Flann O'Brien, as the work of a fellow-countryman of Joyce and Beckett, is a piece of characteristically Irish verbal exuberance and can hardly be considered as a representative English novel. Yet its reputation has developed interestingly since it was first published in 1939; it made no impact at all then, but after the book was reprinted in 1960 it attracted a growing circle of admirers, although John Wain, in a masterly analysis of *At Swim-Two-Birds*, has described it as 'the only real masterpiece in English that is far too little read and discussed' (*Encounter*, July 1967). *At Swim-Two-Birds* both contains a novel within a novel, and embodies the idea of a Promethean or Luciferian revolt against the novelist who, as Sartre said of Mauriac, wants to play God. The narrator, a clever but slothful student, living in genteel poverty in Dublin, is writing a novel about a character called Trellis:

> I was talking to a friend of yours last night, I said drily. I mean Mr Trellis. He has bought a ream of ruled foolscap and is starting on his story. He is compelling all his characters to live with him in the Red Swan hotel so that he can keep an eye on them and see that there is no boozing. . . . Most of them are characters used in other books, chiefly the works of another great writer called Tracy. There is a cowboy in Room 13 and Mr McCool, a hero of old Ireland, is on the floor above. The cellar is full of leprechauns.

In so far as it is a very funny book, *At Swim-Two-Birds*, is more like *Tristram Shandy* than are other twentieth-century novels that juggle with levels of reality. Yet, like them, it is also a continuous critical essay on the nature and limits of fiction. In Trellis's story the characters plot against him while he is asleep, at the same time quarrelling among themselves. One of them is the legendary giant Finn McCool, who tells a beautiful but interminable story drawn from Irish mythology, which counterpoints the naturalistic low-life chat of the others. The narrative is also complicated by two cowboys who had been characters of – or, as they put it, worked for – a writer of cheap Western fiction, Tracy, before coming into

Trellis's novel. Trellis himself has fallen in love with one of his own female characters, ravished her and had a son by her, who, born as a fully grown adult, is called Orlick Trellis. This incestuous union is reminiscent of the birth of Death in *Paradise Lost*; nor is this the only Miltonic echo in *At Swim-Two-Birds* : one of Trellis's characters, Mr John Furriskey, comes into the world, *ex nihilo*, at the age of twenty-five, and describes the experience in terms that recall Adam's memory of his own creation. In fact, at this level *At Swim-Two-Birds* is an extended pun on the word 'creation'. Orlick Trellis is himself a writer of highbrow inclination, and revenges himself on his father – or 'creator' – by humiliating him in a story, in which he is vehemently encouraged by the other characters.

Flann O'Brien's imaginative and verbal exuberance dominates the whole work, which is a magnificent piece of ludic bravura. John Wain, who sees the novel in slightly more serious terms than I do myself, has effectively shown the way in which it is about the culture and destiny of Ireland (*Encounter*, July 1967). The influence of Joyce is, of course, paramount, although absorbed by an original intelligence. In the naturalistic parts of the novel the situation of the seedy young narrator, spending long hours lying on his bed and occasionally drifting into a class at the National University, recalls Stephen Dedalus, while the ribald conversations of Shanahan, Lamont and Furriskey, although rooted in the speech of Dublin, also remind us of stories like 'Grace' and 'Ivy Day in the Committee Room'. And the prevalent encyclopaedism of O'Brien's novel, the collage-like introduction of extraneous fragments of information (a sure way of short-circuiting the distance between fiction and the external world), the tendency to present information in question-and-answer form, all derive from *Ulysses*, particularly the 'Ithaca' section. *At Swim-Two-Birds* is one of the most brilliant works of modern English fiction, which was fortunately given a second chance to establish a reputation. In the 1960s critical opinion, however averse to heavily experimental or innovatory works, has been more inclined to look sympathetically at novels which depart from the established norms of fictional construction.

Without doubt the most ambitious novel of this kind to have appeared in England in the last decade was Doris Lessing's *The Golden Notebook*, a book which I find very fascinating but not at all easy to place or evaluate. Part of the difficulty lies in deciding just what kind of book *The Golden Notebook* is : more than any other modern novel it dissolves the distinction between fiction and direct autobiographical statement. George Steiner has demanded: 'What is Doris Lessing's *Golden Notebook*, that acute portrayal of woman and urban society: a novel or an autobiography, a political essay or a psychiatric case-book?' (*Language and Silence*, p. 421). Walter Allen, though thinking well of the book, concludes that ultimately 'its main interest seems to be sociological' (*Tradition and Dream*, 1964: p. 298). Yet part of the disturbing achievement of *The Golden Notebook* is to make the traditional distinction – once so firmly understood, and so much part of the basic vocabulary of critics, including this one – between literary and sociological ways of looking at the world a good deal less easy to sustain. *The Golden Notebook* follows Doris Lessing's earlier novels in the Martha Quest sequence; if those books showed the struggles of a young woman for independence, then *The Golden Notebook* shows the harder though less dramatic struggles of a woman in her thirties who has long since achieved it. Anna Wulf, the heroine of *The Golden Notebook*, is like an older version of Martha. Though born in London, she too lived in Rhodesia during the war years, where she was involved in left-wing politics and contracted a brief, unhappy marriage. After the war she returns to England, and in 1957, when *The Golden Notebook* opens, she has made a name as the author of *Frontiers of War*, a best-selling novel, has been a Communist for a few years, and has undergone psychoanalysis. She has never married again, though for five years she was the lover of a Central European refugee and has had many minor affairs. On the face of it Anna Wulf has achieved a degree of personal freedom that the New Woman of Ibsen and Shaw could scarcely have dreamed of; she is as free as any man in all the major spheres of life, professional, intellectual and, above all, sexual. Only her deeper emotions remain unliberated; she is conscious of a surviving need for dependence, and the clash between her desire to control her own destiny and her passionate love for a young American writer takes her to the brink of insanity and provides a major theme of the novel.

The perilous situation of the emancipated woman has become a common enough topic in Western society, although it has not so far received very significant literary treatment. Doris Lessing links her interest in this question with a profound dissatisfaction with the kind of novel form that she used with a good deal of competence in her earlier fiction. *The Golden Notebook* offers, not incoherence, certainly, but a systematic fragmentation, which seems to echo the fragmentation of Anna Wulf's own life, although to say this might suggest that one has adopted the so-called 'heresy of expressive form'. (Yet all these distinctions are relative: compared with, say, William Burroughs, Doris Lessing is a remarkably controlled writer.) Only a small part of *The Golden Notebook* is taken up with the conventional narrative of Anna's life in the year 1957; most of it consists of the contents of her four notebooks: the black, in which she recalls the Rhodesian experiences that provided the source material for *Frontiers of War*, and also sets out the financial fortunes of that book; the red, in which Anna Wulf describes her comic and pathetic experiences in the Communist party; the yellow, in which she is writing another novel; and the blue, which contains a personal diary of her day-to-day life. Finally, there is a short section headed 'The Golden Notebook', in which Anna, using a dream or cinematic narrative tries, without much success, to synthesise these disparate strands. In a book so dedicated to exposing the fragmentariness of existence, integrity is not so readily attained, even in fantasy. *The Golden Notebook* is a work of great, if cold, brilliance. It is dominated by Doris Lessing's hard, analytical intelligence, a quality which at once sets her apart from such lesser frank exponents of the woman problem as Edna O'Brien, and which is always evident, even at the very brink of hysteria; as, for instance, the many intelligent passages of parody and assured mimicry.*

One of Anna Wulf's problems is that she is suffering from a writer's block, and cannot produce an effective sequel to *Frontiers of War*; hence, presumably, her ceaseless preoccupation with her notebooks. Presumably *The Golden Notebook* reflects some similar crisis in Doris Lessing's own life. At a particular point in their careers, novelists sometimes turn inward to write about the creative process or its difficulties: one thinks of James's short stories about novelists, and more recently of Graham Greene's *A Burnt Out Case* and Evelyn Waugh's *The Ordeal of Gilbert Pinfold*. *The Golden Notebook* clearly belongs in this category. (David Lodge has argued, though not quite convincingly to my mind, that Amis's *I Like it Here* should also be read as a novel of this kind.) Yet *The Golden*

* Such as, for instance, the alleged reviews of *Frontiers of War* in English-language Soviet magazines, the spoof journal of a young American wandering around Europe, and the piece called 'The Romantic Tough School of Writing', quoted on p. 69 of this book.

Notebook leads beyond this personal dilemma to larger general
questions about the nature of fiction. It is very much a novel about
process, which is something that preoccupies a wide area of contemporary Western culture, ranging from action-painting, or 'happen-
ings', to the literary scholarship that is much less interested in the
finished work than in the source material, notebook outlines and
early drafts that went into it. The process that most concerns Doris
Lessing is the way in which 'experience' is transformed into 'fiction'.
In *The Golden Notebook* we see the source material for *Frontiers of
War*, but not the novel itself; we are, however, able to read the draft
of a novel about a girl called Ella that Anna Wulf is composing in
the yellow notebook (Ella is herself writing a novel about a young
man who commits suicide; the Chinese-box effect becomes positively
vertiginous in places), and this enables us to see (a) how far this
novel reflects Anna's own experience, as described in the blue notebook, and the intercalated sections of 'straight' narrative; and (b)
how muffled, unfocused and generally inferior this draft novel is to
Anna's direct accounts of her own experience. Her own difficulty is
involved with her loss of belief in Art as a viable cultural activity :
traditionally the novelist is supposed to transform the raw stuff of
his experience into art, but Anna comes increasingly to feel that
this is distortion and evasion. She is about to turn an incident she
has witnessed into a short story when she reflects : 'It struck me
that my doing this – turning everything into fiction – must be an
evasion. Why not write down, simply, what happened between
Molly and her son today?' When writing is seen as primarily com-
munication rather than making, then the nature of fiction must
change radically, even to the extent of no longer seeming at all like
fiction. *The Golden Notebook* reflects precisely such a change, and is
accordingly hard to get into critical focus.

Within the confines of *The Golden Notebook* our attention is
directed from source material to its literary rendering and back
again. Yet attention is also led outwards, beyond the confines of
the book. Inevitably, if we have read Doris Lessing's other novels,
such as *The Grass is Singing* and the Martha Quest volumes, then we
will be aware that all these books are rooted in the same area of
experience. It is here that questions about the relation of fiction to
autobiography, which in more traditional novels can be ·either
ignored or regarded with detached curiosity, become exigent. *The
Golden Notebook* cannot be read with the established canons of

impersonality in mind; yet to attempt to follow up the speculations it inevitably triggers off might cause one to fall foul of the laws of libel, not to mention offending common delicacy.

The notion that the literary transformation of experience is a form of mystification or lying is to be found in two accomplished recent novels, by authors who certainly do not share Doris Lessing's impatience with the established conventions of fiction. Thus, Margaret Drabble, in *The Millstone*, lets her heroine discover the manuscript of a novel that a supposedly loyal friend has been writing about her; she reads through it with mounting horror at the copious distortions and misrepresentations it contains. In A. S. Byatt's *The Game* one of the two sisters who are the central characters publishes a novel in which experiences involving the other sister are improved on and written up for literary purposes, with, in the end, disastrous results. For orthodox twentieth-century criticism the source has no rights and need not be considered. What counts is the finished work, in which disparate materials are transmuted by the author's imagination into a new aesthetic unity; this, certainly, is the critical tradition in which I feel most at home and which I would struggle to defend. Nevertheless books do not come into the world *ex nihilo*, and questions about the experiences that went into them, like questions about the author's personality, are not easily suppressed; especially in a cultural climate which, as I have remarked, is less interested in the finished artifact than in the processes that went into it.

The idea that fiction is lying, and in other respects undesirable, has been propagated by another English novelist, B. S. Johnson, whose considerable talents seem to me unnecessarily limited by his doctrinaire attitudes. For an English writer Johnson is remarkably conscious and theoretical in his ideas about what he wants to do. His first novel, *Travelling People*, opens with a stately 'prelude' in which the author offers his reflections: 'seated comfortably in a wood and wickerwork chair of eighteenth-century manufacture, I began seriously to meditate upon the form of my allegedly full-time sublimations'. Johnson continues this prelude with an exposition of his ideas about the novel:

> Furthermore, I meditated, at ease in fareastern luxury, Dr Johnson's remarks about each member of an audience always being aware that he is in a theatre could with complete relevance be applied also to the novel reader, who surely always knows that

he is reading a book and not, for instance, taking part in a puni-
tive raid on the curiously-shaped inhabitants of another planet.
From this I concluded that it was not only permissible to expose
the mechanism of a novel, but by so doing I should come nearer
to reality and truth . . .

Travelling People is an extremely entertaining novel with an
obvious debt to Sterne in its typographical eccentricities: as, for
instance, when one character has a heart-attack and Johnson illustrates its effect with a blank page printed entirely in black. The
novel contains a lively parade of stylistic improvisations, including
passages printed as letters, a television script, extracts from obscure
early writers, and interpolated digressions by the author. If its
manner is fairly dazzling, the matter tends to be thin: in essence
Travelling People is a familiar kind of first novel about a young
man's picaresque adventures, in this case set in a shady country
club in North Wales. There is a lack of conviction about the more
conventionally narrative section, and it is evident that much of
Johnson's energy went into the stylistic innovations. Yet this novel
showed that Johnson had unusual talents and some disconcerting
and provocative ideas about the novel; unlike most young English
writers he had learnt a great deal from Joyce and Beckett and was
trying to move beyond the conventions of realism. In his stress on
the formal and artificial elements in fiction, and his preoccupation
with eighteenth-century models, Johnson has something in common
with John Barth, although he comes nowhere near Barth in intellectual stamina and obsessive power. Johnson's second novel, *Albert
Angelo*, also showed a wealth of stylistic variety, and a high degree
of comic inventiveness. It describes a short period in the life of a
young Londoner called Albert, who has been trained as an architect
but has been unable to find work in that profession, and who supports himself by supply teaching in a variety of tough London
schools. Albert's life in and out of school is described in the first person, realistically and comically, until a point near the end of the book,
when the consistent surface of the narrative is violently shattered.
Part 3 ends with a measured paragraph of calculatedly fine writing:

After fifteen hours of rain, in the late afternoon the sun slashed
through, lightening first over the south-westward houses of the
Circus, glinting silver on the wet courses of the chimneys and
throwing the dormers into shadowed mystery. A patterned flight

of sparrows was scattered in reflection from the polished roof of a car outside.

Albert lazed at his drawingboard before the great window. Nearly seven weeks' summer holiday lay ahead of him in which to work; and he could not work today, always tomorrow was the day he was going to work. Part of the trouble, he thought, was that he lived and loved to live in an area of absolute architectural rightness, which inhibited his own originality, and resulted in him being – OH, FUCK ALL THIS LYING!

After this brutal interruption of the fictive illusion, *Albert Angelo* moves into its fourth section, headed 'Disintegration', in which the author tries desperately to tell the truth about himself, after all the lying fiction that has gone before:

— fuck all this lying what im really trying to write about is writing not all this stuff about architecture trying to say something about writing about my writing im my hero though what a useless appellation my first character then im trying to say something about me through him albert an architect when whats the point in covering up covering over pretending pretending i can say anything through him that is anything I would be interested in saying
— so an almighty aposiopesis
— Im trying to say something not tell a story telling stories is telling lies and I want to tell the truth about me about my experience about my truth about my truth to reality about sitting here writing looking out across Claremont Square trying to say something about the writing and nothing being an answer to the loneliness to the lack of loving

Although it would be possible to assimilate this effect to familiar modes of fiction by saying that the author's 'second self' has undergone a rapid and violent change of persona, this is surely to soften its impact excessively (in private conversation B. S. Johnson has violently protested against any such interpretation). This part of *Albert Angelo* continues with the author correcting, for the reader's benefit, all the fictional lies about himself that he has told in the rest of the novel.

Albert Angelo contains an epigraph from Beckett's *The Unnamable*:

When I think, that is to say, no, let it stand, when I think of the time I've wasted with these bran-dips, beginning with *Murphy*, who wasn't even the first, when I had me, on the premises, within easy reach, tottering under my own skin and bones, real ones, rotting with solitude and neglect, till I doubted my own existence . . .

In his next novel, *Trawl*, Johnson seems to take up Beckett's hint, and abandons all attempts to invent fictional characters, concentrating on his own experience. (One might remark in passing that *The Unnamable*, which is a series of reflections on what possible meaning or meanings can be given to the pronoun 'I', hardly gives direct warrant to the fusion of fiction and autobiography.) *Trawl* is a more sober and more limited work than Johnson's two previous novels, lacking their humour and verbal exuberance. The title has a double significance: the narrator spends some weeks as a passenger on a trawler fishing in far northern waters; he has deliberately undergone this isolating experience as a means of dredging, or trawling, through the memories of his past life in an attempt to find some pattern in them. *Trawl* is an immensely serious book, which Johnson describes as being 'one hundred per-cent true'; the writing is always acute and sensitive, and there are many fine descriptions of life on the trawler, but the narrator's memories are often uninteresting, and the whole novel is marked by a curiously invariable flatness of tone, which may indeed stem from the author's determination to remain faithful to the facts, and abandon the lying rhetoric of fiction.

Johnson has asserted that he is not at all interested in 'invention' or 'imagination', nor indeed in 'fiction', in so far as it involves these qualities:

> I'm certainly not interested in the slightest in writing fiction. Where the difficulty comes in is that 'novel' and 'fiction' are not synonymous. Certainly I write autobiography, and I write it in form of a novel. What I don't write is fiction. (BBC recording 1967: 'Novelists of the Sixties')

He argues that such a novel is distinct from a fragment of autobiography, by virtue of its form: 'it has a certain shape and impetus and construction which an autobiography wouldn't have'. Johnson is perhaps aware that this is a vulnerable position – with possibly defensive irony, he has called one of his short stories, 'Aren't You Rather Young to be Writing Your Memoirs?' – but he adheres to it with great firmness. In one sense it might be argued that Johnson has taken to a logical conclusion the example of such great twentieth-century novelists as Joyce and Proust, whose work contained a very high proportion of autobiographical material, even though transformed by the imagination that Johnson so rigorously disapproves of. As he states it, his position seems to me oppressively solipsistic and narcissistic; the reader may not find anything like the same degree of interest in the author's personal experiences as the author himself, as parts of *Trawl* make apparent. Johnson seems to have been prompted both by a demand for total moral honesty, seeing novel-writing as a means of reproducing experience as faithfully as possible, and by a strangely positivistic dislike of imagination. Here his views chime interestingly with those expressed by Wells more than thirty years before; Wells, too, had come to prefer documentary record to fiction : 'Who would read a novel if we were permitted to write biography – all out?'

Johnson also assumes that the novel – even the novel that does no more than recall direct experience – differs from autobiography by its shape and organisation and impetus, so that the novel is literature while the autobiography is not. This is surely fallacious. Any autobiography will also admit those formal and organising elements which Johnson would confine to the novel, and which, however committed the author may be to total fidelity to the facts, will inevitably distort his original evanescent experience. And this is to leave out of account the gap between language, as a necessarily inexact system of codification, and the unknowable reality which it labours to describe : 'the limits of my language are the limits of my world'. A complete answer to B. S. Johnson has been given by another English novelist of the 1960s, Julian Mitchell :

> we read autobiography exactly as we read fiction, to enter imaginatively into other people's lives and so to explore the world and ourselves. What distinguishes autobiography is the ease with which we accept its illusion of authenticity. But it is only an illusion, and we should distrust an autobiographer just as much as a novelist – because his memory is human, and thus fallible, and because we can see his alleged facts being shaped, selected, highlighted and improved for aesthetic reasons right under our eyes. Perhaps we should – and do – distrust him even more than a novelist, since what interests us is his personality, of which far more is revealed by his presentation of the 'facts' than by the 'facts' themselves. The 'authenticity' is simply a trick to make us suspend our disbelief. Autobiography, in fact, is an art form which plays with illusion and reality just like the novel.
> (*New Statesman*, 15 March 1968)

All this is very well said, and far truer than Johnson's positivistic simplifications. The corollary of Mitchell's statement is that, once the similarities between fiction and autobiography are recognised, the novelist can take upon himself a great deal of freedom in blending and counterpointing these two forms. And this is what Mitchell has attempted in his most recent novel, *The Undiscovered Country*. This book is divided into two sections. The first part seems purely autobiographical – and much of it is verifiably accurate, as the present writer, who is fleetingly referred to, can confirm – in which Julian Mitchell traces his friendship from his schooldays with a young man called Charles Humphries, an enigmatically attractive figure, to whom Mitchell is intensely attached. Charles dies at an early age, and leaves Mitchell a sealed box-file, which, when opened, is found to contain the manuscript of a novel called 'The New Satyricon'. This thoroughly eighteenth-century touch leads us to the second part of the book, which contains 'The New Satyricon'. It is a collection of fragments – rather like *The Man of Feeling* – which Mitchell tries to edit with introduction and commentary. The style is a fair pastiche of eighteenth-century prose, and the story of 'The New Satyricon', so far as Mitchell can piece it together, is outlined in his 'Introduction':

> The 'hero', Henry, arrives in a new country, immediately sees and falls in love with someone whose sex, age and character are all quite unknown to him, and spends the rest of the novel trying to find her or him. His pursuit of his beloved leads him into ludicrous situations which give Charles an opportunity to satirize modern life.

After we have read 'The New Satyricon' Charles's personality remains as enigmatic as ever, and the precise nature of his significance in Mitchell's life still eludes us. Nevertheless, as a kind of satirical vaudeville, incorporating a series of stylistic parodies, 'The New Satyricon' reads entertainingly enough, and contrasts effectively with the rather staid autobiographical narrative in part one. As a technical experiment the novel seems to me very accomplished, although the manner is too relaxed and good-humoured to demolish the reader's incredulity, in contrast with, say, the obsessive force of *The Golden Notebook*. At the same time Mitchell's novel raises questions about the relation between reality and its fictional rendering. I have referred to the way in which Doris Lessing's book implicity directs our attention beyond its own covers, as it were, back to her own earlier novels. Mitchell does the same thing, explicitly:

It will not come as a surprise to anyone who has read a novel called *As Far As You Can Go* that the character there called Eddie Jackson was based at some distance on Charles, or that some of the book's scenes of looseish California living are fairly faithful accounts of the society in which he moved.

As Far As You Can Go is Mitchell's third novel; there is also what looks like a version of Charles in his first book, *Imaginary Toys*. And while following up these speculations, I might remark that Julian Mitchell's second name is Charles, which might support the idea that Charles is the author's *alter ego*.

These novels, to which one might add such further representative English works as Michael Frayn's *The Tin Men* and David Lodge's *The British Museum is Falling Down*, and, in America, the novels of John Barth, are all examples of what Wells called 'the frame getting into the picture', where the author's act of writing is included in the field of the novel. By their shuffling of levels of reality, their reliance on *collage* and pastiche and parody, they point to possible redefinitions of the novel, in which, as I have suggested, the distinction between fiction and other kinds of writing could become blurred. Yet all these novels depend for their effect on violating assumptions which have been previously established by existing kinds of fiction. In so far as they depend parodically on the realistic novel, then their relation to it is also parasitic. By their playing with representations of reality, and their deliberate shattering of the narrative surface, they provide plentiful shocks and surprises, often of a comic kind. Yet, despite the arguments of an *avant-garde* aesthetician such as Morse Peckham, I cannot believe that shock and surprise can ever be anything other than a very minor aspect of art. Art must be essentially the impression of form on flux; or, to phrase it rather more exactly, the raising of a low degree of order to a much higher degree. Within such broad definitions one needs as much freedom and sympathy as possible, in understanding what the reality to be transformed might be, and what possibly unimagined modes of transformation might ultimately be feasible. We may have to understand, on the one hand, that the author could be involved in his work in a far more direct way than the familiar canons of modern criticism will allow; and, on the other, that since all writing is a symbolic breaking down and codification of experience, it must include some degree of stylisation and distortion. In practice this may simply mean agreeing to extend the definition of 'literature' to take in many non-fictional, or non-inventive kinds of writing, a practice for which there are well-established, if slightly old-fashioned, precedents.

Again, however tentative our aesthetic views are, and however much we may need to expand our concept of the possible forms of order, I remain convinced that some form of unity and order are essential to art if one is to use the word meaningfully, however contrary may be the theory and practice of the contemporary *avant-garde*. I would like to conclude this chapter with a brief consideration of two works which both illustrate the ideas raised in it and point beyond them. Both have a deceptively conventional appearance, without obvious stylistic tricks or distortions of narrative manner. One takes the form of a novel, the other of a volume of autobiography; but both, I believe, accomplish similar things. The first is Evelyn Waugh's *The Ordeal of Gilbert Pinfold*, a short and characteristically elegant story, about a respectable man of letters on the edge of a nervous breakdown, who takes a sea voyage for his health and is subject to a macabre series of hallucinatory persecutions which, at last, he succeeds in defeating. The opening sentences of Waugh's novel crisply epitomise the situation which I have tried to discuss in the course of this book :

> It may happen in the next hundred years that the English novelists of the present day will come to be valued as we now value the artists and craftsmen of the late eighteenth century. The originators, the exuberant men, are extinct and in their place subsists and modestly flourishes a generation notable for elegance and variety of contrivance.

It would be perfectly possible to read *The Ordeal of Gilbert Pinfold* without knowing anything of Waugh's other novels, or of the personality of the author. In which case one would certainly enjoy it as a bizarre and entertaining novel. Yet one does, I think, find more in this work, if one reads it with a knowledge of Waugh's total *œuvre*, and of the public persona that he was at such pains to present in his final years. If so, one is forced to conclude that Pinfold, a cantankerous, middle-aged Catholic writer, very much a social recluse, who is totally out of sympathy with the modern world, is essentially Waugh himself. And yet, throughout the narrative, Pinfold is kept at a certain distance; we may sympathise with him, but at the same time we see him as a distinctly ludicrous figure, who is both pathetic and comic. In this novel, which is, I believe, based on personal experience, we see Waugh both establishing in greater and greater detail his public persona, and at the same time subjecting it to detached scrutiny. It is a magnificent though wholly unpretentious piece of writing.

The other book is by an American, Norman Mailer's *The Armies of the Night*; here, too, Mailer incorporates his public persona in a narrative which, although autobiographical, is organised like a novel. This book, which describes Mailer's participation in a great anti-War march in Washington in October 1967, looks like the conclusion to a project that occupied Mailer's literary career over several years, and which the customary categories of 'fiction' or 'non-fiction' are inadequate to contain: it includes collections of essays and other miscellaneous prose pieces, such as *Advertisements for Myself*, *The Presidential Papers*, and *Cannibals and Christians*, as well as works of fiction which are as much written against the form of the novel as within it, such as *An American Dream* and *Why Are We in Vietnam?* Both kinds of book were dominated by the author's personality, and reproduced his obsessive myths and towering romantic egotism. In *The Armies of the Night* all these previously disparate elements converge into a satisfying whole. The book shows the narrative power, the concern with character and the feeling for dialogue of the practised novelist; it also incorporates the essayist's interest in ideas and the expert reporter's ability to catch the precise feel of fleeing events. The greater part of the book is taken up by Mailer's detailed account of the march and demonstration, his subsequent arrest and brief period in prison. Mailer writes of himself throughout in the third-person with total, even harsh objectivity. Nothing is left out of his freakish vanity, snobbishness and irascibility. Yet one sees that Mailer's driving egotism involves more than a romantic assertion of the Self; this quality is humanised and even offset by a Montaigne-like curiosity about the human being one happens to know best – oneself – down to every minor mental quirk and physical peculiarity. And throughout the book there is a constant interplay between Mailer's inner visions and fantasies, and the desperate reality of politics and history in modern America. He succeeds, in fact, in bringing the private and the public into the same focus, in a way that someone like Doris Lessing – who, like Mailer, has been deeply affected by Marxism – has striven for but never been able to achieve. *The Armies of the Night* is, I think, the finest book

Mailer has written; in its colourful, sensitive and outrageous way, it shows that it is possible to fuse the fictional, the autobiographical and the documentary within a single seamless narrative.

Yet both Waugh and Mailer were masters of language, writing at the peak of their careers : with the best will in the world one cannot conclude that such ways of developing the possibilities of the novel beyond its present situation are generally available. Such books must, indeed, be fantastically difficult to write, and the attempt to combine direct personal experience and literary form is likely, if undertaken by inferior talents, to produce results as dismal as the reams of bad confessional verse that followed the publication of Robert Lowell's *Life Studies*. For the most part it looks as if novelists are likely to continue making variations on familiar themes, or carrying out intricate stylistic manoeuvres within a basic *impasse*. Yet I shall resist concluding on a note of prediction; most prophecies are false, which is one reassurance that history can offer us, since most prophecies are also gloomy. Beyond that, I feel too much a part of the situation I have described to be able to see very far beyond it.

An Appendix on the Short Story

THE short story is a paradoxical form in that it is both common and neglected: one or two specimens, at least, are to be found in any self-respecting intellectual quarterly or glossy monthly, yet no one seems very interested in the theoretical justification and possibilities of the short story, a situation that contrasts with recent strenuous attempts to erect a poetics of the novel. It is true that collections of short stories, overlaid with commentary and annotation, are popular as college textbooks: the New Critical assumption that all literature is really poetry, or at least can be read as poetry, is difficult to apply to the novel, but can serve very well with a few pages of self-contained fiction that can be gone over in class and given the theme–symbol–image treatment just as though it *were* a poem. Yet this approach, illuminating though it may be, and pedagogically useful, is surely remote from the way most readers receive the short story, and, for that matter, how most writers conceive of it.

One of the few useful critical studies of the short story that I have come across is an unpretentious book by Frank O'Connor (*The Lonely Voice*, 1963) in which he remarks that in its essence the short story deals with life's victims, the insulted and injured, the forlorn and alienated. This seems to me a shrewd remark, and one borne out by several recent collections of short stories by American writers: Meyer Liben's *Justice Hunger*; James Leo Herlihy's *A Story that Ends with a Scream*; Sallie Bingham's *The Touching Hand*; and Paul Bowles's *The Time of Friendship*. These contain uniformly accomplished renderings of the defeat of human aspiration by brutish circumstance, whether the victims are Moroccan peasants, as with Mr Bowles, or American middle-class housewives, as with Mr Herlihy. No one would want to deny that such defeats, whether violent or mild, are a perennial part of the human condition, providing the kind of drama that the fiction writer is always looking for.

Nevertheless there is, I think, a small but highly significant difference between writing about victims and seeing the world as peopled by them. Sooner or later critics of fiction will have to take to heart some of the demonstrations made about the visual arts in Gombrich's *Art and Illusion*, and apply its lessons to literature. Although the writer may aim at a direct rendering of reality, and the reader may believe that this is what he is receiving, such directness is likely to be illusory. Distortion will occur, not just from the author's temperament, which can be recognised and allowed for, but much more insidiously from the inherent presuppositions and limitations of the genre he is employing. It seems to me that the modern short-story writer is bound to see the world in a certain way, not merely because of our customary atmosphere of crisis, but because the form of the short story tends to filter down experience to the prime elements of defeat and alienation.

Again, most stories are written for publication in a limited number of possible places; although their requirements may not be quite consciously in the author's mind when he is writing, they will certainly exert their pressures somewhere along the line: the four writers I am dealing with acknowledge periodical publication in such places as *Esquire*, *Playboy*, *Harper's Bazaar*, *Mademoiselle*, the *Atlantic Monthly* and *Commentary*. Making a possible tentative exception of the last named, one can say that such publications do not aim at a consciously defeated and alienated audience; the short stories they carry, with their sense of humiliation and despair, exist in a curious tension with the editorial and advertising pages, full of messages of hope, worldly success and sexual glory. The fiction provides the necessary touch of astringency, which, though likely to be quickly read and quickly forgotten, may touch some raw nerve of uncertainty or guilt.

In a more narrowly literary way one can say that appearing in these magazines does impose on the writers a very high level of stylistic competence: where space is limited, no words can be wasted. The combination of a sharp economy of narrative means with a profoundly bleak view of the human lot produces a characteristic tone of moral brittleness that I find recurring throughout these books. The basic pattern is predictable. Two or three specimens of humanity, neither very elevated nor repellently wretched at the outset, are shown to the reader and characterised with a few deft touches; their strengths and, far more important, their weaknesses are shown with exactly the right blend of compassionate understanding and clear-eyed detachment. The narrative moves steadily and economically to a crisp moment of defeat; and then, *diminuendo*, to a bleeping finish with, again, just the right mixture of pathos and irony. Here, by way of illustration, are the conclusions of four stories by these authors; the tendency toward a uniform tone is very apparent:

> Tears came to the eyes of Miss Roth as she turned to her work and I to mine. There were no tears in my eyes, nor in the eyes of any man whose heart is drained by delusions and afraid of love.
>
> (LIBEN)

> When she had walked several yards down the lane, she turned to glance over her shoulder and found Mrs Kay standing in the middle of her patio still looking at her with the same, naked, depressing stare.
> Under her breath, Loretta said, 'Die. Disappear. Turn to ashes.'
> But when Mrs Kay waved at her, she waved right back.
>
> (HERLIHY)

> 'Another year, perhaps,' the captain had said. She saw her own crooked, despairing smile in the dark window-glass beside her face. Maybe Slimane would be among the fortunate ones, an early casualty. 'If only death were absolutely certain in wartime,' she thought wryly, 'the waiting would not be so painful.' Listing and groaning, the train began its long climb upwards over the plateau. (BOWLES)

> She turned the three facts over and over, like three pebbles in her hand. They were cool and solid and round, and she did not know what she would do with them. But they were – they existed; and suddenly she felt the weight of her life, of herself, laid upon her bare bones. (BINGHAM)

The tendency to write about life's victims also shows itself in a concern with forms of consciousness that are exceedingly limited: children, imbeciles and persons in a low state of cultural development (to use as untendentious a formula as possible). The writing expressing such states of mind is very adroitly done, but I have considerable doubts about how far it is based on direct observation or intuition, and how far it relies, perhaps unconsciously, on established literary models. There is a relevant instance in the title novella of Miss Bingham's collection, which is about a difficult transatlantic voyage made by a homely children's nurse and her two singularly unattractive charges. We are given an insight into the little boy's mind:

> He began to sing, 'Planks, planks, planks. Tanks, tanks, tanks. If you want to build a tank, you got to have a plank. Planks . . .'

The word began to lose its shape, sagging and stretching like a wet sweater hung from the neck. If he said it once more, it wouldn't mean anything at all. Once when his mother was driving him to Sunday school, he had said 'Gasoline station' so many times it was practically ruined. 'What does that mean I'm saying?' he had asked his mother in a fright, and she had said, 'You know perfectly well what it means, after all, you're almost eight years old.' For months after that, he had avoided saying gasoline station for fear that it would stretch again and lose its shape for good.

This passage demonstrates Miss Bingham's professionalism, and it shows the rather persistently knowing tone that the actual or implied narrators of short fiction seem constrained to adopt. Whether it represents an accurate rendering of the thought processes of a small child is not something I can give an opinion about, even though I have three children of my own; but it corresponds very faithfully to the way we have learnt to imagine those processes, from such sources as the opening pages of *A Portrait of the Artist* and the early stories in *Dubliners*.

Characteristically, both Mr Herlihy and Mr Bowles have first-person stories told by mad narrators. The former has a brilliant little piece about a mental patient who thinks the world is being overrun by the sound that cartoonists denote as ZZZZ, although he cherishes certain private antidotes: 'I'm absolutely certain the Zzzz of the razor did not really penetrate, I kept saying K-K-K-K-K-Kill, K-K-K-Kill over and over again the whole time, and I'm sure those good hard sounds counteracted the Zzzz almost entirely.' I admire Mr Herlihy: he is a superb stylist, as his longer fiction has already made plain; but in his stories everything is liable to be consumed by style. In the parallel story by Paul Bowles a somewhat confused maniac devises a scheme for inserting packets of poisoned gum in the vending machines on subway stations. But he bungles the scheme and is left with all the poisoned gum on his hands; the story concludes:

It is a lovely evening. After dinner I am going to take all forty boxes to the woods behind the school and throw them on the rubbish heap there. It's too childish a game to go on playing at my age. Let the kids have them.

Critics have already placed Mr Bowles as a writer of Gothic tendency with a taste for gamey, melodramatic situations and not much liking for humanity. This is a fair enough description of his short stories; still one must insist on his extreme verbal skill, while finding what he does with it very limited and ultimately monotonous. He places his characters before us and then destroys them in an unerring way: it is a remarkable performance, but one expects something more from literature.

I'm afraid I may have been unfair to Meyer Liben, who is a highly original and interesting writer, and who seems to me to have a good deal more to offer than Herlihy or Bowles, and certainly than Miss Bingham, who is very competent, but who relies heavily on the short-story formula to compensate for the thinness of her material. At least I enjoyed considerably the title story of *Justice Hunger*, which is in fact a short novel of 140 pages. It tells the story of a love affair that doesn't come to very much, between two young New York intellectuals in the thirties, set in a milieu – that is more than a mere background – of eager left-wing activism, and bitter feuding between Trotskyists and Stalinists. Mary McCarthy has described this situation in her early fiction, and Mr Liben must have been similarly involved, although he seems to have waited longer before writing about it. His manner is very much his own; cool but not to the point of coldness; seemingly hesitant, and yet highly articulate. He writes with serenity, a fairly rare quality nowadays. In the shorter pieces he tends to succumb to the limitations I have been discussing, though not invariably; in some of them he shows an admirable tendency to write against the grain of the short-story form instead of going smoothly along with it, and his book is given a certain unity by one's sense of the sympathetic personality and quiet but keen intelligence underlying it.

Many of the characteristics I have ascribed to the short story – in particular, the tendency to what Frank Kermode once called, apropos of Salinger, 'a built-in death wish' – could also be found in novels; but the novelist, although subject to all kinds of generic and cultural factors, can more easily transcend them, and see the world in his own way, rather than the way in which literary form or the presuppositions of an audience make him see it. For all its popularity and apparent necessity to magazine editors, the short story, in its present condition, seems to be unhealthily limited, both in the range of literary experience it offers and its capacity to deepen our understanding of the world, or of one another.

References

THE following books are referred to in the text. Kingsley Amis, *Lucky Jim, I Like It Here, Take a Girl Like You, One Fat Englishman, The Anti-Death League*, Gollancz, 1954, 1958, 1960, 1963, 1966; *A Look Round the Estate*, Cape, 1967. John Bayley, *The Characters of Love*, Constable, 1960; *Tolstoy and the Novel*, Chatto & Windus, 1966. William Peter Blatty, *John Goldfarb, Please Come Home!*, Gibbs & Phillips, 1963. Wayne C. Booth, *The Rhetoric of Fiction*, Chicago University Press, 1961. Anthony Burgess, *The Right to an Answer, The Wanting Seed*, Heinemann, 1960, 1962; *The Novel Now*, Norton, New York, 1967. Stanley Crawford, *Gascoyne*, Cape, 1966. Nigel Dennis, *Cards of Identity*, Weidenfeld & Nicolson, 1955. Ralph Ellison, *Invisible Man*, Gollancz, 1953. Richard Farina, *Been Down So Long It Looks Like Up to Me*, Random House, New York, 1966. L. P. Hartley, *Facial Justice*, Hamish Hamilton, 1960. W. J. Harvey, *Character and the Novel*, Chatto & Windus, 1965. B. S. Johnson, *Travelling People, Albert Angelo*, Constable, 1963, 1964. Herbert Marcuse, *One Dimensional Man*, Routledge & Kegan Paul, 1964. Leonard B. Meyer, *Music, the Arts and Ideas*, Chicago University Press, 1967. Alberto Moravia, *Man as an End*, Secker & Warburg, 1965. Flann O'Brien, *At Swim-Two-Birds*, Macgibbon & Kee, 1960. José Ortega y Gasset, *The Dehumanization of Art and Notes on the Novel*, Princeton University Press, 1948. Anthony Powell, *Afternoon Men*, Duckworth, 1931; *A Question of Upbringing, The Acceptance World, Casanova's Chinese Restaurant*, Heinemann, 1951, 1955, 1960. Thomas Pynchon, *V., The Crying of Lot 49*, Cape, 1963, 1967. Alain Robbe-Grillet, *Snapshots and Towards a New Novel*, Calder & Boyars, 1965. Robert Scholes, *The Fabulators*, Oxford University Press, New York, 1967. C. P. Snow, *The Light and the Dark, The Sleep of Reason*, Macmillan, 1947, 1968. George Steiner, *Language and Silence*, Faber, 1967. Lionel Trilling, *The Liberal Imagination, A Gathering of Fugitives*, Secker & Warburg, 1951, 1957. Ian Watt, *The Rise of the Novel*, Chatto & Windus, 1957. H. G. Wells, *Experiment in Autobiography*, Gollancz, 1934. Angus Wilson, *The Old Men at the Zoo*, Secker & Warburg, 1961.

Index